EMBROIDERING LIVES

SUNY series in the Anthropology of Work
June C. Nash, Editor

EMBROIDERING LIVES

Women's Work and Skill in the Lucknow Embroidery Industry

CLARE M. WILKINSON-WEBER

State University
of New York
Press

Portions of the text have previously been published by the journal *Ethnology*, in an article by Clare M. Wilkinson-Weber, titled "Dependency and Differentiation: Agents and Embroiderers in the Lucknow Embroidery Industry." Volume 36(1), Winter 1997, pp. 49–65.

Published by
State University of New York Press, Albany

Production by Susan Geraghty
Marketing by Nancy Farrell
Photos and figures by Clare M. Wilkinson-Weber and Steve Weber
Maps by Karen Williams

Printed in the United States of America

For information, address State University of New York
Press, State University Plaza, Albany, N.Y., 12246

Library of Congress Cataloging-in-Publication Data

Wilkinson-Weber, Clare M.
    Embroidering lives : women's work and skill in the Lucknow
Embroidery Industry / Clare M. Wilkinson-Weber.
        p.   cm. — (SUNY series in the anthropology of work)
    Includes bibliographical references and index.
    ISBN 0-7914-4087-7 (hardcover : alk. paper). — ISBN 0-7914-4088-5
(pbk. : alk. paper)
    1. Women embroidery industry employees—India—Lucknow. 2. White
work embroidery—India—Lucknow. I. Title. II. Series.
HD6073.T42I483 1999
331.4'874644'09542—dc21   98-16883
                                                                 CIP

10 9 8 7 6 5 4 3 2 1

CONTENTS

MAPS

FIGURES

TABLE

A NOTE ON TRANSLATION

A translation of all Indian words in this text follows their first occurrence, and successive occurrences too if the word is of special importance
and enough space separates it from the first. Exceptions are words that
can be found in English dictionaries, names of religious festivals, and
castes. Complete transliteration with diacritics is given at first occurrence
(except in the case of proper names). The system of transliteration, a
guide to sounds, as well as meanings of select words, is provided in a
glossary at the end.

ACKNOWLEDGMENTS

I have been fortunate enough to receive assistance, advice and encouragement from many people at every stage of the preparation of this book, and I am pleased to recognize them here.

My research was funded by the American Institute of Indian Studies. In the stages of writing up, I was supported by grants from the University of Pennsylvania and supplementary funds from the Department of Anthropology. My dissertation, upon which this book is based, was written under the supervision of Dr. Arjun Appadurai, with the guidance of the other members of my dissertation committee, Dr. Peter van der Veer and Dr. Kris Hardin. Needless to say, there would be no book without their many contributions to my research over the years. I am especially grateful to Arjun Appadurai for encouraging my interest in India, and suggesting this topic. Among the scholars who advised me during the year of my fieldwork were Barbara Daly Metcalf, J. Mark Kenoyer, Sandra Barnes, T. N. Madan, Shahid Amin, Gail Minault, Harold Gould, Jasleen Dhamija, Jyotindra Jain, and Nita Kumar. I am also grateful for the help of the faculty of the Anthropology Department at the University of Lucknow, and of the Giri Institute of Development Studies in Lucknow.

While I was in India, I particularly appreciated the help of Dr. P. R. Mehendiratta, director of the American Indian Institute of Indian Studies in New Delhi. Sarla Sahni, Leila Tyabji, Runa Banerjee, the staff of the Uttar Pradesh Export Corporation, the District Industries Commission and the Central Design Centre, as well as numerous traders and consumers of chikan, were good enough to talk at length. I am particularly grateful to Anita Singh, my assistant, discussant and conscience, and the ever-resourceful Ram Advani. Others who assisted me in various ways while in Lucknow were Moira d'Souza, Ranjan Misra, and Brigadier K. C. Sharma.

In the protracted stages of interpretation and writing, Lee Horne, Deborah Swallow, Susan Bean, Emma Tarlo, Douglas Haynes, David Ludden, David Rudner, Anita Weiss, Michael Billig and Margaret Wiener offered critiques and insights. I am grateful to the anonymous reviewers of this book for their thoughtful comments and suggestions. Ajanta Jain assisted in practical details of translation and transliteration.

Karen Williams drew the maps for this book and Wy'East Color of Portland developed and printed my photographs. I would like to thank the support staff at Washington State University Vancouver, particularly Vickie Darnell and Ginny Taylor, for their patience and hard work.

On a more personal level, there are many people whose encouragement and friendship over the years have been indispensable. I would like to acknowledge the late David Brooks, my inspiring undergraduate advisor. My parents and parents-in-law have been a constant source of support. My husband, Steve Weber, has been both mentor and companion through all phases of researching and writing this book. Most of all, I acknowledge the embroiderers and artisans of Lucknow, and above all, Saliha Khatun, my teacher, to whom I still owe a considerable debt.

MAP 1. Lucknow in relation to Banaras and New Delhi.

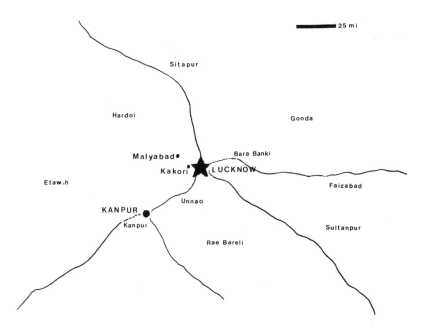

MAP 2. Lucknow and its region, showing districts and some settlements referred to in the text.

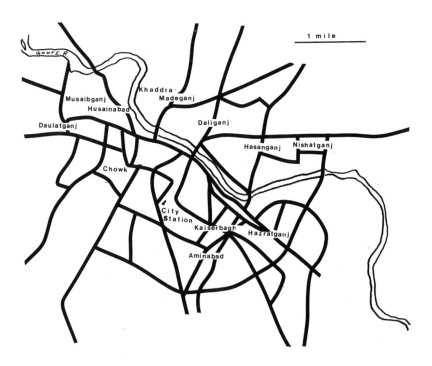

MAP 3. The city of Lucknow and some of its neighborhoods.

INTRODUCTION

This book is about work and workers. It is about the people who make chikan (*čikan*)—a style of hand-embroidered clothing from Lucknow, North India. Chikan is made in a large-scale, low-technology industry where hand-powered labor predominates, piece wages are paid, and there are no factories. Embroidered garments are made in stages, starting with fabric cutting and tailoring, followed by block printing and embroidering, and finally, laundering. In all stages but one, male specialists predominate. However, the embroidery stage is completely dominated by women, almost all of them poor, with few other job opportunities. They do embroidery out of necessity, not as a hobby. The wages they make from chikan are, for some, the only resource they have against utter destitution. In the following pages, you will learn why this is, what work embroiderers do, and what broader lessons we can learn from their example—about gender, about class, and about the transformation of skills in capitalist development.

A few years after I returned from fieldwork with embroiderers in Lucknow, I presented a paper about embroiderers' skills and knowledge. When my presentation was over, I sat down next to one of my fellow panelists. I noticed the sum of his notes on my talk; "Woman talking about nice embroidery." The subject of embroidery seems to bring out the worst prejudices about women's work and women's research. No matter the progress of women's studies and gender studies in anthropology, certain kinds of research seem doomed to be regarded as trivial and uninteresting.

There is a rich irony in these reactions. The plight of embroiderers, as I shall show in the succeeding chapters, stems largely from an ideology in which their work is regarded as a leisure-time activity, unworthy of serious attention and serious wages. Anthropologists help perpetuate these stereotypes when they respond dismissively toward the study of handicraft and, in this case, embroidery.

So why should you be interested in the women whose lives fill these pages? I can give several answers. First, we shouldn't delude ourselves this is a precious art form done only by women with time on their hands. Embroidery is business, first and foremost. It is one of the biggest industries of Lucknow, employing tens of thousands of people and generating millions of rupees in sales. Its organization and productive relations fit wholly within the contemporary capitalist world. Whole parades and streets in Lucknow's major retail and wholesale markets are occupied by shop after shop specializing in chikan goods, and chikan-embroidered goods are worn by Indians all over the country.

Of particular scholarly interest is what embroiderers can teach us about how people learn their work skills, how they use them, and how skills are changing. Almost all of us worry sometime about what we know, what use it is, and whether it can bring us the social rewards our world has led us to expect. Embroiderers work in an industry in which low skills and intensive labor are becoming the norm. In 1989–90, chikan clothes ranged in price from as little as ten rupees for a child's shirt to several hundreds of rupees for a finely made *sārī* (women's garment of wrapped cloth). Women make the finest, as well as the crudest work. Since chikan is currently a mass-market commodity, most items, including men's shirts and women's tunics and trousers, cost under or around a hundred rupees.[1]

While there is little superficial resemblance between the best chikan work and the commonplace product, they are connected in that the makers of fine work derive their basic living either from making inferior work for the mass market, or subcontracting it to less-skilled women. The potentially vast numbers of women capable of low-skilled work mean that not only is high-skilled work endangered but that embroidering as a whole is becoming a deskilled, low-status occupation, typified by low wages and a sporadic work flow as many women compete for limited work. This book captures a moment in that transition, a moment at which high skills still exist but in a complex relationship to low skills.

Last, but not least, embroiderers are people who are important both for what they do and for the outlooks they bring to their society and their times. The way in which embroiderers make a living is increasingly the pattern for many workers around the world who are underemployed, poor, and exploited (e.g., Beneria and Roldan 1987; Singh and Kelles-Viitanen 1987; Collins and Gimenez 1990; Prügl and Boris 1996). What we can learn about life and work among embroiderers can provide a glimpse into the lives of many more millions like them.

This is by no means the first study of an industry like chikan. Foremost among earlier analyses is Maria Mies's (1982) work on lacemaking in Andhra Pradesh. Unlike Mies's study, however, this book is about a commodity and production process that is almost entirely South Asian in finance, organization, and taste. I do not mean to suggest there have been no outside influences on chikan. In fact, I suggest later that the chikan industry in its essential form was a creation of colonialism. I stress the very South Asian nature of chikan because the capricious trends of the export market that are blamed for the problems of so many native handicraft industries cannot be invoked in this case.

To date, there have been two kinds of studies of chikan. First, there are a few, short economic analyses of chikan as an informal-sector industry employing female labor (e.g., Rai 1975; Mathur 1975). These studies do not acknowledge the diversity of products and skills, and do not make much of the fact that embroiderers, while they are all women, are differentiated in terms of the work they do, the training and abilities they have, and the relations they have with one another. The second kind are technical and descriptive accounts of embroidery that focus almost wholly upon work of the very best kind. By ignoring the entire range of chikan embroidery, these studies fail to place even the very best work (and its makers) in a historical and social context. Clearly, what is needed is to examine the production process and productive relations in which chikan as commodity or art object is created.

I have two preeminent goals in this book. The first is to explain why the embroidery stage, alone of all the stages that make up the chikan production process, is almost completely dominated by women, when only half a century ago there were both male and female embroiderers. A satisfactory explanation of this historical shift requires stepping beyond (or, at least, to the edges of) the anthropology of gender and into the analysis of class. Female seclusion, sexual segregation, and ideologies of gender difference inhibit self-assertion among embroiderers, and entrench many embroiderers' ignorance of the market for, and prices of, the products they make. But it is also necessary to consider the "rise" of female embroiderers as an example of labor-force restructuring, or a strategy of global capitalism, which ideology tends to obscure.

Women have always been a cheap source of embroidery labor, but only recently have they come to dominate all skill levels in the craft, from the lowest to the highest, as chikan has been transformed into a mass-market commodity. Male embroiderers who used to make fine chikan have largely abandoned the craft, to be replaced by a few hundred female virtuosos. The vast majority of neophyte, unpracticed embroiderers are brought into productive networks through male agents unversed in the techniques of chikan production.

The transformation of chikan embroidering from a craft with a gender division of labor to one in which men have disappeared altogether has occurred simultaneously with an overall decline in quality of chikan products. This decline is ideologically linked to the degradation of Lucknow, formerly renowned as a cultural center dominated by the fortunes and tastes of a hegemonic Muslim elite. Embroiderers, as well as others involved in chikan production, are convinced that there is less "distinction" (Bourdieu 1984) in the makers, traders, and consumers of chikan than there was even twenty years ago. The feminization of chikan production is taken by embroiderers and manufacturers alike to be indicative of decline—but the association of women and low quality conveniently ignores the fact that some women can and do make very fine chikan. So why should the employment of women be so glibly associated with decline in the product? The simple answer is that undervalued female labor suits the needs of a rapidly developing manufacturing industry.

My second concern is to describe productive relations among women themselves. Confronting the evidence of conflicting economic interests and social differentiation among women has forced me to discard any romantic views of gender solidarity among female embroiderers, even though their gender clearly plays into their relations with manufacturers, government officials, and others. I have not found it possible to ignore the extraordinary skills some embroiderers possess, but while the investigation of "what skilled embroiderers know" forms a somewhat separate strand in this book, it is related to the overarching theme of economy because it involves the question of skill: what it is, who has it, and what is happening to skill in the production of commercial chikan. Ironically, those who speak loudest about the decline of chikan skills are the same people that are struggling to wrest some kind of living from the high skills they possess. They are also subcontractors of work to their less skilled neighbors and to the lowliest of village embroiderers. There is little superficial resemblance between fine chikan work and the common commercial product, but a connection exists—since the makers of fine chikan work can only continue to make it if they can obtain a living through working (as embroiderer or agent) for the market.

METHODOLOGY

This book is based on nearly one year's fieldwork in and around Lucknow. I talked to embroiderers, shopkeepers, state and central government officials, and personnel attached to SEWA Lucknow (a nongovernmental organization [NGO] that encourages women's participation in and management of their own embroidery enterprise), as well as craftspeople in all stages of embroidery manufacture. I had many informal conversations with middle-class Lakhnawis—the preeminent consumers of embroidery—about their tastes and preferences in chikan. I focused on urban production and did not see much village embroidery. I visited a handful of embroidering households outside Lucknow but they were not that far from the city, thus falling into an intermediate category that was neither wholly urban nor wholly rural. While the embroiderers in these households may have been typical for a subset of village production on the city's fringes, they were not necessarily like workers in rural areas several hours' journey away. How to survey and understand rural chikan production presents major methodological challenges beyond the scope of the present study. These must be tackled in future so that a critical part of the industry is properly understood.

Even in the city, learning about chikan means getting away from the visible, public world of Indian markets and commerce into the concealed, productive worlds of poor artisans, and still further into the homes of secluded embroiderers upon whose labor a vast hand-powered industry is founded. The scale of the chikan industry can only be guessed at by noting the number of shops and the ubiquity of embroidered garments in the city. One of the most difficult practical challenges in my fieldwork was to draw out details of chikan technique, skill, and social relationships, while keeping the broader picture of the entire industry in sight. One approach—though not the only one I used—was to investigate the knowledge and skills of very accomplished embroiderers, one of whom agreed to teach me chikan. I took this step out of necessity. Participant observation was difficult to do among embroiderers. Apart from the usual disadvantages of youth and ambiguous status that beset many novice fieldworkers, I found that many embroiderers had been questioned in the past by journalists, economists, and social scientists, usually through use of statistical surveys and a few formalized interviews, and there was clearly no novelty to be found in yet another "student" coming around asking questions, even when some of my concerns were genuinely different.

Still, I was quite surprised to hear how many writers and scholars had supposedly been visiting only a few months before me, asking the same kinds of questions. This may simply have reflected a heightened interest in chikan in the media and the academy—as Leili Tyabji, designer for the SEWA Lucknow organization, believed. Another possibility, given the fact that I doggedly stuck around for nearly a year, was suggested by skilled embroiderer (and wit) Ayub Khan, that is, that the person embroiderers remembered seeing was in fact me, and they had simply forgotten who it was.

Chikan embroidery is a subject that women are all too accustomed to expounding upon, even those anonymous, unskilled women who have contributed to many sociological and economic surveys in the past. Through these experiences, embroiderers have formed a good idea of what they think can or ought to be said about chikan, from which many other details of their personal lives are left out. I was often physically excluded from conversations in which embroidery (or the vision of embroidery I was supposed to receive) was not the primary subject, either by voices being dropped to a whisper or the conversants moving away. As an anthropologist interested in delving deeper into the social relationships and experiences of embroiderers, I found these reactions enlightening, though frustrating.

Poor artisans were understandably unwilling to spend any of their time with a stranger unless there were (although often even in spite of) clear and measurable rewards. I cannot say that this was the kind of fieldwork in which I made friends. Instead, I was often the target of complaints and accusations of embroiderers angry that the promises of earlier studies to publicize and improve their conditions had gone for naught. I have probably added to their resentment in the time it has taken to produce my own findings in print. I hope, however, that I am now at least beginning to repay the debt I owe them.

APPRENTICESHIP AND LEARNING (ABOUT) CHIKAN

My teacher Saliha Khatun is a well-known embroiderer, the subject of a handful of articles and recipient of a National Award for excellence in handicrafts. I sought her out when the idea of finding a teacher was already forming in my mind, and when we did meet, I felt immediately drawn to her. I asked her to teach me embroidery, and she agreed. Up to that point, I had found myself limited to fleeting interviews that gave only a taste of what I wanted to know, and where my language abilities were sorely tested. I did not like having to rely upon an assistant to carry on conversation for me and it was clear that independent research could only come about once I had freed myself from this constraint. In becoming an apprentice, I found an answer to many of my research difficulties. I was able to find a mutually satisfactory way in which to recompense someone for her time and her conversation; I was able to establish a daily presence in someone's house that was both appropriate and expected; I became familiar with one woman's knowledge of chikan and gained an insight into the creative process that would have been impossible to achieve in any other way; and I was able to observe the relationships between an active subcontractor of work and her clients and see how the different makers and different forms of chikan might be connected. On a personal level, my teacher's home was the one place where I began to feel accepted.

It is well known in anthropological circles that fieldwork is very largely a process of acquiring competence in the cultural practices of the people one is supposed to be studying. Anthropologists learn things without intending to be taught them; they learn how to dress (e.g., Gold 1988), to veil (e.g., Fernea 1969; Abu-Lughod 1986), even to eat and to talk in ways that are deemed appropriate to their status. With ethnographic methods coming under closer scrutiny in recent cultural anthropology, the conscious effort to acquire knowledge and skills through apprenticeship has attracted fresh interest, although it is by no means something new in the discipline (Coy 1989). Apprenticeship, of greater or lesser length, acquired an early legitimacy in material culture studies thanks to the influence of Ruth Bunzel (1929), who employed this technique in her study of Zuni pottery. Arts and crafts provide the most obvious settings in which an anthropologist can learn new and critical skills (e.g., Blacking 1973; Feld 1990; Cooper 1980, 1989). But apprenticeship has also been invaluable for understanding systems of esoteric knowledge that in western society are categorized separately from the plastic and oral arts, although they may not be so distinguished in other cultures, for example, Dow's (1989) apprenticeship to a shaman, Stoller's difficult experiences becoming a Songhay sorko (Stoller and Olkes 1987), and, of course, Castaneda's famous (and notorious) relationship with Don Juan (Castaneda 1970, 1971, 1973). For some anthropologists, learning to do something oneself is a necessary element in understanding how and why their subjects do it, but is not a prominent element in their analyses. For others, the process of learning plays a more critical role in revealing the processes by which knowledge is shared and concealed, and skill distributed.

In learning in this way from my teacher, I was not only able to ensure daily contact with embroiderers, but I was also able to acquire a familiarity with stitch variability that mere observation could not have produced. The drawback is that I see all chikan with her eyes, so to speak, and tend to interpret it according to her scheme of stitches, where other embroiderers adopt different classifications. Therefore, I do not present my description of stitch names and relationships as a definitive or unimpeachable account of "Lucknow chikan." Many of my teacher's practices of naming and making stitches are shared by other embroiderers, but not by all. It may have been desirable to replicate the learning process with other practitioners, but in the small world of skilled chikan embroidery in Lucknow, once committed to my teacher, I did not feel I could be the pupil of more than one master.

Toward the end of my fieldwork, it became apparent to me that an alternate, and perhaps more expected role for me was that of patron. Several women invited me to commission work from them but I consistently rejected all such offers, convinced that such a role would conflict with my identity as "ethnographer." My refusals were evidently puzzling and annoying to embroiderers. They knew that selected members of the cultured elite of Lucknow individually commissioned work. As a wealthy foreigner, I ought to have behaved in the same way. Perhaps initiating a production process through commissioning work, rather than trying simply to observe it, would have been another acceptable and fruitful way in which to frame my inquiry. But to have been a patron exclusively would have narrowed my perspective on chikan far too drastically. Since I did not adopt this strategy, I cannot speculate further into the specific advantages and disadvantages of such a venture.

In any case, I have been forced to acknowledge the fact that my research uncovered only a small fraction of the world of chikan. It is curious, in contrast, that so many texts about chikan lay out their "facts" with unswerving confidence, and in definitive terms. I have found, instead, that the world of chikan is complex to a degree unhinted at in previous works. In chapter 5, I describe in some detail the ways in which what each embroiderer says she knows about chikan varies. None is any more correct than another, but some have had their work and their knowledge officially recognized while others have inexorably disappeared. Where I do feel it is important to be unequivocal, however, is on the basic reasons why women are employed in such high numbers in embroidery production and why some women can work at the higher levels in the industry, while others languish at the bottom. In any particular area of expertise, there may be many who are far superior to me (I do not consider myself a textiles specialist, for example). However, the synthesis I present in this book is an attempt to go beyond both polemics and dry artifactual description.

SUMMARY OF CHAPTERS

The first chapter is a brief history of chikan and a description of the field setting in Lucknow. The second chapter describes the multistaged chikan production process, the different artisans involved in each stage, and the merchants who finance and coordinate production. The third and fourth chapters provide accounts of the lives, relationships, and work of female embroiderers. The third chapter addresses the question of why women's work is so little valued and goes into detail on the elements of women's subordination. In the fourth chapter, I describe embroidery work, wages, working styles, and the activities of female subcontractors. Knowledge and creativity amongst highly skilled embroiderers is the subject of the fifth chapter, which includes a description of the acquisition and transmission of skills, and the meaning and variability of stitch repertoires. The sixth chapter looks at the influence of the development strategies of the state and the NGO SEWA Lucknow on the craft and its makers. The implications of the study, and suggestions for future work, are summed up in the conclusion.

CHAPTER 1

Chikan in Historical Context

THE FIELD SETTING

Lucknow today is a less important cultural center than Banaras and a secondary manufacturing center compared to Kanpur (Gould 1974). It is still, however, the capital of the state of Uttar Pradesh, and houses the State Parliament and many state government departments. It is also home to a large number of educational and research institutions, including several colleges of art and design, the Uttar Pradesh State Museum, Lucknow University, the Birbal Sahni Institute of Palaeobotany, the Central Drug Research Institute, and the National Botanical Research Institute.

Lucknow's population was recorded in the 1991 census as 1,669,136. In population terms, Lucknow is second only in the state to Kanpur, with a population of just over two million (Census of India 1991). The larger part of the city forms a semicircle on the south bank of the Gomti River (Hjortshoj 1979:27). The north bank is punctuated with poor neighborhoods where crafts manufacture—including chikan embroidery—and industries are located. Some areas, for example, around Daliganj and Hasanganj, are extremely old, dating from the seventeenth and eighteenth centuries (Hjortshoj 1979:85, 117). Currently, Lucknow is expanding much further to the north in new commercial and residential areas such as Indira Nagar and Aliganj, which cluster around the major north-south thoroughfares.

The main city is made up of three distinct sections (Mukherjee and Singh 1961; Hjortshoj 1979:28). The oldest section to the west is centered on the Chowk wholesale market, the newest organized around the Hazratganj retail market in the east, and the third associated with the Aminabad retail market. The last section is impossible to define as neatly and accurately as the Chowk and Hazratganj sections. Since 1900, dense retail markets (of which Aminabad, in the narrow sense, is just one) and residential areas have clustered around nineteenth-century roads built to connect Hazratganj to the south and east. Today, the Aminabad section extends as far south as the railway station at Charbagh. Many of the twentieth-century immigrants to Lucknow have

1

settled in this area and the population of the section is heavily Hindu (Hjortshoj 1979:29).

Aminabad aside, Lucknow conforms to King's (1976) model of a colonial city. New Lucknow confronts Old Lucknow, the two areas of the city organized according to different ideological principles of space, order, and morality. In almost all parts of the old city, buildings and neighborhoods abide by ideological rules that demand separation (of men from women, and of different ethnic, religious, or family groups from each other) and enclosure (containment of internal diversity while presenting external anonymity) (Hjortshoj 1979:36). In this respect Old Lucknow is like most other "Islamic" cities throughout North India, South Central Asia, and the Middle East (see Gilsenan 1983, Kostoff 1991). The population of the city's older sections has been relatively stable over time, with families living in the same place for several generations. Even in *hawelīs* (traditionally constructed mansions) that have been subdivided into accommodations for many families, people still try to maintain a lifestyle in tune with the principles of separation and enclosure. The immigrants who swell the *bastīs* (slums) and squatter settlements in Aminabad and New Lucknow, cannot (Hjortshoj 1979:65–66). The newest arrivals even live their lives openly on the streets (ibid.).

While the consumers of chikan come from all areas of Lucknow, embroidery production is almost entirely contained within its oldest sections. I never heard of any of the new immigrants into the city doing embroidery. Most of the city's chikan embroiderers live in the old city and chikan businesses are concentrated in the Chowk market. However, the two areas with which I became most familiar were both north of the river. Madeganj is a community in an area known as Khaddra. Madeganj is built around a *pakkā* (constructed, paved) but badly deteriorated street that runs directly off the main road, about half a mile north of Hardinge Bridge. Like other lanes in the *moḥallas* (traditional neighborhoods) the street is bounded by open drains covered with stone slabs. North of Madeganj is a largely open, rubbish strewn area dotted with ruins. Most homes in Madeganj are partly *pakka* (made of baked brick), although some are entirely *kaččā* (made of sun-dried brick). One Madeganj house with which I became familiar was entered through a broken wooden door, opening onto a small courtyard. To the right of the door was a latrine and washing area. To the rear of the courtyard was a kitchen area partially roofed with thatch and canvas, and inside was a mudbrick oven for cooking. Two rooms led from the courtyard, the farthermost with a curtained doorway. A single light bulb hung in the covered kitchen area and water had to be drawn from a pump outside the house. The house, in size and upkeep, was moderate for the neighborhood. In Khaddra, houses ranged from small *kacca* dwellings to two-storeyed, spacious, *pakka* ones, situated closer to the main road. Ayub Khan, the foremost male embroiderer and agent in Khaddra, lived in a larger *pakka* house a few *galīs* (narrow lane) over from the house just described. I did not see the house in its entirety, but what I did see included a large room set up for *zardozī* (gold and silver embroidery) work, a back room for receiving guests, a large sunny courtyard, and family rooms. In contrast, the poorest houses were single-roomed, *kacca* dwellings, covered with a rotten thatch and a few sackcloths.

Daliganj is a large area made up of several *mohallas*. It is very close to Khaddra and lies on the main road leading from Iron Bridge. I spent most of my time in Bandho Mohalla, which was reached either by a tortuous rickshaw ride or on foot through small *kacca* streets that led off the main road. The journey took one past small general stores, sewing workshops, vegetable stands, all interspersing old, and mostly *pakka*, residences. At one point, the way led beneath the railway line, where the rickshaw had to negotiate a path to the side of a vast, stinking garbage dump. Approaching closer to Bandho Mohalla, a large open area lay to the right of the road, site of the Idgah (festival grounds for celebrating Id-ul-fitr, the Muslim festival that marks the end of the month of fasting known as Ramadan).

The last part had to be done on foot, through narrow, uneven, and sometimes muddy *galis*. Several possible routes existed to the house of my teacher, with whom I spent most of my time. The routes took one past the two prominent institutional features of the *mohalla*, the school, and the mosque. The *galis* were busy places, where people visited and shopped at the permanent food stands or mobile vegetable carts. Goats and dogs were also familiar inhabitants of the *galis*. At dusk, a herd of water buffaloes wended their way through the neighborhood after being watered at the river.

Homes in Bandho Mohalla were better made than homes in Madeganj. The kinds of embroiderers who inhabited these two neighborhoods were also different from a social standpoint, and did different kinds of work. My teacher's house was completely *pakka*. There was a front room with two curtained doorways to a backroom, where the family spent most of its time. The backroom contained personal items, mementos, chests of finished chikan work collected over the years, and bundles of chikan to be embroidered. To the rear of the backroom was a courtyard and adjoining it three small rooms, a kitchen with a kerosene stove, a latrine, and a washing area. There were at least two electric light bulbs in the house, and an electric ceiling fan that because of power brown-outs could never be used at the time it was most needed. A water tap, which carried only an intermittent water supply, was in the courtyard.

WHAT IS CHIKAN?

The most satisfactory definition of chikan today perhaps would be "any cotton embroidered article that comes from Lucknow." Its Lucknow origin is the strongest and simplest element in the definition, since chikan includes garments—both Indian and western in style—and table linens, a range of stitches, articles entirely white and some using color, as well as handwork and machine work. Scholars have been defining and classifying chikan for over one hundred years. Their efforts span several changes in the kind of embroidery being produced and the conditions in which it has been made.

Several writers have tried to probe the word itself for clues as to the essential nature of chikan. But there is no certainty, and certainly no consensus as to what "chikan" means. I have heard chikan described as a "Bengali" word meaning "very nice thing." Some have translated it as "fine" (Lucknow Magazine 1988:16), while still others have termed it a Persian word meaning "to put in bold relief" (Lucknow City Magazine 1988:21). Paine (1989:16) gives a range of Persian possibilities, from the 1651 Burton's classical dictionary definition of "kind of embroidery with gold thread, quilting," to "embroidery in various kinds of silk on garments and other items," in later dictionaries. She also writes of Richardson's 1806 Persian/English dictionary terms *chikan/chikin* "a kind of cloth worked with the needle in flowers." Finally, she notes that chikan has a possible linguistic connection to the physical barriers of purdah through the Persian word for "a blind" (*chick/chiq*) (ibid.).

The very range of embroidered textiles to which the word "chikan" has been applied in the literature no doubt contributes to the difficulty in settling upon its meaning (see especially Watt 1903:398–406). The category "chikan" is essentially the product of British classification of the last century and it is unclear at what point the analytic categories of British critics diverged from names and descriptions given by makers and consumers of embroidery. British (and other subsequent) writers' own prior ideas about how embroidery was to be understood and their familiarity with European styles of needlework, were highly influential in shaping their classifications (e.g., use of terms such as "satin-stitch," "buttonholing," and so on). In most lexigraphical definitions, chikan appears as a class of objects, neither connected specifically with Lucknow nor entailing an entirely distinctive form of embroidery.[1] Watt's (1903:398) classification gives chikan the status of a "division" of embroidery, with subdivisions of chikan-work proper, satin-stitch on white-washing material, and *kāmdānī* or gold and silver embroidery on white cotton cloth and muslin. Watt therefore writes about chikan in such far-flung places as Peshawar, Madras, and Calcutta as well as Lucknow, although the work differed in each location. One must conclude from that the word "chikan" is loosely associated with needlework of various kinds, a collective noun with either no specific referent, or shifting referents. What relationships there may have between chikan in different locations, whether chikan's appearance was an accidental product of similar politicocultural conditions in other locations, or whether the apparent ubiquity of chikan is simply an artifact of classification, cannot be dealt with adequately here.

STITCHES AND "WORK"

Defining chikan in terms of its stitches usually produces exercises in abstruse categorization rather than illuminations of how embroiderers themselves think about their work. Occasionally, traders—and less commonly, embroiderers—are cited as local authorities or sources of information. Aesthetic and technical analysis is cumulative, drawing heavily upon previously published work. Sources are not always cited, but George Watt's volume on the Delhi Art Exhibition of 1903 is clearly a starting point for many descriptions (Watt 1903: 399–406). Categorizations are many and each is invariably presented as definitive. On the contrary, they are inevitably partial, drawn as they are from only a few informants or from previous analyses. A "complete" list is in any case hypothetical, since there is no one who subscribes to such a list.

A recurrent discrimination is made between flat and embossed stitches, in which the chikan stitches *bakhyā*, *kaṭā'o*,[2] and *tepćī* are termed flat, and most forms of *murrī* embossed. Sharima (1959:47) describes *bakhya* as a smaller version of *murri*, but this seems to be an aberration. *Jālī* is always treated separately as a kind of "network," in accordance with indigenous discriminations. Again, Sharima (1959:47) is alone in his description of *jali* as *katao*. While the segregation of *jali* is well established, I found no evidence that embroiderers make a distinction between so-called embossed and flat stitches.

All stitch forms are described with reference to named western-style stitches when possible, for example, "stem" or "chain" stitch. For many reasons, certain chikan stitches are *not* stem stitches or satin stitches—not even the technique is commensurate. In appearance, there are similarities, but appearances are no guide to the forms of design, construction, and naming employed by embroiderers. Naqvi (1971) eschews broad western classificatory categories and simply presents the stitches as a list. He recognizes the names given to stitches by embroiderers but is still inclined to describe them in terms of western technique. The descriptions he gives are, in turn, heavily dependent upon an earlier article by Pande (1968).

Short descriptions tend to pinpoint a few details of chikan that make it distinct. *Bakhya, katao,* and *tepci* are invariably mentioned, grouped together as "flat" stitches according to Watt's categorization. Chattopadyaya (1964:9) also refers to *kalai,* which I cannot identify. Dhamija (1964:25–26) also traces the *bakhya, tepci,* and *katao* triad, but inserts a discussion of *murri* and *phandā* before going on to *jali.* Saraf (1982) is clearly unaware of the basic difference between "shadow-work" (broadly used as a synonym for *bakhya*), which is worked on the reverse, and stitches that are worked on the obverse. He does, however, utterly distinguish *katao* and *bakhya.* Paine (1987:7–9) gives one of the most extensive and satisfactory accounts of chikan but again tends to couch it in definitive terms. She writes that there are six basic stitches, five derivatives, and seven stitches "that in themselves form an embossed shape," and that this fixed repertoire is the basis of discipline and constrained creativity in the craft. However, this cannot be an exhaustive list since none of the embroiderers I met subscribed to such a narrow and precise classification of stitches.

The most highly skilled embroiderers possess a broad repertoire of between twelve and seventy-five stitches. Although there are major areas of overlap, there is no consensus among the most highly skilled over how stitches are named, nor does knowing more stitches *necessarily* translate into greater skill. Describing chikan on the basis of its stitches is therefore a somewhat fruitless task. However, a critical distinction between the most accomplished embroiderers and the mass of workers lies in the fact that while for the former there are only a range of stitches, for the latter, there are only different forms of work. I believe that this discrimination is critical for developing a truly useful definition of chikan. Forms of work are named for the stitches that are used in them; for example *bakhya* work and *phanda* work contain *bakhya* and *phanda* stitches, respectively. Most embroiderers know only one form of work that employs, typically, no more than five stitches, and commonly only one, often sketchily executed. The main forms of work are *bakhya* work, *murri* work, *jali* work, *phanda* work, and *tepci* work. Women tend to specialize in one form of work or another, and this in turn reflects their skill level and position in the industry's structure. All forms of work are regarded by highly skilled embroiderers (and traders) as debased derivatives of "authentic" work based on knowledge of many stitches.

Bakhya work is the most ubiquitous form of work and uses only one stitch. In appearance, *bakhya* most closely resembles the western herringbone stitch, done on the reverse of the cloth. Ideally, tiny, closely packed stitches should yield, on the obverse, opaque petals and leaves rimmed by contiguous stitches. In the simplified work prevalent in the market, the stitches are so loosely applied that no opaque areas show up at all on the right side and stitches rarely touch one another (figure 1.1). The rudiments of *bakhya* can be mastered very quickly and an acceptable standard of work for the market achieved in comparable time.

FIG. 1.1. Detail of *bakhya* work.

However, the difference between *bakhya* as a stitch in the repertoire of the highly skilled, and as a form of work done by women with few or no skills at all, is so great that it is difficult to view them as being at all alike. *Bakhya* work is regarded by skilled embroiderers as coarse and crude. "It is poor man's fare next to real chikan," said one. It is made almost entirely by low-skilled villagers, although neater and less sketchy forms of *bakhya* work are made in the city.

Bakhya work is conventionally opposed to another form of work, *murri* work. *Murri* is considered higher in status than *bakhya* work and typically includes between four and six stitches (e.g., *gol murri, lambī murri, phanda,* and possibly *joṛā, kauṛī,* and *kīl*). The very finest pieces, in which stitches are counted distinctly, are also known as *murri* work (figure 1.2). But the most accomplished embroiderers insist their kind of *murri* can readily be set apart from the *murri* work of ordinary embroiderers. Even run-of-the-mill *murri* work requires a higher degree of skill than *bakhya* work and thus takes longer to master. It is almost exclusively a city specialty.

Phanda work is made almost entirely in villages and uses only one, knotlike stitch. *Tepci* work is made by villagers and city-dwellers, and

FIG. 1.2. An example of fine work. This kind of work is collectively known as *murri* although it is finer quality than commercial *murri* work.

is characterized by a large quantity of stitches distributed all over the garment, often a *sari*. The *tepci* stitch, which is the only one found in *tepci* work, is made with a thin thread and is most like a running stitch.

Jali always appears alongside *bakhya* or *murri* work, but like them is done by a separate set of workers. *Jali* involves opening up spaces in the base cloth and holding them apart with taut stitches, creating the effect of a net. In theory, *jali* demands a skilled technique (although some *jali* is extremely crude) and uses a different kind of needle and thread from *bakhya* and *murri*. Except for an increasing number that feature *bakhya* work alone, most articles of chikan embroidery are made in two separate production circles: first the rural embroiderers make the *bakhya* work, then the urban embroiderers finish the garment by making the *jali* work.

ORIGINS AND HISTORY OF CHIKAN

Scholars generally admit that little can be said about the origins of chikan with any certainty. This has not stopped some from indulging in speculation. The most ambitious trace chikan to references by Megasthenes to "flowered muslins" in the third century B.C.E. (Pande 1968:43), or to dress in the seventh century C.E. court of Harsha, ruler of much of North India (Saraf 1974:213; Chattopadhyaya 1963:8). Curiously, these claims assert a Hindu identity for a craft that throughout its existence has been most associated with Muslim makers and, until recently, a group of elite consumers heavily influenced by Muslim tastes.

The majority of origin stories recited by embroiderers, traders, and scholars go back only a few hundred years. No single origin story predominates and each is delivered with the same finality by their various proponents. Nobody denies that chikan reached its most elaborate and distinctive form in Lucknow, applied with spectacular results to Indian garments such as *topis* (caps), *saris, cogas* (a kind of scarf), and so on (Hoey 1880:88; Paine 1989:13–15). Watt (1903:399) specifically terms Lucknow chikan "the most artistic and most delicate form of what may be called the purely indigenous needlework of India." However, there is disagreement over whether chikan began in Lucknow, or came from some other location. I do not intend here to speculate upon the possible accuracy of any origin stories. This kind of historical study was outside the scope of my research. However, origin stories are encountered so often in literature and in embroiderers' accounts of their craft that they merit special consideration.

Bengal

The majority of written accounts (government publications and scholarly books on handicrafts and embroidery) trace chikan back to Bengal and to male artisans who came to Lucknow from there to take advantage of courtly patronage (Irwin and Hall 1973; Chattopadhyaya 1963:43–44; Dhamija 1964:25; Coomaraswamy 1964:206; Mukharji 1888:371; Naqvi 1971).[3] Most writers are vague about when this migration occurred, referring broadly to the period of the *nawābs* (rulers of the territory called Awadh [roughly coterminous with present-day Uttar Pradesh] from 1720 to 1856). On the whole, most subscribe to a later florescence in Lucknow rather than a sooner one (e.g., Mukharji 1888:180). Watt (1987:399) puts its arrival in Lucknow during the second half of this period, referring specifically to the patronage of *shāhs* (kings), the name that replaced *nawab* in the early nineteenth century. In a vague and tantalizing reference, Sharar (1975:172) also portrays chikan as a late arrival in court culture. After describing the invention by Shah Nasir ud-Din Haidar (1827–37) of a cap made expressly for members of the Shia sect of Islam, Sharar writes,

> A little later, a very attractive embroidered cap of the same type was created for the winter. The five panels were covered in thin muslin upon which gold and silver crescents and designs were stitched in different colours. In winter one saw no other covering on the heads of men of fashion. Later, when chikan [embroidery on muslin] became popular, it was used for this purpose.

Paine (1989:26) remarks candidly that no clear-cut evidence exists for the Bengal origin thesis. However, she and others subscribe to it on three major grounds. First, the richness of indigenous textile traditions in Bengal compared to what was found at a comparable time period in Lucknow—asserting in essence that a tradition of embroidery like this could not have arisen spontaneously in the city. Second, a possible relationship between chikan and *jāmdānī* (muslin with an interwoven design that was particularly associated with the Bengali city of Dacca) (Mukharji 1888; Watt 1903:283). Some surmise that chikan evolved from *jamdani* either as a conscious imitation or as a means to repair flaws in the woven cloth (Paine 1989:19), although Watt makes a strong argument for the autonomy of embroidery working its own unique influence on loom fabrics (Watt 1903:371). Third, forms of embroidery called chikan appear in accounts of Bengali textiles in the nineteenth century (Taylor 1851; Mukharji 1888). Bengali products with this name were intended either for export or for use by Europeans living in India. Lucknow chikan was used in the past for the production of European-style clothing and table linens (Coomaraswamy 1964:206) but chikan embroideries have always included indigenous forms of clothing and nowadays almost all production is dedicated to Indian apparel. How a kind of embroidery so adapted to European usage as Bengali chikan might have been adapted to the decoration of indigenous clothing in Lucknow is unclear. Paine (1989:24–25) suggests that chikan's unique form might have been influenced both by Bengali flowered muslins and by European embroidery.

Without in-depth knowledge of historic textile collections, it is difficult to judge the validity of some of these propositions. But it is important to note that like other origin stories, the story of Bengali origin is not just a hypothesis but is instead an ideological construct that tells us as much about gender as it does about actual "facts." The Bengal thesis stresses the male, artisanal nature of chikan, eliminating the work of the women from consideration. It also downplays the significance of Lucknow as a place of origin in its own right. No contemporary embroiderer endorses the Bengal story, preferring instead an exclusively Lucknow history, or tracing chikan to a courtly genesis in Persia.

Lucknow

Most embroiderers insist upon a Lucknow origin for chikan, at some vaguely distant time anywhere from one hundred to three hundred years ago. A story that includes elements of both a Lucknow and a Bengali origin that is occasionally encountered in written accounts, describes how a woman from the cultured Bengali town of Murshidabad became bored with life in the court *zanānā* (separate and secluded women's quarters) at Lucknow, and embroidered a cap for amusement that she presented to the *nawab*. Other women in the *zanana* followed her example, and the competition that arose among them helped elevate chikan into a unique artform (Hasan 1983; Dhamija 1964:25). Indeed, Hasan attributes the employment of so many impoverished but high-status women in the later industry to the courtly beginnings of the craft, when so many women learned to make it. Dhamija attributes the story to shopkeepers in the city. I did not hear any embroiderers relate it, however.

Courtly patronage is paramount in accounts of Lucknow origin (Sharima 1959). The original *shauq* (passionate interest, love) for chikan grew among kings and nobility, in short, the *ra'īs log* (rich, important people) of the city. Saliha Khatun, in her version of the origin of chikan, said that it was the whimsical conceit of a court servant (again, male) to embroider a flower upon a nawab's *topi* that had just been washed. Once the *nawab* had given his approval, this proto-embroiderer made increasingly elaborate designs until chikan came into being. In contrast to the previous story, this one reasserts a "male" origin to chikan. However, unlike the Bengal stories of origin, there is no "industry" evident. Indeed, the story denies a role for any of the other artisans involved in chikan production today. In casting full aesthetic responsibility for chikan upon the embroiderer, this story is more like the tale of the bored Murshidabad lady. Another feature of this second story is that Saliha located the proto-embroiderer firmly in Daliganj. Embroiderers all over the city tend to agree that Daliganj was one of the earliest centers of chikan production in the city.

When relating their family histories, some embroiderers claimed a diverse craft background, most often in *zardozi* and *kamdani* (light embroidery with gold and silver wire—contrasted with the heavier *zardozi* form). Others spoke of chikan being the first craft activity acquired in the family. In a story that uniquely unites family history and chikan origins, Ayub Khan, son of one of the most famous embroiderers of this century, Fyaz Khan, retold his father's version of how their ancestor, Mohamad Shair Khan, became an embroiderer (for Fyaz Khan's version, see Dhamija 1964:25). According to Ayub Khan, his ancestor was resting outside his house when he was approached by two men. "What are you doing here?" they asked. "Do you know any craft?" He replied that he knew none, and they answered that they would teach him one. The next day they returned with needle and thread and taught him chikan. He in turn instructed his family and his neighbors, and thus chikan was born. The men who gave him his initial training were never known, and family lore refers to them as angels. Although I did not hear any other embroiderer repeat this story, or any variation of it, Dhamija (1964:25) found embroiderers respectfully visiting a tomb of Mohamad Shair Khan at the time of her research.

Persia

A major alternative to local stories of origin among embroiderers shifts the emphasis away from male originators to female ones. This story attributes the invention of chikan to Empress Nur Jahan (transformed into Empress Mumtaz Mahal in one version), consort of Jahangir, an emperor in the Mughal dynasty that dominated North India from the early sixteenth century to around the early eighteenth century. It is unsupported in scholarly literature, but has a few adherents in the lower levels of the government hierarchy who have received the story directly from embroiderers, specifically the family of another famous embroiderer of the mid-century, Hasan Mirza. In Persia, Nur Jahan was said to have seen stone tracery[4] on a monument that she found particularly beautiful. She wanted the same designs to be replicated on her clothing and she got an embroiderer to make them for her. In a version told to me by Rehana Begum (daughter of Hasan Mirza), Nur Jahan gathered together blockmakers and printers, as well as embroiderers, to recreate the design. Here we see a distinct "industry" being established—a solitary feature this story shares with tales of Bengal origin. The empress's own interest in the craft then set a trend that spread to the rest of the Mughal court. According to Akhtar Jahan, Rehana's sister, the man who did the first embroidery for Nur Jahan was the *ustād* (master, teacher) of the first embroiderer in her own family. In another version cited in *Lucknow City Magazine* (1988), it was a female handservant of Nur Jahan who brought the craft to Awadh. Others who quote the Nur Jahan story make no mention of how the craft became established in Lucknow. They do, however, emphatically deny that chikan came from Bengal. With a female originator, organizer, and transmitter of skills, and the use of chikan on female garments, this story contrasts starkly with tales of male embroiderers completely immersed in a public, market-oriented system of production.

There are also intermediate forms of the Bengal/Persia stories. Some Bengal stories of origin credit the Mughal emperors with having encouraged the development of chikan on Indian soil either through their own patronage, or indirectly through their courtiers. In general, like the Persian thesis, these theories tend to dilute the Indianness of chikan by referring to an external source, but return the emphasis to royalty, women, and personal patronage over and above commercialism and trade.

Historical Reconstruction

So much for legends. But what can reasonably be inferred about the history of chikan in Lucknow? A major problem in historical reconstruction is that chikan embroiderers simply do not feature prominently in histories of the city or of its region. Identifying the sociopolitical events that helped produce the conditions in which early industry flourished is not too difficult, and there has been plenty written about the kinds of people who have worn and enjoyed chikan over the years. Unfortunately, we know much less about the people whose production made accumulation and elite consumption possible.

Lucknow has ancient associations but is not usually thought of as a city of antiquity. Different legends associate it with Lakshman, brother of the divine hero Ram, for whom the Lakshman Tila area in the old city is said to be named (Hjortshoj 1979:17), or Lakhna, the builder of the Macchi Bhavan palace complex on this same site (Sharar 1974:37). By the sixteenth century, Lucknow was a thriving commercial town (Oldenburg 1984:6). Chowk was one of its oldest streets, its southern end (and the southern extent of the city) bounded by the Akbari Darwaza (Llewellyn-Jones 1985:18). A number of routes connected Lucknow with important transregional centers and it was a stopping place on the imperial highways to the East. Around the Chowk clustered *mohallas* and markets, some of which were built at the behest of Mughal emperors Akbar and Jahangir (Oldenburg 1984:7).

As the Mughal state slid into decline at the beginning of the eighteenth century, Lucknow became a prominent city, seat of the *nawabs* of Awadh who came to power in the Mughal rulers' wake (Cole 1989:42). Although not all the *nawabs* of Awadh resided in the city, all had some impact on the form the city took in this period (see Hjortshoj 1979; Llewellyn-Jones 1985). Above all, Lucknow became home to thousands of artisans who supplied the sophisticated demands of the *nawab* and his retinue.

The old city, with its *mohallas*, markets, and religious monuments, has always retained a level of independence vis-à-vis the palace complexes that began to dot the city from the mid-eighteenth century onward. It was the home of craftspeople, bankers, courtesans, and merchants. By the mid-1700s, Europeans visitors never failed to remark upon the splendor of the palaces and the vibrant commercial life of the city. They also noticed its congestion and filth, and the wretchedness of the poor (Llewellyn-Jones 1985:11–12; Oldenburg 1984:11).

In the latter half of the eighteenth century, the British East India Company supplanted the *nawābī* lineage as the preeminent regional power. The *nawabs* continued to rule in name and the nobility remained, but the achievement and perpetuation of status took new forms. Some grew wealthy as revenue contractors and bankers, and streamed their income more and more into patronage of the arts and crafts (Cole 1989:93–95). The most famous of the *nawabs*, Asaf ud-Dawlah, moved his court to Lucknow from Faizabad and helped raise the settlement to artistic and architectural prominence. Hjortshoj (1979:20) dates Lucknow's status as a true city from the succession of Asaf, citing the feverish building activity that took place in his reign, and the growth in Lucknow's population.

From now on, the court became more famous than the rest of the city, leading to the impression that the city *was* the court. Asaf was a lavish patron, supporting scholars, architects, and artisans on a scale unmatched by his predecessors, and generally without regard to sectarian or communal differences (Oldenburg 1984:4; Fisher 1987:75; Cole 1989:94–95). Asaf's courtiers emulated his example in other areas of the city, with the result that mosques, *imāmbārās* (religious buildings of Shias, especially associated with the observance of the Islamic festival of

Mohurram), and mansions began cropping up in affluent *mohallas* all over the city (Hjortshoj 1979:49; Oldenburg 1984:14). Asaf's building projects included a major refashioning of the Macchi Bhavan site and the construction of the Daulat Khana complex. Major landmarks of what later became "the old city" were built at this time, including the Rumi Darwaza and the Asafi (or Great) Imambara, the latter conceived as a kind of "work for welfare" project during the famine of 1784 (Sharar 1975:47). Recent estimates put the population between 350,000 (Llewellyn-Jones 1985:12) and 400,000 (Oldenburg 1984:19) by 1856, with between 50,000 and 100,000 people migrating into the city during the court's heyday.

A few of the monuments built in Asaf's reign stand today, including the Great Imambara, the Rumi Darwaza, the Baoli of the defunct Macchi Bhavan complex, and a few buildings of his huge palace compound, the Daulat Khana. None of these stands in the context of its original construction, and only the Great Imambara and Rumi Darwaza are prominent stops on the tourist trail. But nostalgia for the "golden age" of Asaf ud-Dawlah (famines notwithstanding) is as strong as ever, so much so that it is not at all surprising to find a contemporary advertisement for a chikan store headed by the famous couplet that reads, *"Jis ko na de Maulah, use [tis ko] de Asafu'd-Dawlah"* (Who from the heavens naught receiveth, to him Asaf ud-Dawlah giveth).[5] In fact, chikan is casually assumed by many Lakhnawis both inside and outside the industry to have been one of the many craft specialties that blossomed under the *nawabs*. Some sources even make deliberate reference to Asaf ud-Dawlah himself as an early patron.

At the death of Asaf ud-Dawlah, the British moved swiftly to become the new superregional power, taking a greater role in *nawabi* affairs and seizing more land (Metcalf 1964; Barnett 1980:236). The *nawabs* had little more to do than indulge consumption habits that were paid for with revenue they were still allowed to extract and keep for themselves (Barnett 1980; Fisher 1987:7). Under the first *shah*, Saadat Ali Khan, Lucknow's "consumer aristocracy" was boosted again (Bayly 1983:205). Accounts written by British visitors, attendants, and residents described life at court as indolent, indulgent, and extravagant, utterly distinct from the world outside its walls (Knighton 1855, 1865; Sleeman 1858).

It is quite possible that this was when chikan embroidering was first introduced in Lucknow. Mrs. Meer Hassan Ali, a European woman writing in 1832 about her twelve-year stay in the city, writes of poor Sayyid (high-status Muslim) women making "jaullie (netting) for courtie's [*sic*] (a part of the female dress), which, after six days' close application, at the utmost could not realize three shillings each" (Meer

Hassan Ali 1973[1832]:9). She makes no elaboration upon this remark, either in a discussion of productive activity or of fashion. However, it is possible there was an early specialist role for female *jali* makers, and that there was production for exchange of one of the present-day forms of work.

At last, Awadh succumbed to British annexation (Metcalf 1964), an event swiftly followed by the anti-British uprising (also known as the mutiny, or first war of independence) of 1856–57. The uprising's causes are complex and beyond the scope of this book (see Metcalf 1964; Brown 1985:83–89). Ranged against the British was a diverse group including disgruntled landowners upset at British reallocation of land rights (Metcalf 1964; Fisher 1987:238), religious figures (particularly Shias) who lost financial support and judicial standing with the annexation of Awadh (Cole 1989:271–72), and people with interests in commerce and handicrafts, both of which had suffered a decline with annexation (Bayly 1983). Lucknow was literally in the middle of the uprising; there was a harrowing succession of sieges and reliefs of the city and considerable portions were devastated in the course of the conflict. The sociopolitical, economic, and even psychological effects of the uprising have been amply documented (e.g., Metcalf 1964; Spear 1984; Brown 1985). In Lucknow, construction of a "new" city for Europeans to live in marked the shift of political power from the old city (Oldenburg 1984).

"Loyal" citizens were rewarded. *Ta'alluqadārs* (large landowners), deemed the ultimate "natural" authority and appropriate beneficiaries of a new land settlement, were brought by British patronage into the milieu of urban life from which they had previously been isolated, helping to buoy existing patterns of elite consumption in Lucknow, particularly at the occasional *darbār* (ceremonial celebrations of authority and deference, see Cohn 1983) held in Lucknow between 1867 and 1876 (Oldenburg 1984). The privileged supporters of the *nawab* that they replaced included Shia nobles, pensioners, and retainers, as well as the courtesans and royal wives. Many courtiers left Lucknow altogether after 1858 (Freitag 1990:261). Some with pensions and vested rights eked out a living and perpetuated, in genteel poverty, some last remnants of *nawabi* culture.

William Hoey, writing in 1880 of the "trade and manufactures" of the United Provinces, states that chikan was "always a favourite employment of women of some castes" in the domestic sphere, but refers to chikan explicitly as a Lucknow *industry* of the post-uprising period, being "almost unknown in the Nawabi" (Hoey 1880:28). Hoey describes two tiers of workers. On one hand, there were male "professional chikan workers" doing the best work and getting paid the highest piece wages (Hoey 1880:89). In another reference to chikan in the nineteenth century, Abdul Halim Sharar (1989 [1975]:172) writes that a delicate chikan cap took up to a year to make, "and even the most ordinary ones cost anything from ten to twelve rupees." On the other hand, there were women and children (whose numbers clearly impressed Hoey), working long hours for very small amounts of money, on lesser-quality work, including Indian-style garments, handkerchiefs, and pieces for inserting into separately prepared articles (Hoey 1880:88). Hoey does not elaborate upon the particular type of work each "tier" was doing, but his reference to women and children embroidering *būṭās* (round floral motifs) and *bels* (lit., creeper, a decorative embroidered flower stem) implies that it was neither *jali* work nor *bakhya* work. Watt (1903:399, 402) refers to both *phanda* and *tepci* "work" in his description of Lucknow chikan. He describes *phanda* as high-status work along the lines of what "*murri*" refers to today, while tepci was dismissed as the simple, cheap work of women.[6] Perhaps it was *tepci* work Hoey observed women making.

Taken together with the earlier observations of Meer Hassan Ali, this strongly implies the existence of a sexual division of labor in chikan work some one hundred years ago, in which men's work was elaborate and well-paid and women's work, while detailed, was low-paid. Chikan was a prodigious industry that flourished in the disturbed social conditions of the postuprising period. In this "fertile ground," chikan as an export industry grew, producing goods for populations outside Lucknow, instead of only for the local elite, with the labor of impoverished women and children desperate even for small wages (Hoey 1880:88; Oldenburg 1984:165; Mukharji 1888:180). In order to support a few vestiges of their previous lifestyle, they sold their personal property to pawnbrokers who themselves had withdrawn from banking in the face of competition from British financial institutions.

Providing the organization and finance for the chikan industry were members of the Hindu commercial castes who had transferred their activities from banking to moneylending and manufacturing. Among them were Rastogis, and Sunni and Hindu Khatri businessmen, who began to set up *karkhānās* (workshops, companies) to cater to the awakening tastes of the new elite (Oldenburg 1984:211–14). A present-day Muslim shopkeeper flatly suggested that the same families who pawned their belongings to Rastogi moneylenders were later compelled to make chikan for them (see also Oldenburg 1984:169)

Numerically dominant among the classes in decline were Muslims, moreover the same Shia Muslims who had been in the ascendancy less than two decades before. On the other hand, Sunnis, who had been unable to grasp power under the *nawabi* but could now claim privileges under the British as the larger minority, fared better in the changed conditions. The precipitous decline in elite Shia fortunes relative to Sunnis, coming as it did on the heels of the establishment of Sunni separateness and superiority, helped consolidate emergent communal identities and resentments in the city (Cole 1989).

In 1877, the Northwest Provinces and Awadh were amalgamated into a new territory called the United Provinces, with its capital in Allahabad. Lucknow's population had fallen after the uprising and the city faded into a political obscurity that lasted for nearly forty years (Hjortshoj 1979:26). In the 1920s, the capital of the United Provinces was finally shifted back to Lucknow. By this time, Lucknow had become known as the only place where "chikan" was made. According to the embroiderers Ayub Khan and Saliha Khatun, three or four male-run *karkhanas* filling orders directly for patrons were the primary source of chikan work in the first decades of the twentieth century and the places in which chikan in its finest form was developed (see also Chattopadhyaya 1963:44–45). While rooted in the household, *karkhanas* were open to a wider circle of young boys to learn the craft. Both Ayub and Saliha emphasized Daliganj, with two *karkhanas,* as an important production center, notwithstanding that it was, in their words, *dehāt* (country) surrounded by "jungle." Other embroiderers put the figure of *karkhanas* at ten to fifteen, referring to locations in Husainabad, Muftiganj, Musaibganj (near Takkurganj), as well as Daliganj. The number of men employed in the *karkhanas* was not given, although Ayub Khan said that five men had held positions in his grandfather's *karkhana* at the beginning of the century.

Karkhanas were still important when women began to replace men as practitioners at the highest level. Although I did not systematically collect oral histories from embroiderers, it was apparent that many present-day female embroiderers, especially those with high skills, were at least second- and more often third-generation artisans, whose grandmothers and great-grandmothers had been the earliest family members to take up chikan. Among the highly skilled, it was also common for embroidery skills to have originated with male ancestors, then shifted to female ones. Skilled embroiderer Anwar Jahan had a *nānī* (mother's mother) who had learnt from her own husband, the first embroiderer in that family. Hasan Mirza instructed all his daughters in chikan, and their mother had learnt from her own father Ali Nawab. Asiya Khatun, daughter of Saliha Khatun, had learnt from her father, but this is unusual today. The prevalent pattern was that once a female ancestress had learnt the craft, the skill had been passed on thereafter in the female line from mother or _khālā_ (mother's sister) to child.

What exactly provoked this shift is still unknown and can only be discovered through further research. That it coincided with a period of global depression certainly seems suggestive. By the 1930s, boys had stopped taking up the craft in any numbers and the *karkhanas* closed. Ayub Khan described his father's earnings from chikan in the 1930s and 1940s as "low . . . only twenty rupees per month." Ayub's account was seconded by a *mahājan* (lit., "big man," businessman, in this context, chikan manufacturer and shopkeeper) who said that the 1930s was when women entered the workforce in high numbers and shopkeepers flourished. In fact, as early as 1923 there were reports the *karkhana* system had come to an end and that male and female members of a household now formed the core productive unit, the better skilled men acting as agents (Ghosal 1923:22). Men continued to have a stake in the fine work that they still made but had an increasing stake in the work that they gave to female embroiderers.

Lucknow retained its position as a regional capital with Indian independence and the creation of the new state of Uttar Pradesh in 1947. The population of Lucknow, which had been depressed for many decades after the uprising, began to increase again after Independence and the partition of India and Pakistan (Hjortshoj 1979:27). Many Muslims left the city for Pakistan, but substantially more immigrants came from the Punjab and other northwestern states (Mukherjee and Singh 1961). Those who left came largely from the middle and upper classes, stripping the city of a layer of elite consumers whose absence may in part explain Lakhnawis' sense that the city has gone into a decline. Perhaps this was when nearby villages began to give way to the city itself as the only location for "real chikan."

Women were already important producers in the industry before Independence, and by the 1950s they were in the majority. According to chikan embroiderers, *mahajans* and Lakhnawi laymen alike, the history of chikan, particularly since the mid-century, is essentially a story of inexorable decline. No embroiderer that I met denied that the quality of embroidery had declined over the years. Embroiderers, even those who can do exquisite work, all swear that the work is *moṭā* (thick, i.e., crude) today, and that fine work is *khatam* (finished). When I asked about changes in chikan clothes at one shop, the proprietor presented me with a stark contrast. "Look at this," he said, casting down on his left a contemporary lemon yellow *sari*, covered with thick *bakhya* work, and on his right, a muslin *kurtā* (an Indian shirt), embroidered carefully and delicately in *murri*, its stitches strikingly clear and precise, slightly worn in a few places. "This," he said pointing to the *kurta* on his right, "was made only twenty years ago. It was commonplace work then. But now, you can't get it at any price."

Old examples of fine work may be fetched from the shopkeeper's private collection upon request, but they are shown only as items beyond price and without contemporary equal. Without exception, these pieces are delicate, detailed, and are remarkable for a profusion of intricate *jali* work. They may include *saris, kurtas,* and *dupaṭṭās* (shawls) ranging from twenty to fifty years old. But the majority are unfinished *topis* that were used as samples for individual clients to choose the designs they wanted on commissioned work. They are not always as elaborate as the scores of outstanding examples of richly embroidered *topis* that have already found their way into private and museum collections. But the standard of work on these *topis,* even if no more than twenty years old, is far superior to what is considered good quality (if not the very best) *murri* work made today. One prominent *mahajan* said there was no present-day market for these kinds of caps, and a sizeable consignment of old caps that the shops could not sell had been packed up and dispatched for sale in Pakistan in the late 1970s.

In the 1960s, the chikan product range shifted toward *kurtas* and *salwar-qamiz* (women's pants and tunic) and away from *topis* and more elaborately tailored apparel. English goods like table cloths and table linens continue to maintain a foothold in the market, produced either for export or for consumption by upper-class Indians. In the same time, *bakhya* work came to prominence, part of the growing commercialization and cheapening of chikan, and the move away from what *mahajans* refer to as an "artistic industry." Newer *mahajans* came into the business with no background in, or knowledge of, chikan. In the 1960s and 1970s, the numbers of shops began to increase dramatically. Sharma (1959) recorded around twelve dealers in the old city. Today, there are dozens of independent shops all over Lucknow.

Not coincidentally, this has also been a period in which the embroidery stage has been totally feminized. No male embroiderer has ever been associated with producing *bakhya* work. With a fall in the demand for superior *murri* work, men have found their productive skills unrewarding, and have either gravitated toward agent roles, or left the industry altogether. Women now make the best and most expensive, as well as the coarsest and cheapest chikan products. They are both the industry's cheap labor and its master craftspeople, and make up an increasing, if still small, proportion of the agents who subcontract work.

The differences between otherwise coincident stories of decline lie in where the blame is laid. Art critics and connoisseurs of fine chikan have denounced the debased tastes of an India-wide consumer class that craves *bakhya* work. Traders and embroiderers agree that there has been a decline in the discernment (and thus the distinction)[7] of chikan consumers. "There aren't as many people who respect chikan and who know it the way the *nawabs* did," said Rehana Begum. Chikan has become, for visitors to Lucknow, the souvenir *par excellence*. As one *mahajan* said derisively, "It's name [chikan] is now enough for people to buy it" or to quote Rehana Begum again, "Real chikan is dying. Only the name goes on. There's just shadow-work now." Buyers lack interest in, or knowledge of, true embroidery, and they refuse to pay the top price for the very best work, stimulating the craft's decline. Ayub Khan added that even in the cases where people knew what good chikan was, they would not spend the money for it. Refusal to pay good prices for chikan was indicative of the lack of *'izzat* (respect) for the embroiderer.

Lucknow customers for chikan were particularly faulted on this point, whereas Delhi and Bombay markets were supposedly made up of people better able to appreciate (and thus prepared to pay for) good chikan. The nongovernmental organization SEWA Lucknow, whose efforts to assist women by producing chikan under its own banner are discussed in chapter 6, specifically targets the "sophisticated urban consumer." Designer Laila Tyabji, who has worked with SEWA Lucknow, states that *"the fundamental lesson that craftsgroups and voluntary agencies using craft for income generation must learn is that the consumer does not buy out of compassion. A craft product, like any other merchandise, must be competitive in aesthetic, utility and cost"* (Tyabji 1990:2, emphasis in original). The customer she is referring to is essentially the *metropolitan* consumer. The Lucknow sales center for SEWA Lucknow goods is a small room adjacent to the production headquarters, in a part of town little known to middle-class residents. The organization itself admits that it does not anticipate an expansion of the Lucknow market. Instead, the innovative SEWA Lucknow designs are predicated upon the existence and tastes of a consumer who is *not* a Lakhnawi.

Local *mahajans* are also blamed by embroiderers (and officials in the government hierarchy) for the decline of chikan, accused of giving work to whoever will take their paltry wages, regardless of the quality of the results. Most skilled embroiderers try to make a handful of items that they hope to sell direct to customers or to bigger dealers in the major cities, bypassing the Lucknow *mahajans* altogether. A male embroiderer argued that Delhi traders were generous and had *izzat* for chikan. They paid more for the work, and they paid up promptly. He showed me many examples of the kind of work he shipped to Delhi— much of it intended for export, so he said. One was a square piece of cloth, embroidered with four circular patterns, in fine *bakhya* work. "In Delhi, they give sixteen rupees for this, four rupees each piece. *Mahajans* in Lucknow won't give one rupee for it." Of another article, "From Delhi, twenty-five rupees. In Lucknow, they give no more than ten." As embroiderers see it, the Delhi businessman views chikan as an exotic and rare artform. But to the Lucknow shopkeeper, chikan is banal and ubiquitous. Rehana Begum was equivocal about the absence of discerning consumers, but agreed that local shopkeepers simply did not stock good work. "In Chowk, all you'll find is shadow-work. You won't find this work [i.e., fine work] on the market. You may be prepared to spend even one lakh (Rs. 100,000) for a chikan *rūmāl* [a square of cloth] but if it's not available, what's the point? You can't buy good work now."

For their part, local *mahajans* accuse metropolitan "outsiders" of knowing nothing about chikan, and blame them for spurring an export boom in the 1960s and 1970s that jeopardized the livelihoods of other *mahajans* when it deflated. As for the tastes of consumers, *mahajans* from the older businesses say that there are customers interested in fine work but there are no embroiderers capable of it. The embroiderers I met were certainly correct that there was little evidence of *izzat* for the embroiderer in the conversations of *mahajans*. "Today, the talent to do really fine work is lacking. There's no interest in knowing the real, old stitches," said one shopkeeper. Store proprietors insisted on their own appreciation of fine work, but were emphatic that "chikan art is vanishing." Yet the most skilled embroiderers' own existence and continuing productivity attests to the inaccuracy of statements that good chikan work is truly dead, although the circumstances in which such work can be made are indeed constrained.

Critics and *mahajans* alike see a clear connection in the development of an exclusively female workforce and the prevalence of poor-quality work—a connection that is based on false perceptions of female skill. The days when men were the embroiderers are viewed nostalgically. It makes no difference that highly skilled women display equal and sometimes superior talents to those of men. In a classic restatement of how gender stereotypes can influence perceptions of skills, chikan is now defined as women's work and as such, can never be regarded with the respect that is given to men's work (see Phillips and Taylor 1980). In fact, it is not even believed that women can exhibit comparable skills to men. Several *mahajans* even argued that there was no difference between the work of women and the work of children.

Mahajans also complained that embroiderers' manners were undergoing a deterioration comparable to the decline of chikan embroidery itself. Embroiderers were described as rough and uncultured, with no sense of *ta'alluqāt* (good faith, loyalty) or of trust. One shopkeeper was resentful that embroiderers showed him no deference, particularly if they were skilled and had received any recognition for it. Embroiderers, however, were cynical about *mahajans* and refused to express the gratitude that *mahajans* felt they were owed. All the women I knew argued that low wages had preceded other developments in the industry, adding that men simply would not work for the low wages typical of this branch of the industry and had thus left it.

Explanations of decline notwithstanding, at base the production of cheap, coarse chikan serves *mahajans'* economic interests. Competition among *mahajans* is now intense and value is more intensively extracted in the embroidery phase, meaning that more and more low-skilled women are being employed to make *bakhya* work for very low wages. If purchasers have come to regard *bakhya* work as the "authentic" chikan, it is probably as much to do with the fact that is increasingly the *only* kind of chikan that anyone sees.

CHAPTER 2

The Division of Labor

Chikan is made in a multistaged production process of which embroidery forms only a part. The division of labor in chikan is distinct and predictable. Productive specialists in each stage may know very little about specialists in others, but the work of each stage is intimately connected with the work of others, so that change in one invariably affects the others. Every stage of production has been affected by the rise of *bakhya* work, the most apparent changes being a consistent decline in the necessary skill needed to complete it and the sheer increase in the quantity of goods that are being produced. At present, though, many, perhaps most, producers lay claim to some special knowledge and skill that marks them out as craftsmen (or craftswomen) rather than automata in a system of production.

THE PRODUCTION PROCESS

A chikan garment must go through several stages of production before it is finished. Most chikan goods, with the exception of *saris* and table linens, are specially cut and tailored clothes. So first, cloth must be cut into the various pieces that make up a *kurta*, a *salwar-qamiz*, or whatever is to be made. Mastercutters usually work in-house for *mahajans*. The pieces are then taken away to tailors for stitching. Tailors are usually men who work in their houses in the older settlements of the city. They are referred to as *darzīs* but a more frequent usage is *silāi karnewāle* (lit., those who sew).[1] Sewing can be taken up by persons without hereditary roots in tailoring. In almost all cases where I found women tailoring garments, those garments were destined for chikan embroidery. After being returned to the *mahajan*, the garments' next destination is the printer, where they receive the design on which the embroidery will be worked. The clothes come back to the *mahajan* once again and are dispatched to embroiderers. When the embroiderers have completed their work and the garments have come back to the shop, it remains for them to be washed and pressed. Only after the laundry stage is finished do the chikan clothes return to the shop for the final stages of production. Buttonholes are stitched, flaws are repaired, articles are folded up and stacked ready for sale. Although the production process is well defined, there is relatively little information about the artisans who populate its stages.

When *mahajans* describe the production process, they refer to cloth purchase and marketing as though they were equivalent to the work done by artisans in the stages in between, although it is clear they are not value-creating activities.[2] Work within the production process is carried out in socially distinct settings, including the artisan's own homes, shops and shopfronts, workshops and semipublic areas of the city, including the riverbank. The chikan industry is not at all centralized. Many of these settings are at some distance from the others.

Each set of specialists has been to some degree affected by progressive deskilling in key phases of production, associated with the rise of *bakhya* work. In most cases, the specialists who make chikan have occupations that were part of a precapitalist division of labor based on caste (see Goody 1982:5). When the labors and products of separate specialists must be coordinated in order to create the final commodity, a functional division of labor can be said to exist (ibid.:2). The entire process may be organized by a third party, the holder of capital, who provides the material to be worked on at each stage and makes a profit by selling finished products for more than the cost of production.

But chikan production, organized by the *mahajan*, is not exactly like this. In fact, it corresponds better to Marx's (1977:457, 464) description of early manufacture. Now that *bakhya* work, with its formulaic, stripped-down designs has become the dominant form of chikan, there has been a concomitant simplification in the tailoring, the printing, and even the laundering required. Young men and women with little previous experience, still less a hereditary background in embroidery-related occupations, now can take jobs in the various stages of chikan production. Artisans finish their tasks in each stage quicker than when they are working on a piece destined to be *murri* work. Putting thousands of specialized workers to work simultaneously has made it possible to turn out garments on a mass scale. The various makers of what ultimately becomes chikan are formally interdependent, in that their jobs can only be done as and when workers in the stage prior to theirs complete their own. They do not do any other kind of work that could provide them with a living. The printer only prints chikan cloth. Tailors do not sew garments for a client to wear, but make articles destined for further modification as chikan clothes. Washermen do not wash the soiled clothing of ordinary clients but devote their entire effort to washing chikan. Chikan embroiderers and almost all other specialists who contribute to the final form of chikan goods work to order for the *mahajan* and are paid piece wages. While they do not have any claim to the chikan product, they do own their own tools; print blocks, needles, washing materials, and so forth. There have been, as yet, no efforts to collect labor together into factories, or to rationalize production in other ways.

KNOWLEDGE AND THE DIVISION OF LABOR

Howard Becker's (1982) concept of "art worlds" connects knowledge with cooperation between categories of artists and artisans. Becker takes as his starting point the division of labor, but sees it primarily in terms of the conventions that characterize its social and aesthetic articulation. To Becker, therefore, "division of labor" refers to cooperative clusters in the wider social division of labor that straddle class, including producers and nonproducers like audiences, critics, or past practitioners of artistic activity who together provide a sociocultural context for the comprehension of art. Becker's basic point is that all forms of art are fundamentally constrained by the conventions that bind art worlds. The artist is not free to produce whatever he/she wants, either because of the force of conventions governing what art is thought to be, or because of the compelling agendas and defendable activities of the other occupants of the art world (and the former is essentially a product of the latter).

Routines and conventions structure a social network of producers and artists, creating "patterns of collective activity" that are involved in the production, reception, and appreciation of art. An art world is an "established network of co-operative links among participants," which at some juncture features someone who is acknowledged as the artist (ibid.:34). Not all activities are considered equal, in that some are considered quintessentially "artistic" while others are the domain of mere "support personnel." Yet all activities are necessary if the art object or performance is to take its place in social life.

If we turn to the art world of chikan production, we find that producers have more or less clear ideas of the skill and technical-aesthetic qualities of their craft that are to some extent in competition with the abilities of (generally unknown) others in different stages. Their knowledge is equivalent to what Stephen Marglin (1990) terms "techne"—the tacit "knowing" that all craft producers possess. Producers implicitly reveal the ways that change has affected the work of each stage in what they have to say about themselves, and about each other.

One important, shared belief of many specialists is that design—of the printing block pattern, the print, or the configuration of embroidery stitches—issues "from the mind" (*dimāg/man se*). The fewer the actions that come between mental inspiration and its material effect, the greater the accomplishment of the artisan. Inspiration and effect are regarded as essentially simultaneous. Thus, the blockmaker's mental design takes shape under the chisel, the printer stamps the cloth without apparent forethought, and the greatest embroiderers can embroider without a print at all. Assertions of creative autonomy in each stage consistently appeal to the origin of designs "in the mind," that is, "*my* mind," and continue to be heard even as deskilling proceeds and as *mahajans* begin to claim creative as well as organizational preeminence.

PRODUCTIVE SPECIALTIES

Print Blockmakers

Print blockmakers (known as *ṭhappākars*) are not integrated into the process of chikan production and have no relationship with the *mahajan*. They deal only with printers, and possibly embroiderers who come to them to purchase blocks. The blockmaker is thus a rather different economic character from others who populate the world of chikan. He is an independent craftsman who does not work for a capitalist (Marx 1977:463). His products are commodities and are directly exchanged, under his supervision. His work is an end in itself and not a stage of a production process. It is difficult to gauge how many blockmakers are still working in Lucknow. Printers refer to only two or three blockmakers in Takkurganj and Musaibganj when asked where they purchase their blocks. Another is said to live in Khaddra.

Mushtaq Ali is a second-generation blockmaker who lives in Musaibganj. His father, Ahmad Ali, was the first to learn the craft of blockmaking in his family. Ahmad Ali's own father (Mushtaq Ali's grandfather) was a chikan embroiderer. Using a word I came to know well, Ahmad Ali said that even as a child, his "*shauq*" (love, interest) was for the blocks rather than the embroidery itself and he asked to be apprenticed to a blockmaker. He learnt the craft from a man named Abdul Hamid, and in turn his son learnt from him. Ahmad Ali no longer makes blocks owing to his poor eyesight.

Without hesitation, Ahmad Ali said his designs had come *dimag se* (from the mind). Mushtaq Ali said the same thing, adding that he drew his designs immediately onto the prepared surface of the wood, without sketching them on paper first. Blocks are made out of *sal* wood (also known as *sisam*, botanical name *Dalbergia sisso* [Wealth of India 1952:7–8]). The blockmaker cuts the block to size, and paints it with emulsion before carving it with a hammer and chisel (Paine 1989:46). At least one skilled embroiderer and a *daraz* (appliqué often found with chikan) maker insisted the blockmaker was no more than a workman who made blocks according to their design and specifications. Mushtaq Ali, for his part, admitted that a few people come to him with their own designs but that this was rare. He professed not to know any embroiderers but dealt exclusively with printers who came to order and buy his blocks. When he demonstrated his work, he set to on a block that was obviously not for chikan. Mushtaq Ali's work is in fact more diverse, and although he makes many more chikan blocks than anything else, he also makes blocks for cloth printing, including designs that can replicate tie-and-dye effects.

As the chikan market has shifted heavily toward *bakhya* production, so the nature of the blocks used in printing has changed. Old blocks, besides being dustier and deeply dyed, have wholly different contours from those made more recently. The raised edges to which the ink adheres are more densely arranged on the block, in patterns that embroiderers immediately identify as specific to *murri* stitches. New blocks have large leaf motifs that are distributed more openly over the block surface. Large blocks with animal motifs and elaborate patterns also seem to belong to the older set. Ahmad Ali confirmed that block designs had fundamentally changed in his lifetime. Old blocks were *māhīn* (fine) but demand in the present day was primarily for *mota* (thick) blocks featuring designs that lent themselves to *bakhya*, rather than *māhīn ṭankā* (fine stitches).

Is the blockmaker the premier "designer" in the chikan production process, since it is his carving, reproduced as a print, upon which the embroiderer works? While Mushtaq Ali denied that embroiderers ever approached him to make *their* designs, he did not specifically claim that he was the creative pivot of chikan. The connection of blocks to chikan is well understood, but I did not gain any sense of the blockmaker's conceiving of his "design" growing beyond the completion of the block itself. Meanwhile, a small, emergent, elite market in blocks as completely aesthetized objects further separates blockmaking, as an independent artisanal activity, from the process of chikan production.

Printers

Fabric printing is a craft of long standing in the Lucknow area (Saraf 1982:200). Chikan printers made up one of three divisions of printers in the United Provinces in the late nineteenth century (Crooke 1896). Of the printers I met or was told about, not one did anything other than chikan printing. All were Muslim men. The number of chikan printers had increased significantly, even in the few years preceding my fieldwork.

A number of printers operate in small shopfront/workrooms clustered around Chowk Bazaar. They were all young or middle-aged men.

Printing is the quickest stage of production, owing to the speed at which it is accomplished and the fact that no preparatory or finishing techniques need be done on the cloth to complete the work. The printer's speed comes from the store of tacit knowledge of spatial design he possesses after years of experience (see Bunzel 1928; Polanyi 1967; Marglin 1990). Printers rarely seem to pause for reflection as they work. Echoing the blockmaker, printers said that designs came from their minds in the very act of printing.

Some print designs are set by convention. For example, on a *kurta* (the most common item) a narrow block, about three to four inches long, is used to make two stamps forming a tapered point at the bottom of the placket, then two vertical stamps are made on either side. A *kurta* can be finished in a matter of seconds. Consequently, a single printer can claim to be able to complete a couple of hundred *kurtas* a day. *Saris* and table linens require more ingenuity and a good grasp of spatial organi-

FIG. 2.1. Print blocks.

zation. They take more time to do but the wage rate per piece is higher.

All the printers talked in terms of a working day (giving the hours at which they commenced and finished work), although I did not make the kinds of observations that would lead me to conclude that they did indeed work a consistent set of hours on a daily basis. I was quoted a variety of wage rates for printing work, the lowest wages going to the youngest and most inexperienced practitioners of the craft. For example, where older, established printers (one working for over thirty years) quoted rates of up to 25 paise for a *kurta*, a youthful printer of only a couple of years experience was only paid between 10 and 15 paise for the same work. For a larger amount of work on a different kind of garment, the maximum rate quoted by the same young printer was Rs. 1. On the other hand, older printers with many years of experience said they could get up to Rs. 1.50 for a *salwar-qamiz*, or from Rs. 4 to Rs. 10 for *saris*, the higher rate being reserved for *saris* with *pallū* (portion of *sari* worn over the shoulder) designs.

The young printer's low wages reflected both his relative lack of skill and the less complex, quicker work he was expected to do. When superior printing skills are not needed, *mahajans* are strongly inclined to shift printing work to young practitioners and away from older ones who demand higher piece rates. The young printer got orders for work on *kurtas* destined for *bakhya* work practically to the exclusion of all other types. He lacked, therefore, the necessary training and experience to do more complex jobs. More experienced printers do a wider variety of work (including printing *saris* and table linens) and can make variations upon standard patterns. For these kinds of work, they expect, and appear to get, higher piece rates. However, skilled printers may not be able to maintain their higher wages per piece for straightforward *kurta* printing as newcomers accept lower rates. For skilled printers, then, further homogenization and simplification of chikan clothes, and the related downgrading of skills in both printing *and* embroidery, represent a distinct threat. Even among the young printers, competition for the cheapest and simplest kind of work has intensified.

Besides the *mahajans*, government development schemes and embroiderers also use the printer's services. The wages for printing garments for the government development schemes are believed by many printers to be better, but an actual government contractee said they were only fractionally higher, although he declined to name figures. Embroiderers may also approach the printer to do a design specifically for them, although several printers flatly denied such a thing occurred. In these instances, embroiderers told me, the cost is higher than the rate per piece paid by the *mahajan*. For example, a *kurta* may cost an embroiderer Rs. 1.50 to have printed. I paid Rs. 20 for printing the piece used to teach me embroidery, a figure I am sure had been adjusted in accordance with my relative wealth. It is not difficult to believe, though, that embroiderers are forced to pay more for a small printing job than a *mahajan* who has greater leverage over the printer and can give mass orders. An embroiderer may also be expected to pay more for a printer to take the time to make a complex, customized print.

Printing is usually segregated from the productive and organizational operations of the *mahajan*. However, one printer occupied a workshop adjacent to his younger brother's own chikan shop. His grandfather was the first printer in the family, and the trade had passed from father to son ever since. Of the printers I met, only this individual claimed it was his traditional occupation, and that he had been printing since he was a child—all the others had taken it up in young manhood.

My questions about how the business had expanded and diversified to include chikan production were not adequately answered. But it seemed to me that it was more likely for a printer to have expanded his enterprise to include the activities of a shopkeeper/manufacturer with agency as an intermediate stage (since I heard of least two other printers who had done this), rather than shopkeepers' acquiring the means of printing as a step toward greater direct control of the production process.

I encountered one other case where printing had provided a starting point for further occupational diversification. A family of printers a few steps off Chowk Bazaar had a workshop behind the main printing area, where machine buttonholing and embroidering were done. The cooperative labor of related men had permitted them to diversify their productive activities. Their involvement in machine embroidery, a recent introduction, showed their awareness of and ability to exploit a new trend in chikan.

Besides the possible combination of printing and entrepreneurial activities, printers may have female relatives who do embroidery. No printer I met had a wife currently working at the embroidery, although some *mahajans* volunteered printing as a possible occupation of embroiderers' husbands. One printer said his wife had once specialized in *jali*, but had given it up when the family's fortunes improved. In any case, husband and wife will not work in the same space, given that the semipublic nature of a printer's workshop makes it an inappropriate workplace for a woman. Nor can they work in any sense cooperatively, since his work proceeds at a much faster rate than hers. My conclusion is that in this, as in most other functions to do with chikan, producers are largely socially and spatially separated.

Printers work alone on one garment at a time. Printing is done with one, or several wooden blocks. A block is pressed onto a dye-soaked cloth wad in a tin of dye, then rolled swiftly on the cloth (see also Paine 1989:49). There are two kinds of dye, one blue (*nīl*) and one pink (*gulābī*). I was unable to find a printer, young or old, who could describe for me the ingredients of the two dyes, implying that this kind of knowledge is unimportant to printers' own practice.

The pink dye is much harder to remove from cloth than the blue dye. Pink is conventionally used on cottons, from which it can only be removed by protracted boiling. Blue is used on synthetics, for which it seems to have been specifically developed. Blue comes out easily in water and is thus better suited for fabrics that cannot undergo the rigorous bleaching and boiling to which cotton is subjected. In practice, blue dye is now found on cotton as well as synthetics, but the association between pink dye and cotton cloth is a compelling one to those involved in chikan. Skilled embroiderers prefer to work on cotton and choose pink dye because it stands up better to the repeated handling that complex embroidery entails. Blue dye is *kamzor* (weak). It dissolves readily in water and fades rapidly on elaborately printed cotton. Because pink dye is used on the kind of material used traditionally for fine chikan embroidery, it has a higher status than blue dye. With the diminution of the skill and amount of work needed for mass-market items, pink dye is beginning to lose its raison d'être. On a simple *kurta*, the work is scant enough that a hardy dye is not required.

Printers recognize a clear difference between blocks for *bakhya* and blocks for *murri*. They also distinguish between *bārīk* (thin) blocks and *mota* blocks. This contrast can also be expressed with the opposed terms *mahin* and *mota*, in which case a distinction between subtle and coarse is intended. Good printing requires sharply defined edges and ridges on the block. Blocks that have outlived their usefulness have had their lines somewhat blunted by age and use, and to transfer intricate and dense designs to cloth requires a more distinct, thus *barik* line. But the difference between *barik* and *mota* is not at its root one between newly made and used blocks. Instead, printers recognize the same differences between *mahin* and *mota* blocks that blockmakers do. One printer did indeed say that the difference between new and old blocks was simply one of repair and disrepair. But after some reflection, he added that the blocks that are made today are for *moṭā kām* (coarse work), whereas blocks from the past had designs for thin, shorter stitches. Thus, whatever their physical state, old blocks are quintessentially *barik* and *mahin*, while new ones, designed with *bakhya* in mind, are *mota*.

Two printers seated in their workshop against racks filled with old, dusty blocks, pulled two or three currently unused blocks from this collection to show me, saying that the people who made these were "*khatam*" (finished, dead). In theory, the blocks are still usable. That they were not being used implies a dwindling requirement for them, as opposed to their being unfit for the purposes of printing. At the same time, truly worn-out blocks for fine-lined *murri* work are not being replaced at the same rate—nor to the same level of excellence—as thick-lined, *bakhya* blocks.

Printers said they chose the blocks and created the subsequent design. They conceded that the *mahajan* sometimes told them what he wanted, indicating, for example, whether he wanted a *bakhya* design or a *murri* design, or even choosing the blocks he wanted used. But print-ers never admitted to having the design minutely directed. Most *maha-jans* claimed instead that it was they who directed the design, by choos-ing the blocks to be used as well as telling the printer where to place them. *Mahajans* wished to emphasize their own control and direction of the clothes' designs, and in so doing, relegate the printer from craftsman to mere technician. Some *mahajans* are explicit in stating this view, arguing that a piece with a careful print of the printer's own design will cost them as much, if not more than, an item printed more quickly with a standard design.

This disavowal of the printer's own skill is surely related to the increasingly minimal demands placed upon the printer by *bakhya*-style chikan. And yet no printer conceded that rates of pay differed accord-ing to who was believed to have originated the design. Instead, almost all insisted on their own creative autonomy—their designs coming from their own minds.

The embroiderer is another specialist who competes with the printer over whose skill and judgment is most important in producing a piece of chikan work. One of the first clues to their differences came in con-trasting remarks about flaws in the print. Printers do not seem to be con-cerned about smudging and faintness of the printed lines. Asked if these irregularities would cause problems for the embroiderers, one printer responded that it scarcely mattered, since chikan embroidery was *ćālū* (commonplace) *kām*. In essence, the printer was disparaging the petty skills of embroiderers whose work conforms so modestly to the print that they simply plow on through obscured areas. Embroiderers, on the other hand, stress that it is only because they possess a high level of skill that they can make up for shortcomings in the print.

In fact, even less-skilled embroiderers contend that their work involves a creative engagement of the printed pattern, smudged or oth-erwise, that is unacknowledged by the printer. Failure to work sensi-tively with the print was regarded with humor and scorn, as when mod-erately skilled urban dwellers scoffed at village women's tendency to follow a print literally, even if that meant embroidering the manufac-turer's stamp on the edge of the fabric. City women's jibes aside, however, village women may take the same view of the print as their urban counterparts. In the nearby village of Kasmandi Kalan, an embroiderer said that she and other village craftswomen were often called upon to do *dandī dār phandā*, a stitch requiring the execution of a knot upon a stalk, or stick, over a pattern which showed only a series of circles. This adjustment, they said, was a common one, which they knew well.

At first, I thought these disagreements between printer and embroiderer stemmed from a contrast between print-as-design and print-as-guide, where the printer sees the print as a unique aesthetic product that the embroiderer takes only to be a template for the creation of her own, embroidered designs. For the printer, the variability that issues from printing is a technical modulation that does not impinge in a fundamental way on his own, unique design. The embroiderer on the other hand, must muster additional resources of skill when what she sees as the minimal requirements of a print are unmet. However, only the least-skilled embroiderers seem to be uninterested in the print as design, seeing it as a pattern or model only. The highly skilled are supremely conscious of the design that a print represents, but strive to claim the motivation and vision behind the design for themselves, saying it comes from *their* minds. Some dismiss the printer completely from the process of making truly fine work, claiming that they get blocks made and print the fabric themselves.

Merchant/Shopkeepers

The men (there were no female *mahajans* to my knowledge) who finance and coordinate the production of chikan are far from invisible, and occupy shops in public, market areas all over the city. Merchants have very little to do with the actual way in which the various stages of work are done and their authority over all the laborers engaged in making chikan is quite limited. On the other hand, the decentralized nature of chikan production is fundamental to the survival and success of Lucknow chikan businesses.

While Chowk and its adjacent streets are centers of production, as well as of wholesale and retail activities, chikan retail shops can be found in almost all major bazaars. They appear in Hazratganj along the main thoroughfare and an adjacent shopping center called Janpath, and in Aminabad and surrounding areas, including Mohan Market and Nazirabad. There are outlets in places like Nishatganj on the north of the river, Murli Nagar on the Cantonment Road, and in markets off the main road leading to the Main Railway Station in Charbagh to name but a few. Some of these are more like "showrooms" attached to storage and organizational centers located off the main street. Others are exclusively retail branches of a business whose organizational center is elsewhere.

Some *mahajan* families have been involved in the chikan industry since the beginning of the century, and in some cases, over a hundred years. At the other end of the spectrum, some businesses have been functioning for only five to ten years, others even less. Chikan manufacture is usually a family business, with perhaps adult brothers acting under the authority of their father or uncle. Even sons-in-law may be drawn into a business. Partition of the business often follows upon the death of the senior relative in the business. The majority of *mahajans* are of the Rastogi subcaste, whose traditional occupation is moneylending. Many Rastogis still occupy enclaved neighborhoods of the city. Although *mahajans* are an important source of credit for the craftspeople they employ, they were reluctant to acknowledge this role. So strong is the association of Rastogis with chikan sale and manufacture that *mahajans* are often called by craftspeople and Lucknow denizens in general as simply "Rastogis" without further elaboration. Many chikan enterprises were started only twenty years ago, at a time when Sahai (1973) noted a general pattern of diversification in Rastogi enterprise. New educational and occupational opportunities have drawn members of the community into technical and professional jobs in other areas of the city. Young men with formal business training have also brought specialized talents into the chikan industry. *Mahajans* agree that the rapid pace of change in commercial chikan production is best understood and managed by young men with "modern" business skills.

The shop is a center both of productive organization and of sales. But many businesses are started in homes and continue to operate out of them. Merchants may then supply chikan directly to traders outside the city. If they open a shop later, many aspects of productive organization are retained at home, at least at first. The longer a shop has been established, the more likely that organizational functions have shifted there. While one store is common, some manufacturers have up to two or three in different parts of town. Successful family businesses may have a number of stores, although some "chains" actually represent separate businesses, the results of tense family partitions.

A careful distinction needs to be drawn between export meaning "outside Lucknow," and export out of the country. Overseas export is much touted in both the literature and in some *mahajans'* rhetoric. However, demand for chikan inside Indian is high, and *mahajans* have enough to do competing over this internal market. Where *mahajans* are involved in overseas export, it is usually as suppliers of goods to Delhi and Bombay merchants who dispatch them out of the country. Wholesalers also mail goods to secondary outlets throughout North and South

India (at a rate of Rs. 8 per kilo in 1989) or via visiting retailers who buy in bulk. I observed one transaction of the latter kind in which the retailer, over several hours, picked out goods whose total worth was around Rs. 20,000. Family networks may also be used to establish chains of retail shops in major urban centers throughout India.

On the whole, Lucknow *mahajans* largely confine their productive and marketing operations to the city. The profusion of shops in Lucknow caters to a steady, yearlong stream of visiting and local consumers. Out-of-towners are brought to stores by various means: rickshaw pullers bring in customers for a small fee and may carry the name of a particular store in the back of their vehicle; or business cards and adverts are distributed among touring or business groups. These are important strategies for the owners of the "showroom"-type shops, who might otherwise be bypassed for the more visible stores in the main shopping districts.

A small number of shopkeeper/merchants are Muslim, although chikan production is regarded by the artisans, and also by these same Muslim traders, as a principally Hindu (and the *only* Hindu) domain within chikan. Embroiderers would only admit that there were Muslim merchants when pressed, and only *"do, cār—bas,"* ("two, four—that's all") at that. There are certainly more than four Muslim merchants, although I do not know exactly how many. One Muslim merchant estimated that Muslims made up about 10 percent of all *mahajans*.

The corresponding conviction that production, specifically embroidery, is a Muslim category, was acknowledged by most producers, Lucknow denizens in general, and most *mahajans*, irrespective of whether they were Hindu or Muslim. Hindu *mahajans* might equivocate for a moment or two over the Muslim character of the craft, drawing attention to its supposed intercommunal and intercaste features today. However, this attitude was rarely sustained throughout the conversation, and ultimately they would return to talking about their workers as "Muslim ladies."

While Muslim *mahajans* do not differ in terms of their role in production from Hindus, their anomalous position (as Muslims in a "Hindu" role) sometimes led to the expression of a slightly different set of opinions about chikan. This might be couched in terms of accentuating, and disparaging, the strong association of Hindu *mahajans* with commerce. For example, one Muslim merchant's account of the history of chikan went that while Muslims had everywhere brought craft and industry to India, Hindu moneylenders had emerged to dominate them and their work. Another observed that while his children would be educated and given a free choice of occupation, "Rastogis and Agrawals" always directed their children to study commercial subjects. These kinds of statements were often followed by comments about the lack of knowledge and sensitivity of Hindu *mahajans* to culture, which was explicitly or implicitly meant to be Muslim. A Muslim manufacturer who operated out of his home belittled "those Lalas, those Rastogis . . . they don't know about the history [of chikan]."

Another Muslim shopkeeper with a twenty-year-old chikan enterprise complained that manners and culture had declined in Lucknow. He attributed this decline to a spatial and metaphorical "constriction" of Muslim life. Punjabi and Sindhi refugees in the post-Independence period who opened shops in the crowded Mohan Market were, in his opinion, ignorant about indigenous Muslim culture and too complacent to help regenerate it. They too had hemmed Muslims in, depriving them of the space and air (*hawāī*) needed for their culture to flourish.

The older the chikan business, the greater the claims to knowledge of its proprietors. They usually have elaborate, treasured chikan pieces and they can recite accounts of chikan's origins, and of the earliest relationships between their ancestors and chikan embroiderers. Most are able to articulate some judgments about what makes certain kinds of chikan good and some bad, and most can produce items to demonstrate their arguments about changes in taste and embroidery quality. Those *mahajans* who have been in the business the longest are most familiar with what goes on at each stage of production. Old manufacturers also stress their close, paternalistic relations with producers, remarking that neither do they exact penalties over spoilt or late work like newer *mahajans*, nor do they hold back wages. Whether these latter statements are true or not, the implied empathy with embroiderers seems to reflect business roots in agent activity, which would have entailed direct relationships with producers, at least in the past.

On the other hand, the relative newcomers who largely sell village-made *bakhya* are sometimes barefaced about their ignorance of certain stages of production, specifically what happens to the clothes, or who works on them, once they have left the shop. A young man working for his older brother in a shop selling nothing but *bakhya* goods appeared unaware that most embroiderers were women. Others confessed complete ignorance of the circumstances of village production, and of how much embroiderers received of the wages they gave their agents. They seemed to have had no experience as agents.

As the examples of newer businesses seem to imply, being an agent is not a necessary pathway to becoming a *mahajan*. These days it is sufficient to have capital, and to know other agents. In fact, with more agents becoming involved in chikan, it appears that it will become harder in future for any of them to acquire the financial means to propel themselves into the ranks of the *mahajans*.

Mahajans do not directly supervise the production process. Only a few procedures are carried out in the shop, including cutting, finishing, and sizing. In general, specialists are left to do the work unsupervised, and the small scale of these tasks, which are entrusted to a small number of individuals (in the case of finishing, two or three women) who work on their own, makes it impossible to call the shop either a workshop or a factory.

Mahajans see their aesthetic contribution as controlling design and selecting product ranges. One young man employed in his brother-in-law's business said he adapted designs from catalogs and movies. However, even the most active manufacturers cannot assert their creative authority beyond the very earliest stages of production. *Mahajans* are directly responsible for selecting and acquiring cloth, and possibly, though not necessarily, supplying thread. They can specify exactly the kinds of articles they would like cut and tailored. Once the garment reaches the printer, however, the *mahajan's* ability to control creative decisions is lost. *Mahajans* may claim to take an active interest in the choice and layout of print designs but, in practice, they probably do not. In turn, the embroiderer, with whom the *mahajan* has minimal contact, looks to predictable qualities of the printed pattern to suggest the range of stitches to be used. The agent cannot have much to say to the embroiderer on the *mahajan's* behalf, since most stitches used in commercial work are easy to make and largely repetitive.

Yet, as with printing, *mahajans* often claim a continuous and untrammelled control over *all* creative decisions throughout the production process. *Mahajans* seek to wrest aesthetic responsibility for the product from the artisans who make it, primarily the embroiderers. Yet this assertion of creative control (and concomitant reduction of artisans to technicians) occurs side by side with the manufacturer's *lack* of direct control over the circumstances of household production.

Most producers are linked to several different *mahajans*, either in sequence or at the same time. *Mahajans* do not have direct contact with embroiderers, dealing with them instead through agents. *Mahajans* who deal only with male agents are those who have the minimum of work performed in the city, if at all, while those who get work done inside Lucknow see female agents/producers also. *Mahajans* do not seem to take the initiative in finding either agents or embroiderers. Agent connections are acquired informally, through the introduction of a potential agent by another. *Mahajans* put great store in references for potential agents from workers already known to them and they like to know something about the would-be agent's family background. An agent's trustworthiness can also be vouchsafed by fellow *mahajans*. Agents, the *mal* (goods) they have been given, and payments that have been made, are all noted in ledgers. Few written contracts (if any) are made between shopkeeper and producer in any stage of the industry.

The number of agents a *mahajan* works with varies according to the size of his enterprise and the range of goods he gets made. One manufacturer whose products were restricted to village *bakhya* used the services of twenty to twenty-five agents, each working a single village. Another who got work done both inside and outside Lucknow, employed only five or six agents for the village work and one to distribute *jali* and *hatkatti* (subsumed under *jali*) work in the city. At the upper end, large enterprises might have dozens of agents carrying work to and fro, a large proportion of them urban women collecting *jali* and *murri* work on their own or others' behalf. A proprietor of an old store in Chowk estimated he had two hundred male and female agents working for him. This figure seems so high compared to others that if it is not an exaggeration, it can only be explained by reference to the rise of female agents, who operate on a much smaller scale than their male counterparts.

It is difficult to figure how much a *mahajan* spends to get chikan work produced. The single biggest expenditure is for cloth. A manufacturer might, for example, purchase one and a half meters of cloth for a *kurta* at Rs. 20 per meter. His total investment in cloth would be Rs. 3,000 for sufficient cloth for 100 *kurtas*. He may pay Rs. 350 for cutting, sewing, and printing altogether. Before embroidery, the investment of the *mahajan* would be around Rs. 3,350. He will spend about Rs. 1 to Rs. 2 per item on embroidery (most of this going to the agent), adding up to Rs. 200 altogether. Added to this would be Rs. 250 for washing and no more than Rs. 200 for finishing. The total investment at this point would be Rs. 4,000.

The above estimate applies only to the most common items and is probably on the high side. However, *mahajans* also carry a limited stock of goods, often *saris*, that are very expensive in comparison, up to Rs. 1,000 in some cases—although the prices quoted to me were probably upwardly adjusted because of my being a foreigner. While the cloth in these items is always superior, and therefore costs the *mahajan* more than the cloth he would usually buy, it is the payment to the embroiderer that is much larger than the norm. Wages rise into the hundreds of rupees and the *mahajan* must be prepared to pay more if he wants better-quality work. But customers for these kinds of products are few and so not many are made. I was unable to find a woman who was working on an item like this for a *mahajan*, and so I cannot confirm the payment quoted. *Mahajans* claimed to be making on average a 10 percent profit. Prices in stores varied according to several factors, such as the location of the shop in a wholesale, retail, or upscale retail area, and other costs that the *mahajan* must take into account but which I was unable to measure (for example, rent, utilities, and so forth).

The amount of capital needed for chikan production is modest compared to what businesses with machinery, factory space, and so on demand. Instead, the *mahajan* contributes capital and waits until the final product is sold to realize his profit. The *mahajan's* chief initial investment is in cloth. The better the cloth the heavier the investment (for example, ranging from Rs. 20/meter to Rs. 45/meter). In a race to get a return on his investment, a *mahajan* would presumably favor the production of *bakhya salwar-kamizes* and *kurtas* (the fastest items to print and embroider as well as the items that draw the lowest wages) in synthetic or synthetic-mix materials (the quickest and cheapest to launder). And indeed, these kinds of items are increasingly prevalent in the chikan market. Older shops carry larger stocks of table linens and all kinds of *murri* work on cotton, the most time-consuming products to make. A *sari* from one of these stores may take up to six months to complete, from the time of cloth purchase to laundering and folding. However, these older shops rely strongly on name recognition and a reputation for quality (for which they charge high prices) to sustain a market for these products.

The entire production time for even the simplest items ranges from just under one month to one and a half months. This period is markedly lengthened in the rainy season, when the washing stage takes much more time. At other times of year, delivery of items at several stages can be delayed by marriages, as well as miscellaneous family misfortunes and ill-health among artisans. Surprisingly, specific Muslim festivals and observances were never cited as presenting obstacles to the *mahajan's* business—not even the Muslim holy month of Ramadan, when observation of *roza* (fasting) might be expected to limit artisans' productivity.

Of all the stages of production, the embroidery stage takes the longest and causes the most worry to the *mahajan*. The cloth is never so far away, and for so long, as in this stage, and items are usually returned in a piecemeal fashion, as and when they are completed. Some articles never come back at all. One prominent *mahajan* complained that if an agent were to say that a whole batch of embroideries had been destroyed there would be no way to refute him. *Mahajans* also expressed concern over the amount of poor-quality embroidery that they were saddled with, although the complaint over quality is moot, since *mahajans* freely admitted that chikan work of highly variable quality can be sold to undiscriminating customers without great difficulty. Interestingly, the washing stage, which is the most ostensibly tricky and potentially destructive stage, was never acknowledged as a difficult one by *mahajans*.

Mahajans do not seem to have made extraordinary efforts to speed up the embroidery stage. They frankly term embroidery a household task that is subordinated to domestic work—a kind of "free-time" activity that is neither a priority for women nor a "real" occupation. While *mahajans* in the older stores were more likely to stress their paternalistic relationships with embroiderers, stating that embroidery was a good way for poor women to get some extra money for the household, the proprietors of newer businesses were evidently less sympathetic. One went so far as to say that the embroiderer had an easy job compared to the *mahajan*. "They just sit around and they get work, and they get money. All in their spare time! I'm the one with all the headaches."

Not interfering in the production process and maintaining the agent system instead is, however, advantageous to the *mahajan*. He incurs no long-term obligations to his employees and he can leave much of the responsibility for managing labor to his agent. *Mahajans*, particularly ones who have entered lately into chikan production and are beginning the process of accumulation, are unwilling or unable to invest in the fixed costs of workspace, equipment, and labor of the "typical" capitalist enterprise. A workforce to which the *mahajan* has no fixed contractual obligations beyond the paternalistic duties he takes upon himself voluntarily and which bind workers to him more effectively, is easier to deal with than a collectivized and organized one.

The most recurrent complaint of *mahajans* during my fieldwork was about the intensification of competition among all the newly opened businesses in Lucknow. Several *mahajans* complained of a shrinking profit margin, from 10 percent to only 3 or 4 percent. With the cost of cloth on the rise, some feared they might not survive. *Mahajan* after *mahajan* also complained of a shortage of embroiderers. This cannot reflect any direct experience of the labor market, since mahajans do not recruit directly from among embroiderers. Rather, this illustrates the limitations of a system in which the *mahajan* depends upon agents and in which labor can be tapped only indirectly. Interestingly enough, while there is no doubt the *mahajan* is eager for products, he is not so eager that he is willing to pay substantially higher wages to procure them. What *mahajans* mean when they complain of labor shortages is that there can sometimes be a shortage of labor at the prices they are willing to pay. The industry is at an interesting point of development where the potential and implications of the shift toward rural production are just beginning to be realized.

Agents

The overwhelming majority (maybe as many as three quarters) of chikan embroiderers do not deal directly with manufacturers and probably do not know for whom they are working. Instead they collect their work and their wages from agents of some kind. In order to access the rural labor pool, *mahajans* must rely upon agents. Some *mahajans*, but not all, refer to male agents as *ṭhekedārs*, and *bīć-wāle* (go-betweens) is also a term that recurs with some frequency. Otherwise agents are simply known by name and not given a collective term. The expansion of chikan embroidery to include secluded women in rural areas could not occur unless there were agents to traverse the physical and social space between *mahajan* and embroiderer.

Marx (1977:695) described two kinds of subcontracting systems in which piece wages prevail, or what he calls "hierarchically organized systems of exploitation and oppression." In the first, an agent comes between capitalist and laborer, which is what happens when men act as intermediaries in chikan production. In the other system, a worker is contracted to supply work to others, as it is with female agents. In both cases, agents extract a profit from the difference between the price of labor, and what the worker actually receives.

Mahajans were reluctant to arrange introductions—and in any case, agents do not stop long inside the doors of the chikan shop, nor can their visits be anticipated with any accuracy. My meetings with agents were thus a matter of luck, as when, for example, I came across one or two who happened to be waiting for goods at a shop (and on these occasions I was prevented from asking a lot of questions by the presence of the shopkeeper), and another spending time with his friend, a printer. It was as hard for embroiderers to say exactly where a given agent was to be found as it would have been for *mahajans* had they wanted to give me the information. Wherever male agents were heads and members of embroiderers' households, they were usually out of the house when I called, "carrying on their business." It is probably true that the male agent's activities are more an appearance of "busy-ness" than genuine "business," the more so because what they do is so simple and essentially unproductive. However, as the means of bringing together the home-based embroiderers and the *mahajan*, their significance is immense.

Discussing "jobbers" of the colonial Bombay textile industry, Kooiman (1983) points out some of the practical advantages to capitalists of intermediaries as the recruiters and overseers of labor. The formal employment relationship between the holder of capital and the laborer is effected and sustained between agent (or jobber) and worker. Exploiting kin and neighborhood relationships, intermediaries locate and recruit labor that is otherwise inaccessible to the holder of capital, either because it is geographically distant or because of cultural barriers (for example, community, ethnic, linguistic, or, in the case of chikan, gender differences). By providing elementary work discipline, agents relieve businessmen of the responsibility for handling labor relations—a job for which they have little experience. Occupying this lynchpin position means that the agent is an important channel of communication between businessman and worker and can stand to benefit financially from each relationship. By bridging two distinct worlds (the world of unequal relations based on wages and the world of unequal relationships based ultimately on ideologies of kinship and patriarchy), the agent helps perpetuate the second set of relationships and releases the entrepreneur from the need to bring labor formally under the control of capital (see Kooiman 1983:140–46).

Many men derive their livelihood from delivering work to and from *mahajans* and artisans, and their social and economic relationships with these two groups, as well as their community identities and class trajectory, are subjects that deserve considerably more attention than I was able to give them. My own focus on female embroiderers and their own ventures into agent activities overshadowed the admittedly larger dimension of the exchange of materials and finished products between the city and the village that is dominated by male agents.

All the agents that I met or heard about were related to at least some of the women to whom they gave work. Since most embroiderers are Muslim, it follows that these agents are Muslim also. Yet, in a book whose focus is minority identities and relations in Lucknow, Srinivasan (1990:59) comments in passing that "the middlemen who allot work to the contract workers are mostly non-Muslims." Unfortunately, she does not present primary data upon which to base this remark, but cites "contact with the concerned people" (ibid.). Agent careers have in the past formed the springboard for chikan businesses belonging to Hindus, whose relatives do not make chikan. Agents in the past, however, distributed work in Lucknow and its immediate surroundings. The "new" agents are heavily involved in the rural areas and are diversifying away from agricultural work. They lack access to capital and seem unlikely to accumulate sufficient means to rise to the ranks of the *mahajans*. On the other hand, it is likely that even in the past there were "ranks" of agents, ranging from those poised, with the requisite funds and expertise, to become *mahajans*, to men who would simply insert themselves between manufacturers and the embroiderers who lived in their own house. Men who were essentially subcontractors for their families were often themselves artisans and they bequeathed their experience in such activities to daughters and wives who have now stepped into their agent shoes.

The full dimensions of the agent sector today—including those individuals who obtain materials from the *mahajan* only to pass them on to *another* agent—are as yet only partially understood. What are the socioeconomic profiles of those agents who are facilitating the expansion of the "frontier" of chikan production deeper and deeper into the countryside? Who conveys work to rural Hindu women who are represented in increasing numbers in the ranks of embroiderers? Learning more about these people and their activities would cast light on agrarian change and class differentiation.

It is up to the agent to relay the *mahajan's* requirements (such as they are) to the embroiderers and to give out materials and wages. He imposes a rudimentary discipline upon them by adjusting the flow of work according to the relative productivity of each woman, and adjusting wages as a means of penalizing deficient workers and rewarding good ones. His job depends upon women completing work to a minimum standard and in a reasonably timely fashion.

Agents whose womenfolk are able to do embroidery (and given the simplicity of *bakhya* work, very few women are exempt from this condition) almost always give work to them first and foremost. For these men, being an agent may become their main source of livelihood, although I heard of cases where men had other occasional jobs, but brought clothes for their wives and daughters to embroider as a secondary activity. This pattern is repeated in households throughout any given village where chikan is made. As agent activities expand, work is given to other relatives and neighbors.

Agents are part of a subset of men with limited industrial and educational skills who are looking for work opportunities generated by capitalization and urbanization (Mies 1982:43). To start out as an agent, a man must seek an introduction to a *mahajan,* normally from another man already involved in production as craftsman or agent. The following account is, I believe, representative of many rural male agents. The agent in question, a Sunni Muslim, had been working as an agent for the last five years in a village six kilometers north of Lucknow, called Motaqipur. His father was the first to diversify his activities beyond farming, becoming an agent about twenty years ago after obtaining introductions from agent friends with whom he spent time in Chowk. (What kind of farming he did and what his class status was, I was not told.) His wife and daughters (the present-day agent's mother and sisters) learned the craft at that time, presumably under his direction. In 1990, his son was an agent exclusively, while his brothers were still "doing agricultural work."

The agent estimated that there were 10 or 15 men like him in the village subcontracting work to about 500 women, of whom about 100 were his clients. Census figures put the total female population of Motaqipur at only 409, meaning that either the entire female population is engaged in chikan embroidery, or that the agent was flatly exaggerating. I believe it is safe to assume, though, that chikan embroidery is an important source of income in the village.

The agent picked up items to be embroidered from three different shops and gave between five to ten *kurtas* to each woman. He said he received Rs. 10 per item, half of which he paid to the embroiderer. Among his expenses were Rs. 1 to Rs. 1.50 for thread and 15 paise per kilo *ćungī* (road) tax to carry the goods into town. From the Rs. 10, he kept Rs. 3.50 to Rs. 4.00 per *kurta*, totaling up to Rs. 1,000 in a month. The Rs. 10 per item seemed a high figure, even assuming these were *salwar-qamizes*, and not *kurtas*. If the true amount were lower (for example, around Rs. 6 to Rs. 8) and his share were the same, then the embroiderer would have been receiving correspondingly less money, as little as Rs. 3 or Rs. 4 per outfit. Making Rs. 1,000 per month in this way would require little work—the equivalent of a single day's visit to two or three shops to collect 250 items. Possibly the agent was making more than he was prepared to admit to me (and giving less to his workers—which may explain the elevated wage figures). On the other hand, he probably did not employ the women outside his own domestic establishment and extended family on a regular basis, and even his own womenfolk might have been underemployed. Competition leading to underemployment among agents may be one factor in the inability of agents to amass capital on a large scale, although their earnings relative to embroiderers are good.

Mahajans regard agent work as easy work, since the agent can make a quick profit for a small investment of time and money. *Mahajans* consistently speak of the agent fee as part of the total wage quoted for a given item and their estimates of the size of the agent's share vary from 10 percent to 33 percent of the total. However, it is much more likely, as the above instance illustrates, that agents pocket more than that. A male embroiderer who had now turned his attention exclusively to subcontracting said that he would pay only Rs. 2.50 to an embroiderer out of a total wage of Rs. 10 for a given item, keeping Rs. 7.50 for himself. At least one *mahajan* described the agent's profit as a "double" one— his "wage" from the *mahajan* and additional skimming from the wages for the women (see also Kooiman 1983:145). Agents may well reward their close relatives with more work and better wages than they give others. But with the added control that agents can exert over the labor that is performed in their own households, it is as likely that they will actually give less wages to their relatives. For example, one strong-willed woman said she had refused to do embroidery work for her brothers-in-law since the standard wage she was paid by an unrelated agent to do sewing was far greater than the pittance she got from them.

The agent usually receives payment from the *mahajan* in parts. Since goods are often returned piecemeal, and because they fear that some pieces may "disappear" altogether, *mahajans* will often keep back a portion of what the agent is owed until all the material is returned completed. In practice, since the agent may take away a new load of items when he brings back even a portion of what he has already received, payments for one batch cross over into payments for another.

For the *mahajan's* purposes, the agent system has definite advantages. He will only reluctantly give out two or three pieces to an individual to work, but with an agent, he can send out hundreds of items at a time. Agents, by distributing work widely and by dropping less productive workers at their discretion, help alleviate the imbalances of productivity that characterize the informal sector (for example, one woman taking a week to do what another takes a day to do). The agent essentially gives the *mahajan* access to large sources of labor without the latter having to expend effort on his own behalf. Moreover, the existence of the agent spares the *mahajan* the costs of supervising production, since workers effectively pay for it themselves through ceding a portion of their wage to the agent (see Kooiman 1983).

The relationship between embroiderer and agent is formally antagonistic (even though, in practice, it is not expressed as such) and the relationship between *mahajan* and agent is itself far from smooth. A predictable upshot of a productive system in which no jobs are permanent, work is irregular, and there is a low level of literacy, is that relations between the parties are highly flexible, and rarely subject to written contracts. On the whole, this benefits the shopkeeper, although the prevalence of informal, short-term verbal contracts is a source of many troubles too. For example, two brothers in business together complained that negotiations with agents over the wages for a bundle of items could be rendered meaningless by a later demand for more money. One agent had demanded an extra fee of Rs. 30 for his services long after the original deal had been struck. *Mahajans* have also come to expect that the process of extracting all articles of embroidery out of the agent will be extremely lengthy, and that not all work that is sent out will come back. Whatever kinds of disputes arise between businessman and agent, manufacturers cannot simply punish the agent by dispensing with his services. *Mahajans* do not go out to find agents, and yet agents are absolutely essential to the successful functioning of their businesses. In the newly competitive world of chikan production, the *mahajan* is utterly dependent upon agents to direct new labor from the villages into the system.

In a household where women make chikan and men operate as agents, some chikan items are the property of the household through a member of the household's having bought the cloth and thread, and having purchased other services like printing and washing directly from the specialists concerned. Most agents lack the capital to invest in cloth purchase, or to market finished clothes. However, on my travels around Lucknow to find specific embroiderers, I occasionally saw women peeping from behind their doors, soliciting my business on the assumption that I had come to the area to get a piece of chikan made. Presumably some households can fill small orders for individual clients, perhaps with an advance against purchase of the basic materials and services. In this way, some pockets of chikan manufacture emulate the model of the the cottage-craftsman described by Goody (1982:2–3), where the internal division of labor along lines of seniority and gender allow a household to generate chikan products that it owns. Most likely the client furnishes the cloth, the male agents in the family arrange the printing and washing, and the women do the tailoring and embroidery. Critically, it is the men who control the product and the money that is made from it. These activities represent only a tiny proportion of total chikan production and are insufficient to form the basis for the rise of agents into the ranks of manufacturers.

Washermen

From any of the major bridges in Lucknow it is possible to see washermen at their work at the several washing locations along the River Gomti. As the day wears on, the ebb and flow of their work becomes apparent in the march of lines of wash up to, then away from the river's edge.

Laundering is a traditional, caste-based job and unlike many producers in other stages of production, Dhobis (washermen) have been washing clothes as their hereditary occupation for many generations. One family had twenty persons working at the river on the day I interviewed them. They specialized in washing chikan but they made no distinction between themselves and the families that did regular laundering, saying they had chosen to wash chikan exclusively because it made them more money. A *mahajan*, though, told a different story. He said his own washerman had told him that not everyone can wash chikan. Those *dhobis* that do, like his family, were special because they were washing clothes for the first time. In essence, the washerman was saying that it was better to wash clothes that were new and unworn than those garments stained by the bodily substances that washermen must remove in ordinary laundry. In the past, this *dhobi*'s family had washed the royal family's laundry. They would not wash just anyone's clothes, not even just anyone's chikan.

The story suggests a connection between chikan laundering and status that I cannot substantiate, not least because of contradictory statements from washermen. Many washermen are Muslims, for whom the substance codes of Hindu thought and practice have limited meaning (see Marriott 1976; Kumar 1988). Some embroiderers said that any washerman could wash chikan, while others insisted that only specialists could. "You need a special *dhobi* for this. Not an ordinary *dhobi*. The *dhobi* has to be special because both the thread and the cloth must be clean." If a household of washermen shifts over to washing chikan exclusively, the financial rewards seem evident. Further study might reveal a real change in extra-economic status that I was unable to confirm.

Washing chikan is a multistaged process. The working day starts at about 6:00 a.m. and ends at 3:00–4:00 in the afternoon. In that time, the washermen guessed that they laundered about 40–50 *kurtas* and *salwar-qamizes*. In the summer, when work is particularly intense, they can wash up to a hundred items per day. However, there are several preparatory and finishing operations that entail several days of labor. On average, items stay from four to five days with the *dhobi* to complete the washing process, whether these are individual items or large consignments from the *mahajan*, and irrespective of personal promises that the work will be done quicker.

Immediately following summer, the monsoon rains (*barsāt*) bring a lull in the chikan industry. It becomes difficult to wash clothes, as the river swells and the water becomes dirty and muddy. During this season, washermen may use water tanks to wash clothes, but find them an unsatisfactory alternative to the river. Access to the tanks is limited and there is a charge to use them.

Laundry wages had gone up in the decade just prior to my fieldwork. Whereas twelve years before, a washerman received only 75 paise for a *kurta*, in 1990 *dhobis* were paid around Rs. 2.50 for a *kurta*, and Rs. 3 for a *salwar-qamiz*. The rates I was quoted for washing clothes were reasonably consistent between washermen and *mahajans*, although no *mahajan* mentioned the process of whitening cambric *kurtas*, a four-day job that the washermen said cost an additional Rs. 3. Only one *mahajan* quoted even higher rates for washing, including Rs. 5 for a *kurta* (which he specifically contrasted with the conventional rate of Rs. 2.50), and Rs. 6 for a *salwar-qamiz*, instead of Rs. 3. Otherwise, embroiderers were the only group that seemed to pay on average from twice to nearly seven times as much for washing consignments as small as one piece. The washermen showed me a tablecloth from a *mahajan* they were washing for Rs. 3.35. A skilled embroiderer, on the other hand, said it might cost Rs. 20 to have one of her own tablecloths laundered.

An ever larger proportion of chikan clothes today are easy-to-wash, blue-printed synthetics that can be easily cleaned with commercially available washing products. But pink-printed cottons are still the mainstay of the *dhobis'* washing activity, and the complex and lengthy treatment to which these clothes are subjected is the most widely reported in descriptions of *dhobi's* activities (see Paine 1989:53–54).

Cottons are soaked in what *dhobis* called a *"masala"* (mixture) of washing powder and water, to which additional soap (from soap cakes) may be added if the pieces are particularly dirty. They are then "cooked"—boiled or steamed vigorously in a clay pot (*maṭkā*) placed over a fire. The whole contraption is also referred to as a *bhaṭṭī* (oven). At least two *mahajans* told me that two sessions at the *bhatti* were necessary for the cottons to be cleaned properly. The high heat required can only be produced by burning wood, not dung cakes, often the preferred fuel for fires.

The rest of the process is finished at the riverside, where the entire washing process for synthetics is done. Clothes are soaked in soap solutions in plastic basins or plastic-lined holes in the ground. Large ridged stones set into the edge of the bank are used as washboards, on which the clothes are beaten and scrubbed. Garments are dried by catching their edges between two twisted ropes strung on poles on high ground away from the river's edge. Paine (ibid.) describes the extraction of soap from earth and the production of starch from boiling rice, but the washermen told me that the products they used were all purchased from the market. Besides soap powder, a whitening agent is applied to remove discolor from threads, and hydrochloric acid is applied topically to remove stains and rust spots. Bleach, referred to as *nil* (lit., blue), is used to treat white items. Rigorous bleaching lends a distinct bluish tinge to white clothes. Washermen said they would have liked to obtain washing materials at wholesale, bulk prices but instead had to pay retail prices of Rs. 11 for a packet of "Nirma" washing powder and Rs. 15 for starch. I did not discover how often these materials had to be renewed.

The complaints of the washermen revolved around the injuries and damage to their health caused by their work, and the increasing cost of materials, for example, washing powder, bleach, and firewood for the *bhatti*. Their hands and feet were cracked, their limbs bleached and pinkish in color, and their skin swollen and completely smooth, all from constant immersion in water and exposure to cleaning agents. They also complained of stomach problems and lack of exercise (but agreed that other artisans shared these problems).

The final stages of laundering are performed by washerwomen at their homes. There clothes are pressed, either with hot coal-filled or electric irons. The use of large, hefty irons in clothes pressing is a familiar sight in North India, with men and women pressing clothes at tables at the edge of the street. I have not seen electric irons used in India, either among washermen or women, but they are supposedly becoming more popular, particularly as synthetic fabrics that require only a light press, and not a particularly skilled one at that, become more prevalent.

There is a certain skill to pressing cottons with large coal-filled irons that has been transmitted from mother to daughter. Some *mahajans* who talked to me at length about ironing and pressing stressed that cotton goods of all kinds required technical skill and care in pressing, and that only the heavy variety of iron would do in such cases. This is most apparent in the pressing of *saris*, which must be ironed when damp. Two irons are needed, one pressing in one direction across the *sari*, one going the other. *Saris* must be pressed in one thickness, the border first and then the rest of the *sari* in one go. Several *mahajans* complained that *saris* were not ironed properly these days. A common practice was for women to fold the *sari* first and then press it through several layers of thickness. Electric irons were said to gave unsatisfactory and uneven results. Washermen stress the sheer physical labor of conventional pressing. Irons are hefty tools, made even heavier by the addition of hot coal. Women suffer chest pains and respiratory problems, in addition to the other aches and pains caused by using them.

Many garments fail to survive the washing process. The washerman is responsible for the accumulated value of several other labors and he uses techniques that can easily damage or destroy the clothes. Inappropriate use of materials will ruin the fabric, and a common point at which failure can occur is the steaming of pink-printed clothes. Clothes can get scorched from being in close proximity to a fire that burns all night, especially if the water is lost from the pot. In one instance related to me, twenty or so *saris*, in which the cloth alone cost Rs. 300, were lost.

However, the washerman is also in one of the strongest positions as a laborer in the production process. One *mahajan* said that washermen are the most aggressive and unscrupulous of the workers he had to deal with. Yet few *mahajans* had specific complaints about them. This seems surprising, since washing frequently damages the embroidery and the fabric, or fails to remove stains and blemishes. Very little chikan is free from routine imperfections, not in the embroidery necessarily, but resulting from the way the cloth has been treated in the final stages of production. These imperfections do not appear to impede the sale of chikan. Indeed, one *mahajan* even argued that minute *pān* (a preparation of betel nut enjoyed by many Indians, and especially relished by embroiderers) stains, far from detracting from the beauty of the finest chikan pieces, confirmed their quality. Such flaws attest to the authenticity of a garment handcrafted by a skilled craftswoman and should not be removed by the washerman.

The strength of the washermen's position, and the dearth of complaints about them from *mahajans* can be explained by the fact that washermen, unlike printers, embroiderers, or even tailors to some extent, are not from a potentially expandable workforce. Dhobis make up the most solidary group among all categories employed in chikan production, and a shopkeeper is wise to form a good relationship with one family of Dhobis. Several shopkeepers spoke of the longstanding relationships they had with their washermen, saying that a move to another washerman would inevitably result in higher washing rates (the exact opposite of what happens when a *mahajan* secures the services of a new printer or embroiderer). Even when disaster occurs, as in the example of the *saris* cited above, there is little the *mahajan* can do, since he is constrained from simply seeking out another *dhobi* (an option that is always open to him with other occupations).

Washermen, it must be said, do not view the situation quite so positively. When reminded that washermen are regarded as the best off of the various laborers involved in the chikan production process in terms of wages and bargaining position, *dhobis* seemed unimpressed. They felt that their skills had gone unrecognized and did not see why embroiderers should get special treatment from the government They were particularly interested in being able to obtain washing materials at controlled rates.

Washermen know little about embroiderers. They complained about the state in which embroideries came to them, dirty from lying around the house, used for cleaning up cuts and scratches, and for miscellaneous cleaning: "you don't want to touch them." Having seen women blow their noses and clean their children with embroideries, I quite believed them. I was once given an embroidered (and as yet unwashed) *kurta* on which to wipe my hands after eating. Knowing that all embroideries have to be laundered eventually clearly encourages women to make use of them as all-purpose cloths, should the need arise.

Presented with the views of washermen on the state of unwashed embroideries, one embroiderer stressed that stains came from labor, and not from lack of care or low habits. At most, she said, clothes become soiled with the sweat from fingers as they worked. Embroiderers simply saw *dhobis* as occupational specialists with no particular skills, but whose key task was to enhance the already beautiful embroidery. On an occasion when I praised particularly fine work in progress, the embroiderer answered that it would look much better when it was white from washing. Embroiderers are keenly aware of the possible ruinous effects of careless laundering. These include the cloth coming apart from use of acidic cleaning agents, or the crushing and melting of threads that make up individual stitches when pressed with an excessively hot iron. Some embroiderers (although not all) even said that any *dhobi* could wash chikan if he had the time. The chikan origin story given by my teacher attributed the first embroidery to a man who made a *bel* (decorative stem motif) on a *nawab's topi after* it had been washed, eliminating the role of the *dhobi* altogether. My teacher told me how to wash the cloth on which I learned embroidery using readily available materials, implying the washerman's skills were not indispensable—at least so long as one was dealing with blue-printed clothes.

As the shift to *bakhya* continues, and as synthetic materials outpace cottons, the greatest change in the washerman's activity will be the end of the elaborate processes of boiling and bleaching. Although these tasks are the hallmark of the specialist chikan *dhobi*, laundering only blue-printed fabrics may not alter the washerman's position too much. The job of washing takes the same time irrespective of how much print there is on a garment, and while the washing of blue-printed clothes takes less time, it is also less costly and less prone to disaster than cleaning pink-printed cottons.

Finishers

Mahajans employ between two and five women to correct and finish embroidery in-house. These are usually urban embroiderers with at least a moderate level of skill, who are able to unpick, redo, or modify areas of embroidery that have been poorly executed. Needing to correct work is a consequence of the lack of formal means to ensure consistent quality. The importance of checkers in other informal industries has been documented (Swallow 1982:159).

Mies (1982) writes that women checkers for traders in the lace industry of Narsapur are usually individuals who occupy a position of some trust. I do not know how such women are recruited in the chikan industry. However, one finisher who was pointed out to me in a major wholesale store was a Hindu, a comparatively rare figure in chikan embroidery, implying that the *mahajan* looks for qualities that bind the finisher to him in extra-economic terms. I was unable to talk to any finishers and it is difficult for me to say how much correction was usually required in order to produce a saleable article—after all, garments with noticeable flaws are routinely offered for sale by *mahajans*. Nor was I able to determine how, and in what amounts, the women were paid.

MACHINE WORK

Chikan production has conceded little to mechanization, centralized workshops, or factories. Instead, producers retain many of characteristics of an artisanal lifestyle and work pattern often dubbed "precapital-ist." They have the nominal "freedom" to adjust work patterns to accommodate periodic demands of socializing and festival observances, not to speak of the artisan's own changeable disposition (Kumar 1988). The flip side of this so-called freedom is that artisans, in every stage of labor, experience fluctuations in the supply of work and therefore wages from the *mahajan*.

Where machines have made inroads in chikan production, their impact is muted. Tailors routinely use hand-powered sewing machines but electric-powered sewing machines and irons are practically non-existent. Since the late 1980s, men have been operating embroidery machines to make men's *kurtas*. Machine work has a limited market, maybe 5 percent of the total, according to some *mahajans*. The dearth of machinery represents a coincidence between the economic self-inter-est of *mahajans*, the aesthetic choices of middle-class consumers, and the constraints of India's industrial infrastructure, all of which help to entrench handwork in the chikan industry.

There are no overriding reasons why *mahajans* should invest directly, or encourage investment, in embroidery machines. All *maha-jans* consistently argue that the demand for machine work is too small, and no one seems to think it will ever become especially large. They insist that "no one wants machine work—it isn't important." Of course, should tastes shift, machine work may disrupt the present production process considerably. One manufacturer even feared that a rise in machine work might encourage the re-imposition of sales tax on chikan goods in the state.[3]

The differences between wages for machine work and wages for handwork are difficult to substantiate. My embroidery teacher adhered to a "labor theory of value" explanation, saying that machine embroi-derers got lower wages per piece because they could make ten items a day to her one. But more than one manufacturer said that men using embroi-dery machines demanded higher wages than female hand-embroiderers—perhaps because they were men, perhaps because there are still only a small number of embroidery machines (and thus machine embroiderers) available. One *mahajan* went on to say that whereas he paid only Rs. 8 for a handworked suit, he had to pay Rs. 20 for a similar machine-worked item. He was forced to charge more for a machine-work *kurta* for that reason, but in general I did not find that machine-worked *kurtas* were universally more expensive than handworked clothes.

Complaining about the costliness of machine work may, of course, be a way of rationalizing a situation where the perpetuation of hand-work and its attendant low wages most benefits the manufacturer. How-ever, middle-class Indians, who are enthusiastic consumers of chikan on a national scale, specifically prefer handwork. Only working-class men show any aesthetic preference for machine work. Rickshaw-pullers and washermen stood out in Lucknow as the wearers of machine-embroidered chikan, but how and why this came to be so, I do not know.

When most people buy chikan, they go to a shop and browse through a lot of items before they make their choice. Shops are filled from floor to ceiling with stacks of finished chikan, the products of a compartmentalized, labor-intensive manufacturing process. A large number of customers explicitly ask for *hāth kā kām* (handwork) when they shop—rejecting any machine embroidery that might be directed their way. I have already pointed out that *bakhya* is now regarded by most consumers as the authentic chikan. The rough contours of coarse, village-produced *bakhya*, disparaged though it may be by the connoisseurs of "art work," is actually preferred. It is the quintessential "face" of Lucknow chikan. As one shopkeeper commented, machine work could be done anywhere, but handworked Lucknow chikan, however crude, is still the signature product of the city. Skilled handwork gives chikan its texture, its pattern, and its recognizability. Curiously, machines approximate the intricacies of *murri* work, and machine products look nothing like the cheaper, coarser *bakhya* that overwhelms the market (figure 2.2).

Shopkeepers often said that the more unscrupulous dealers could persuade ignorant shoppers that machine work is true handwork. This is only partly true. The same *mahajans* that complained about "unscrupulous" dealers put machine-work down in front of their own customers. More often than not, the customer would ask for handwork instead. Machine work is used prominently in shop displays, perhaps because at a distance its evenness and homogeneity, as well as the more pronounced visual contrast between embroidery and cloth, were more pleasing than the subtlety and variability of hand worked items. Whether this was the explicit reason I cannot say. When I asked about it, *mahajans* seemed put out that I had recognized it as machine work. Over and again, the only answer to my questions was that people did not buy machine work.

For good economic and aesthetic reasons, it is unlikely that machine embroidery will ever dominate the industry. However, machine embroidery is so new that definitive statements about it are hard to make. Since embroidery machines can easily be used inside homes, their use does not require a substantial change in the essential structure of production. However, it is hard to see embroidery machines supplanting female handworkers while women's labor is so cheap and plentiful, and while machine work and the most common handwork are so different in texture and appearance.

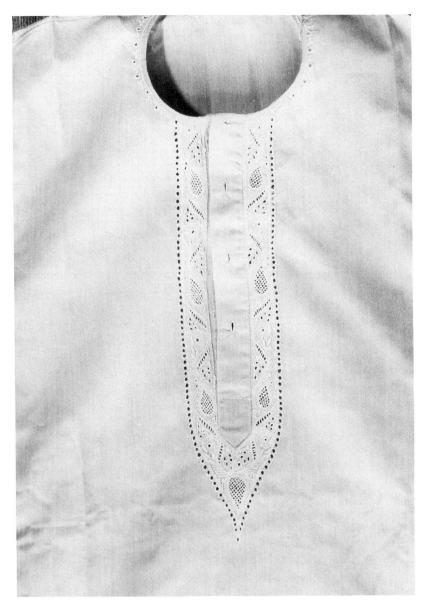

FIG. 2.2. Machine work embroidery on the collar and placket of a man's *kurta*.

CONCLUSION

The contemporary chikan industry thrives on an informal organization of labor, in which artisans work for piece-wages from the *mahajan* without formal wage contracts or assurances of employment from day to day. The levels of skill required in each stage of chikan production are diminishing and tasks are getting simpler. Mechanization has not been introduced because the flexibility, abundance, and effectiveness of hand-powered labor is more beneficial for chikan shopkeepers. The labor pool for chikan production in most of its stages is part of that larger mass of displaced labor, including both men and women, that is unlikely to find itself a permanent niche in industrial production, holding full-time jobs with real wages (Swallow 1982:164; Mies 1982:5). The weak bargaining power of these workers, and potential workers, means that low wages are likely to persist.

The coexistence of cheap and fine chikan goods, and the elaborate division of labor in the industry, have been its essential components since its birth in the colonial era. Now the top end of the market has effectively disappeared, and with the rise of a cheap, popular product, new entrepreneurs, as well as new personnel in other branches of production, have entered production. In these conditions, some specialists have done better than others—the washermen take advantage of the exclusivity of their occupation to protect their wage rates in ways that embroiderers, for example, cannot.

So far, the knowledges associated with each artisan specialty in chikan production remain distinct and complex. Artisans openly voice pride in their skills, expressing aesthetic sentiments that seem to transcend the simple division of artistic and technical tasks. Each stage of production has its own materials, rhythms, and tricks of the trade that are valued and appreciated by the artisans who are so familiar with them. Many of these skills may, though, be doomed as production shifts seemingly inexorably toward simple, cheap *bakhya*.

CHAPTER 3

Embroiderers in Social Perspective

THEORIZING WOMEN'S WORK

In ethnographic studies of female incorporation in, and exclusion from, production, scholars have made a strong case for paying special attention to the different treatment of men and women in capitalist and capitalizing economies. Women have, as in nineteenth-century England, been forcibly relegated to the domestic domain (Lown 1990). At other times they have been the preferred employees at the lowest levels of factory production, as in contemporary Southeast Asia (Ong 1987). Women are also employed in higher numbers than men in home-based production, otherwise known as "homework," which with the increasing decentralization of production around the world has come under close scrutiny (e.g., Beneria and Roldan 1987; Singh and Kelles-Viitanen 1987; Boris and Daniels 1989; Prügl and Boris 1996). As Baud (1987) points out, the supposed development "advantages" of putting-out systems—they are labor-intensive, use so-called appropriate technology— conceal their tremendous disadvantages for those caught up in them, among them the fact that subcontracting is a means for manufacturers to circumvent legal protections usually extended to officially recognized workers.

South Asia has been a fruitful setting for scholarship on women's home-based work. In part this scholarship has been a product of the evolution of an indigenous women's movement. From its beginnings as an advocacy group for education and improved conditions at home, South Asian feminism moved on to tackle constitutional issues, and after Independence, turned toward women hitherto largely sidelined from its activities, that is, working-class women (Lateef 1990). Numerous studies of working women's lives by South Asian scholars together with the research of non-Indians have produced a substantial and growing literature on labor and gender in the subcontinent (e.g., Sharma 1980, 1986; Jain 1980; Bhatty 1981; Feldman and McCarthy 1984; Feldman 1992; Banerjee 1985; Mies 1982, 1987; Hossain 1987; Risseeuw 1987; Weiss 1991; Baud 1992). Home-based work is a recurrent theme in the description of industrialization processes and change in women's working lives. Chikan is only one example of a more widespread phenomenon in South Asia and, increasingly, the world.

The construction of gender difference has been a most useful tool in the extraction of surplus value, and chikan production illustrates this well. Most chikan embroiderers are completely dependent upon agents (and, by extension, *mahajans*) for wage work. They do not go out to work in factories, offices, or workshops. Instead, work from *mahajans* is brought to them at their homes, and picked up when it is done. Only a very few do any work on their own behalf but even these cannot be called "self-employed" since they still depend on work from the *mahajan* for their day-to-day survival. Embroiderers balance work for wages with domestic tasks such as cooking, cleaning, and tending children. Like the Mexico City home-based workers described by Beneria and Roldan (1987), female embroiderers in Lucknow profess a strong identification with the roles of wife and mother. The same identification, made by their employers, casts them in the role of "leisure-time" embroiderers, unworthy of the wages and attention given to "real" workers.

Theorizing the relationship of unpaid, reproductive labor in the household (largely grouped under "housework") with wage labor has been an important, but difficult task (see Beneria and Roldan 1987; Collins and Gimenez 1990; Mies et al. 1988; Prügl 1996). The concept of "subsistence production" has been proposed to take account of labors partially or wholly excluded from regular wage relations (e.g., Mies 1982, 1988; Bennholdt-Thomsen 1988; von Werlhof 1988). Subsistence producers are defined by the fact that they must bear much of the cost of their own reproduction themselves, since wages purposely do not cover it. Subsistence production is not done by women only, although women's work is perhaps its most obvious component. Women's roles in cultivating kinship ties and neighborly relations, making marriages, participating in festivals, and so forth are especially critical for creating vital networks of support and help (Papanek 1982; Sharma 1986; Sacks 1991). Subsistence production includes activities as diverse as childbearing, food processing, petty commodity production, homemaking, and maintaining social relationships (Mies 1988:27–28; von Werlhof 1988:16).

Subsistence production subsidizes wage laborers within a household and when wage labor is scarce, subsistence production is the only way that millions of people, men, women, and children can survive. Subsistence producers will not become "free" laborers in the classic sense, but are likely to remain a perpetually marginalized population, barely able to sustain themselves and without hope of regular employment and real wages. Just as a "housewife" subsidizes her wage-laborer relatives' reproduction, so marginalized subsistence producers subsidize wage labor in a broader transnational context (Bennholdt-Thomsen 1988; von Werlhof 1988).

Jane Collins (1990) objects to the concept of subsistence production on theoretical grounds because it portrays unpaid domestic labor as a form of extraction of surplus labor. As she points out, surplus labor cannot be extracted outside of capitalist wage relations. However, few disagree that unwaged work contributes at least indirectly to the perpetuation of exploitative relations of production. As housewives, chikan embroiderers assist in reproducing male wage workers (Beneria and Roldan 1987; Singh and Kelles-Viitanen 1987). As wage workers, embroiderers are incorporated into productive relations that are profoundly affected by their social status as homemakers and dependents. Time and again, their waged work is described as "spare-time" work, although the formal relationship between worker and employer is no different from that between an employer and "working" male artisan. Described as "spare-time" work, embroidering seems identical to the many and various unpaid tasks that together contribute to social reproduction (see Collins 1990:4).

The language used to describe not just women's work, but all forms of wage labor that take place outside of organized settings, blinds us to its importance. All people who work in the "informal" and "unorganized" sector may find their labor dubbed "casual." The very term "marginal" is problematic, for so many now live productive lives that are "marginal" to classic economic relations that their experience is more properly "central." By using words like "marginal" and "unorganized," lives and livelihoods are discussed in terms not of what they are, but of what they are not (Adams and Paul 1987).

PROBLEMS WITH STATISTICS

Chikan workers are almost all Muslim women, living to some degree in purdah. Doing chikan work for wages is essential to the daily reproduction of embroiderers and their families, but women's status as productive, wage-earning workers is given scant, if any, official recognition. The Indian Census, rightly regarded as structuring, as much as reflecting, the social realities of the subcontinent (Cohn 1984), consistently underestimates the numbers of home-based workers, and female home-based workers most of all (Adams and Paul 1987; Bhatt 1987; Singh and Viitanen 1987:17).[1]

According to the Indian Census, work is "participation in any economically productive activity" (Census of India 1981a:xviii). Workers in any branch of industry are subdivided into "main," "marginal," and, paradoxically, "non-workers." Main workers are "engaged . . . in economic activity for the major part of the year (at least 183 days)" (ibid.).

In both the district and the city of Lucknow itself, there is a strikingly low number of women listed as main workers. Even assuming that female embroiderers are not classified as "main workers" but as "marginal workers" who have worked less than 183 days in one year, fewer than 200 female marginal workers are counted in the census. This is remarkable in light of the fact that chikan is the third most important commodity exported from Lucknow after scooter spare parts, and cement and asbestos sheets (Census of India 1981b). The total value of production, estimated at around Rs. 10 million in 1973 (Mathur 1975), and Rs. 20 million by 1975 (ibid.) rose to Rs. 120–150 million in 1989. Presumably city embroiderers are submerged in the figures for non-workers. According to the census, almost the entire female population does not work for wages, even for a short period during the year. (Although it is fair to say that the heavy weighting of the nonworker category probably reflects general problems of classifying livelihoods of both men and women, as well as the relative invisibility of female labor.)

"Chikan has always been in the village," a *mahajan* once said to me, "and what is today's city was yesterday's village." Certainly the boundaries of the city have expanded throughout history. My embroidery teacher often told me how the areas north of the River Gomti, where many contemporary chikan embroiderers live, were practically "jungle" just a few generations ago. But today the "frontier" (see Mies 1982:73) of chikan production is stretching out farther and farther into the rural heart of Uttar Pradesh, into Lucknow, Barabanki, Hardoi, Unnao, and Sultanpur districts, far beyond the reach of urban expansion. Yet census figures for rural areas of Lucknow district also fail to reflect women's employment in the chikan industry. While women make up the majority of marginal workers counted, again there is no specification of what kind of work they are engaged in. A similar picture emerges from other districts where chikan is made.

There are two primary reasons for the underestimation or invisibility of female labor in these statistics. One is that labor definitions are usually drawn up according to the occupation of the head of household (usually male) without taking into account other sources of income in the family. Women may not even be directly observed by census-takers. The second reason is that the census tacitly agrees with, and helps to perpetuate, the picture of chikan embroidery as little more than a hobby. Women often do chikan on a sporadic basis. This should mean that they are placed within the marginal worker category, but it seems that this is not where they are being counted. Instead, the official view that embroiderers are first and foremost housewives who happen to be doing a little bit of extra work, has tended to relegate them to the ranks of the nonworkers. In this way, their economic contributions to their families, to society, and to the chikan industry, go unnoted.

Estimates of the total number of embroiderers from reports and surveys conducted over the past fifteen years show little agreement, ranging from 30,000 to 75,000 (see table 3.1). The variability is partly due to inconsistency and lack of clarity in defining who is to be counted. For example, do figures reflect the number of workers in the city, or in the city and nearby villages, or all workers in the entire state? In most cases, differences in what figures mean can be resolved by the reader, in which case apparent confusion over the "thing to be counted" does not explain the vast numerical discrepancies encountered in written materials. Most puzzling of all is when the same organization offers two different figures. In table 3.1, a figure of 30,000 is quoted from a *Times of India*

TABLE 3.1
Recent Estimates of Total Chikan Workers

Written Accounts	Date	Numbers
Times of India, Lucknow[a]	1990	30,000
Lucknow Magazine[b]	1988	35,000
Lucknow Magazine[c]	1988	50,000–60,000
SEWA Lucknow[d]	1990	45,000
SEWA Lucknow[e]	?	60,000
Uttar Pradesh State Government (UPEC)[f]	?1987	75,000
Oral Accounts		
Skilled female embroiderer/agent	1990	400,000–500,000
Skilled male embroiderer/agent	1990	100,000
Prominent mahajan	1990	800,000

Sources:
a. "Saviour of Dream Weavers," *Times of India* (Lucknow), May 23, 1990.
b. *Lucknow City Magazine* 1988. Article by Mukesh Shrada.
c. *Lucknow City Magazine* 1988. Article by Angira Vats. Source is given as Uttar Pradesh District Industries Commission (DIC) Report, no date provided.
d. Tyabji 1990.
e. Runa Banerji, personal communication. Figure reported in a survey done for Literacy House, Lucknow.
f. Uttar Pradesh Niryat Nigam (Uttar Pradesh Export Corporation, UPEC), Moti Mahal, Lucknow. Two anonymous and Unpublished reports in Hindi, "Chikankari in Lucknow" and "Chikan Handicraft Industry."

article about a 1990 initiative in women's development by the Women's Welfare Section of the Uttar Pradesh state government. If the figure comes from the section (I assume it does), then the contrast with the Uttar Pradesh Export Corporation (UPEC) and District Industries Commission (DIC) figures are even more astounding, since they imply that even the state government, knowingly or unknowingly, cannot settle upon a single number. It is also virtually impossible to determine the source of quoted figures (except where a writer has simply lifted a number from another text without attribution). Surveys are often packed with a variety of statistical information, government surveys included, but do not give any account of their data-gathering methods.

It is also difficult to quantify the rise of village industry since there have been no longitudinal data collected by any single research institution. Studies by different organizations are unsatisfactory, because of discrepancies in the way they construct their samples. For what it is worth, two separate studies conducted roughly fifteen years apart indicate that while the ratio of village to urban workers was estimated in 1975 to be just over 1:4 (or around 12,000 workers out of a total of 45,000, according to Mathur [1975]), by about 1987, UPEC estimated that one third of a total 74,000 chikan embroiderers worked in rural areas. A reasonable hypothesis might be that not only has the total number of embroiderers increased, but also the proportion of workers from villages farther away from Lucknow.

Embroiderers usually insisted that "in every house, there is someone who does chikan" but could not hazard a guess as to what number there might be. Those who did gave as wide a range of numbers as one finds in texts (see table 3.1). Perhaps the only outstanding characteristic of estimates given me by both embroiderers and *mahajans* was that they were usually higher than those found in printed, official publications.

EMBROIDERY AND POVERTY

Chikan work is not a hobby. It is not done for amusement, or for increasing a woman's stock of personal, material wealth, or for any sumptuary purpose of the embroiderer. It is work for wages, pure and simple. Most chikan embroiderers are extremely poor, meaning that there is a persistent shortfall in money with which to purchase the most fundamental means of life. In the city, most embroiderers live in its older sections ("*purānā* Lucknow") and areas adjacent to them. These are located both south and north of the River Gomti, including Musaibganj, Maulviganj, Kashmiri Mohalla, Chowk, Daliganj, Rajabazar, Muftiganj, and Takkurganj, to name but few. In the classic manner of postcolonial cities, almost all of these are areas that compared to the newer sections have few amenities, poor communications and housing, and, critically, populations that are outside the circles of power and economic decision-making (Hjortshoj 1979; Oldenburg 1984; King 1976).

An explicit ideal (voiced by women as well as men) is that a woman should be supported throughout her life in turn by her parents, her husband, and her sons. All renewable resources of the household are expected to be provided by men's income, as well as the home itself. The woman's responsibilities are primarily those of providing domestic services—cooking, cleaning, clothes-making, and so on—producing children, and doing any preparation associated with festivals. The segregation of gender-specific activities can be radical, and ensures mutuality and interdependence between the sexes—although women's activities are rarely regarded as complementary to those of men, and the necessity of women's work (in all its forms) to the livelihoods and lifestyles of men is seldom recognized by either sex. In accordance with ideals of how relations should be conducted between a woman and the various men upon whom she depends and to whom she submits, most women live largely secluded inside their houses, while men travel openly and freely outside it (Mandelbaum 1988).

The more regular the work and income of a husband, father, or adult sons, the more likely a woman can rely on them completely to supply all the household's money and commodities. But the male relatives of embroiderers are most often engaged in occasional, low-paying, informal-sector occupations. Embroiderers come, by and large, from families whose members are irregularly employed (and irregularly paid). Some of the occupations of my informants' menfolk included: *zardozi* embroiderer; construction laborer; unskilled or semiskilled laborer in a workshop or factory; printer; tempo (large autorickshaw, holding at least six people) driver or cycle rickshaw puller; painter and whitewasher; peon or laborer in shops of various kinds—parts stores, repair shops, *pan* shops. Highly skilled embroiderers' families may include a similarly wide range of occupational variation; the scions of a set of brothers and sisters can include teachers, pharmacists, truck drivers, and storekeepers. Rural embroiderers' male relatives, if they work, have handicraft or laboring jobs, including carpentry, *zardozi*, truck driving, and agricultural labor. Several families of my acquaintance had, in previous generations, possessed farm or orchard land, but had lost it in the last one or two generations. None had any current income from land ownership. Instead, some embroiderers' relatives worked as landless agricultural laborers at a short distance from the city.

Men in informal-sector occupations rarely hold one job for life and cannot always find work. One woman's husband had very recently begun working in a bakery after being a cycle rickshaw puller for several years. Construction, in particular, is very susceptible to delays and layoffs. Menfolk may be unable or unwilling to work because of chronic illness or because, as their wives complain, they are *pāgal* ("crazy") or *bekār* ("useless"). "The children's father" is a common target of biting criticism and expressions of disappointment.

When men have no earnings, small earnings, or have spent most of their income on themselves, women must assume the responsibility of obtaining the most basic provisions for the house—food, supplies, or clothes. Chikan embroidery is one of the only sources of cash for women who lack education, skills, and experience, and are otherwise prevented by the requirements of family honor from seeking jobs outside the home. "What else can I do?" say embroiderers. "If you haven't gone far in school and you have to have money, this work is all there is."

Women who are very reliant upon chikan for an income are not infrequently the mothers of several daughters, with no, or only small, sick, or otherwise unproductive sons. Out of fifty to sixty women I met, sixteen were widowed, separated (because their husbands had deserted them), divorced, or orphaned (by which I mean without a father). In these situations, the woman must take up almost the entire burden of caring for herself and her family. Even when an abandoned wife was taken back by her natal family, she still bore a large responsibility for her keep. Where the husband had died, there was often lingering resentment, certainly bitterness at the inadequate provision for family survival that the man had made for those who have outlived him. For young women, fatherlessness means not simply that they must work for a living, but lack of protection and care in a broader sense.

Urban embroiderers did not, as far as I could tell, have to defer to their menfolk to get permission to do embroidery, although I was told that in villages they had to. Continuing to work for wages also seemed to be under the woman's, or her senior female relatives' control, unless any of the men in the household were agents. What money women get from chikan is theirs to spend. I knew of no case where women handed over their earnings to their male relatives, or even to senior women in the home, unless perhaps they were small or unmarried girls whose wage for a portion of work was sequestered by their mothers.

Chronic lack of money and the obligation to provide for the family's day-to-day needs weigh heavily upon each and every chikan embroiderer. When there isn't enough money, embroiderers are forced into recurrent or progressively desperate measures to reproduce themselves and their families. These include restricted consumption, chronic indebtedness, and the selling of all kinds of personal and household property. The usual diet of embroiderers and their families is vegetables and *roṭī* (bread), with the occasional addition of fruit and a *dal* (cooked pulses), and sundry snacks. Women buy food from vendors who come door to door, or from stands in the neighborhood. The quality of vegetables and fruits is extremely poor compared to produce available in the main shopping areas of Lucknow, Meat, poultry, and fish are relished, but are too costly to be consumed often. Milk is purchased for tea, but is rarely drunk by itself. Even tea is a "luxury," as I realized when it was offered to me on fewer occasions after I became a familiar visitor.[2]

Doing chikan work is perhaps best thought of less as a palliative to poverty, but an activity that, like those listed above, only temporarily averts crisis. The comments of Rashida, a woman who got work from my teacher, illustrated the hand-to-mouth existence of embroiderers and their families: "As soon as you have money, it goes on food. You must eat, so what can you do? The children are hungry whether there is money or not. All your effort goes to eating *roti*. I can't even get new clothes, I get old clothes from [my embroidery teacher's] house—even this *dupatta* and this suit are old clothes from them." Taken together, these experiences are indicative of a slide into pauperism.

An important subset of embroiderers are those whose menfolk are agents. In these instances, women's taking up chikan may coincide with the launching of a man's agent career—and thus women's work essentially subsidizes men's own income. But while they are controlled and supervised by men, they can at least expect to get a large share of the work men bring home. Having, in addition, menfolk with an income of sorts (even if this is essentially at the expense of women's own earnings), elevates the agent/embroidering family above others who embroider only. Agent activity is itself a response to underemployment among men in rural areas, and the fact that women continue to work at their men's bequest indicates that no great social elevation is achieved by being involved in chikan.

LEISURE

Unlike artisans in Banaras (Kumar 1988) few embroiderers enjoy much "leisure" time. In fact, they fall into a kind of limbo where they neither "work" nor really "play." Even when women are not doing embroidery, it is their almost continuous household and wage work that subsidizes the other members of the household (see Mies 1982:117ff.). Such leisure as they do enjoy is reserved for younger women, usually unmarried girls. In female-dominated households, however, women have greater autonomy than they do in male-headed households, and set aside more time for enjoyable activities. Breaks from work might take the form of taking naps and eating light snacks. More structured leisure activities were rare. For example, my teacher had a radio, but I heard it played only a few times. Once, her younger daughter listened to songs on the radio, singing along with the help of a lyric book.

Women in Madeganj had fewer consumer goods. One day, I heard that some women had pooled a sum of rupees (Rs. 1 or Rs. 2 each) to rent a video to watch on one of the few television sets in the neighborhood. The film stimulated some controversy. It was said by the older women to be a "steamy" movie unsuitable for young women. When one of these older women described (and acted out) for nonparticipants a scene thought especially lewd, the narrator and audience (including some of the "young women") were doubled up with laughter. Watching videos or even television is a rare treat, seldom indulged in by women without television sets. (By contrast, my teacher's Delhi-based cousins were well accustomed to video-viewing, as her young cousin's enthusiastic and wordy synopses of the various films she had seen demonstrated.)

Young women might go with girlfriends to the cinema, or tour the shops. For older women, especially those less able to travel outside the house, the most reliable source of relaxation and pleasure came from the attentions of daughters (or more commonly, daughters-in-law) in their personal care, including combing, oiling, and plaiting their hair.

Embroidery seems not to fit into the category of leisure, since it is not an activity that women do for sheer enjoyment, nor does it take the place of the genuinely enjoyed pursuits I have described above. Certainly the word "shauq" (passionate interest) that male artisans in Banaras use to talk about pleasant, relaxing activities and outings appears in embroiderers' own language. But embroiderers use it in a different way. They talk of their "shauq" for embroidery, which for almost all is a means to make a living. Only one woman made the explicit point that her craft was not an occupation, only an expression of her shauq. As far as most embroiderers are concerned, embroidery is unequivocally work, although this does not necessarily mean that women see themselves as workers like men.

RELIGION

Data on the class, caste, and religion of the embroidery workforce are sparse, but the widespread and seemingly correct assumption is that embroiderers are overwhelmingly (over 90%) Muslim (Mathur 1975; Srinivasan 1989). There are two factors at work here: historical contingency (most artisanal specialities in the city are the preserve of Muslims and have been so for many hundreds of years [see Ganju 1980; Cole 1989]); and the affinity between the interests of the chikan industry and the particular constraints upon Muslim women.

Muslims have always been in a minority in South Asia but until the nineteenth century, Islam had had a cultural influence on the subcontinent out of proportion to the numbers of Muslims. After partition, Muslim numbers fell to even smaller levels and a heightened committment to a religious and cultural identity as Muslims came in its wake. As Lateef (1981) notes, Muslim women have borne an inordinate amount of the pressure to preserve an Islamic "community," whether this has meant a purely cultural stance or ongoing wrangling about Muslim women's legal status (Engineer 1987). Most Muslim women are still expected to observe some degree of purdah (veiling, segregation of men and women) and unlike Hindu women who also veil, Muslim women do it in a strikingly public fashion, by wearing a *burqa*ʿ (enveloping overgarment). In appearance, Muslim women "stand" for Muslims in ways men do not and cannot. Embroiderers are no exception. So intimate is the association of Islam and the seclusion of women that where written sources say nothing explicit about the communal background of workers, their categorization of embroiderers as "mainly secluded women" *(mukhyā rūp se pardanishīn mahīlāyen hotī hain)* in effect says that they are Muslims. Seclusion, in turn, is fundamentally bound up with women's weak bargaining position in the labor market. At worst, purdah rules prevent women from moving outside their homes completely, unless they have express permission from male relatives. At the very least, purdah means that work undertaken in public places is considered improper and shameful, even if mobility in and of itself is less constrained. Chikan is only one industry in which home-based work prevails. Other Uttar Pradesh industries that employ secluded women are the *bīṛī*, or beedi (Indian hand-rolled cigarettes) industry (Bhatty 1981, 1987), the *zardozi* (gold and silver embroidery) industry (Jalees 1989), and weaving (Abidi 1986), and they share many characteristics of the chikan industry. Muslim women who want to explore new avenues for work are consistently frustrated by the expectations of behavior that bear down so heavily upon them, and that have political as well as familial and personal ramifications.

Probably the majority of city-based embroiderers today are Sunni Muslims and the minority are Shias. Just as it is in other areas of cultural life in past and present-day Lucknow (see Sharar 1975), the significance of Shias is far greater than their numbers imply. The Shia embroiderers that I met were all living in areas of the old city stretching far to the west of the modern heart of the city. My research was directed early on toward the settlements located on the northern banks of the Gomti, where my interviewees were almost universally Sunni Muslims. When the term "embroiderer" appears in this text, it stands for a Sunni Muslim, unless stated otherwise.

Chikan is not immune from the competitive rhetoric of the two sects. Sunnis did not raise the subject of the relative participation of Sunnis and Shias in embroidery. But when they were asked about Shia involvement in embroidery, Sunnis acknowledged the importance of Shias in the craft's early days but insisted that today both Shias and Sunnis do this work (donoṅ, barābar—"both, equally"). My Sunni teacher said decisively that Shia and Sunni both made chikan, "there's no difference." While Shias did not dispute the fact that Sunnis and Shias both made chikan today, they tended to stress Shia excellence in the craft, contrasting its roots in the Shia nawabi court with its later character as a mass-market handicraft industry staffed mainly by Sunni embroiderers. From this perspective, Shias were the quintessential makers of fine work, while Sunnis were uniquely associated with cheap work—although in reality Sunnis are well represented in the ranks of highly skilled embroiderers. The numerical domination of Sunnis in chikan is, to Shias, a further example of Sunnis' outstripping Shias in many domains, from political influence to cultural leadership and economic opportunity. Only one Shia, Rehana Begum, did not subscribe to the viewpoint expressed by other members of her sect. "Nur Jahan started chikan. Therefore a Shia started it. But there weren't the differences in those days that here are now. Both Sunnis and Shias made chikan; it wasn't just Shias. Possibly one group was doing more—some had more interest, some less."

Urban embroiderers know that new workers include Hindu as well as Muslim women. Hindu embroiderers live in distant districts with small Muslim populations (e.g., in 1971, the last time such figures were available, Muslims made up only 9% of the population of Unnao District, compared to 19% of Lucknow District [Census of India 1971]). But only two Hindu shopkeepers said that Hindus approached equal numbers with Muslims in village production, one going so far as to say that 25 percent of all city workers were Hindu. This figure was repeated to me by a young, city-dwelling Hindu girl whose sisters had been trained to do chikan. However, none of my observations bore this unusually high estimate out.

The women who have recently started making chikan are relatively unskilled and less informed about the market for chikan and producers in other stages. Urban Muslim embroiderers typically dismiss village women's work as crude and coarse. All Hindus' work is criticized in the same breath as village work—"Hindu women are no good at the work. They do mainly shadow-work." Urban Hindu girls were represented in small, but consistent numbers in government training schemes, where they were taught a wide repertoire of stitches appropriate for fine *murri* work. As my teacher told me, "In the last ten years, lots of Hindus have come up. I'll show you registers [of embroidery classes] and you'll see how many Hindus there are. In the past, it was just Muslims. They're [Hindus] learning for same reasons as Muslims—troubles (*pareshānī*)."

While admitting that Hindus were now growing in the ranks of embroiderers, my Muslim embroiderer informants also expressed the view that workers are a community as well as a class apart from their employers. This opinion, in order to be consistent, had to ignore the existence both of Hindu workers and Muslim manufacturers. Once when I asked a skilled embroiderer about Muslim and Hindu students in training programs, she spoke abruptly: "Of course, all businessmen are Hindus. They have the money." "But aren't there Muslim shop-keepers nowadays?" I asked. "Oh, there are no more than two to four Muslim [shopkeepers]," she replied. "*Mahajans* are all Rastogis—that and Lalas." Nor was this opinion confined to the narrow circumstances of chikan production, but was expounded in reference to general occu-pational and class difference. "All of us Muslims, we do the work. We are the craftsmen. The Hindus are the rich people, the businessmen. We are poor." *Pareshani* (suffering, troubles) is freely admitted to afflict all who take up chikan, even Hindus. But as one skilled Sunni embroiderer, said, "*pareshānī meṅ fā'ida kaun uthātā? . . . Hindū log*" (And who profits from suffering? Hindus).

Embroiderers, though, freely complained about the treatment they receive from Muslims as well as Hindus in positions of power. Muslim shopkeepers were never said to treat their employees any differently from Hindu *mahajans*. What is more, whenever a Hindu was part of a group of women discussing the tribulations of embroidery, she was as harsh and unsparing in her criticism of *mahajans* as her Muslim com-panions. Being Muslim is clearly a major strand in embroiderers' lives but it is not the only one. They share with women not their coreligion-ists many of the conditions that make their work undervalued—the fact that they are viewed as housewives, the fact that in practical terms, they endure abuse and discrimination. And they share with all people of their class the distressing problems of making a living in uncertain and poorly rewarded conditions. Often, open discussion of the communal dimen-sion of economic relations followed on my questions about it, rather than arising spontaneously in conversation. Even the embroiderer who spoke so disparagingly of Hindus taking advantage of Muslims later remarked, "I have a student, a Hindu girl. She comes to my house and I embrace her. We are friends. In a temple, we see an idol and ask, 'Is that God?' 'No, it's stone.' Whether you call him Bhagwan or Allah, it's the same." Embroiderers by and large did not use prevailing relations of production to advance a particular view of communal antagonisms and as far as taking up embroidery was concerned, "if there is interest (*shauq*), then there is no barrier."

CASTE

South Asian anthropology was until recently largely absorbed in the study of caste in the subcontinent (see Appadurai 1986). A subtheme has been whether caste exists among Muslims, and if so, what is its nature? Although many writers on caste in the Uttar Pradesh region tend to lump Muslims into a single group, with no further explication, others, notably Crooke (1896), Ansari (1960), and the contributors to Ahmad's important 1978 volume (Ahmad 1978a), drew attention to the differentiated social world of Muslims in South Asia. The emergent picture of Muslim "caste" society, typically, has shown a primary division between so-called Ashraf and non-Ashraf groups; the former distinguished by their purported foreign origin, and internally differentiated according to genealogical proximity to the Prophet; the latter group containing an array of "occupational" castes, thought to be indigenous converts from Hinduism and subject to their own ranking. Organizational subgroupings and forms of marriage among Muslims are again different from those of Hindus. Ahmad (1978b), though, has made a strong case for the shared emphasis of both Muslims and Hindus upon the principle of status elevation and the means to achieve it.

The occupational associations of the non-Ashraf castes are strong but not obligatory (Cole 1989). Even in precolonial and colonial times, Muslims rarely made up the mass of agricultural laborers but were primarily an urban population of artisans and petty bourgeois (Cole 1989; Bhatty 1978). Historically, being an artisan and having high status have not been mutually exclusive (see Cole 1989 on Sayyid weavers).

Chikan embroiderers range from high-status Sayyids, the uppermost of the Ashraf category, to women of occupational groups including Darzis (tailors), Nais (barbers), and Kabariyas (vegetable sellers). The origin stories of chikan also indicate its mixed social heritage, distributed among high-born but destitute women, non-Ashraf male artisans and court servants, and high-status but poor villagers.

There was considerable reluctance to talk about caste. Questions about the informant's caste were time and again deflected or repudiated. A common response was the familiar one that Muslims do not have caste distinctions like Hindus. Even if some notion of status difference among Muslims was acknowledged, for example, in marriage, embroiderers would quickly point out the contrasting lack of constraint on interdining, a social activity strongly proscribed in traditional Hindu practice. Another pointed out that "people take on names today but there are all sorts of people under that name. Julahas come under Siddiqui. Shahs are Siddiquis. Everyone puts Khan Sahib in their name. So if I tell you I'm a Khan, you won't believe me. What can I tell you? If you really ask someone who they are, they can't tell you—it's all mixed up these days." Conversely, appearance is often assumed to be a poor guide to "true status." When I had left one embroiderer's house with my assistant, she and her companion (who had come along to help us locate addresses) discussed the claim that the informant was a Pathan. "They seemed to me like Darzis," said the companion, "but with poverty who can tell?"

There was some correlation between apparent high status and high levels of skill. Those workers whose ancestors to the third generation or fourth generation made chikan, and who were more highly skilled in the craft, all had, or claimed, higher status (i.e., from among the Ashraf groups). But the converse was not necessarily true, that moderately or low skilled women doing the easiest and simplest work were all from the non-Ashraf castes. Anyone inquiring about chikan is told, by almost everyone associated with the craft, that today it is made by all castes ("*sab hī jāt se*"). But I neither met nor heard of women from the lowest-status groups, like Bhangis (sweepers) doing chikan. Indeed, women from low-status occupational groups are more likely to have well-defined and recognized jobs compared to women whose lack of specialized skills leaves only chikan as a source of employment. Two Shia families both claimed Sayyid status. But given the focus of my work upon Sunnis, I cannot say whether most Shias claim this status (or high status in general) or not (for more on caste among Lucknow Shias, see Cole 1989:74–84).

Overall, I believe that among the various reference points for women's self-assessment in their working lives, caste is not especially significant. There is no formal or informal collectivity of chikan embroiderers that functions in any way like a caste or occupational association, unlike what is found among the Dhobis. However, the limited information I obtained on caste and status may reflect my stated interest in embroidery (as opposed to either broader social or political concerns, or narrower familial or neighborhood ones). As the subjects of intermittent, but regular enquiry by scholars and survey-takers, embroiderers have begun to distill a sense of themselves as "chikan embroiderers" that includes some, but excludes other elements of their experience. Caste and status differences are not insignificant to embroiderers. They remain important for the conduct of social relations and, critically, for making marriages. But of the occasions and vehicles of the expression of caste difference, chikan provides few, or none.

PURDAH

The institution of purdah (from *pardā*—lit., curtain) has been extensively criticized as the cause of women's continuing dependency and poverty in the Middle East and South Asia. Indeed, purdah is specifically cited in embroiderers' conversations as a cause of troubles and a barrier to the improvement of their economic fortunes.

The ethnography of purdah in South Asia has increased considerably in the last twenty years, revealing many of its complex economic, cultural, and social aspects (e.g., Mandelbaum 1988; Vreede-de-Stuers 1968; Papanek and Minault 1982; Jeffery 1979). Abu-Lughod's (1986) complex analysis of deference and veiling among Bedouin women in Egypt has influenced my own understanding of purdah. While she refers explicitly to Bedouin values in her interpretation of the implications of *haṣham* (shame, modesty), many of her insights are very useful in the South Asian setting.

Purdah regulates the interactions of women with certain kinds of men. Typically, Hindu women must avoid specific male affines (in-laws) and Muslim women are restricted from contact with men outside the family, or at least their contact with these men is highly circumscribed (Papanek 1982:3). In practice, many elements of both "Hindu" and "Muslim" purdah are shared by women of both groups in South Asia (Vatuk 1982; Jeffery 1979), and Hindu and Muslim women both adopt similar strategies of self-effacement, like covering the face, keeping silent, and looking down, when in the company of persons to be avoided. However, the ideal of confinement within the home is a more consistent feature of purdah among Muslims of all statuses, and wearing a *burqa* when traveling outside the home distinguishes Muslim women in purdah most of all.

The separation and seclusion of women, whether Hindu or Muslim, is justified by and in turn reinforces strong moral convictions about the nature of sexuality and the disparate natures of men and women (Abu-Lughod 1986; Jeffery 1979; Mandelbaum 1988; Papanek 1982; Vatuk 1982). No one expects that sexual drives can or ought to be repressed. However, sexuality is a threat to the integrity of the descent group and the authority of its senior members, and so the social pressure to control sexuality is intense. Honor (*'izzat*) can only be wholly realized by men, but honor itself depends upon women maintaining *sharam* (lit., shame—"sense of shame," modesty). Central to *sharam* is knowing how, when, and where to act with diffidence and restraint. Women do not need to be coerced into modest behavior. Its principles are internalized. Women emphasize their own respectability and piety in taking on the veil, and are eminently comfortable with at least some of the restraints that purdah places upon them (Abu-Lughod 1986; Jeffery 1979).

Many female Muslims are effectively cut off from public life. Most embroiderers cannot conduct relationships in the marketplace openly and face to face. They know little about how the things they make are used or how much they are sold for. The recurrent description of chikan embroiderers as *"pardanashin"* primarily refers to the fact that they do not work outside the house, and rarely go to collect embroidery work themselves. Instead, they rely upon relatives, neighbors, or agents to bring the work to them. The necessary networks to bring work to women at home are so well developed that seclusion and chikan are indelibly related in thought and practice.

Embroiderers state openly that only women in purdah are interested in learning chikan in the first place, and because of purdah, they learn no other skills, and find themselves trapped in embroidery. Just as seclusion prevents women from acquiring other skills, it prevents them from knowing even about chikan. Ayub Khan said of his wife, who worked at his behest, that she could not be expected to know anything about chikan since she never went out. What a woman knows or does not know is, though, difficult to determine when modesty requires that a woman curb her speech in the presence of men. Among the most skilled embroiderers, those who were widowed or divorced overtly contrasted their present outspokenness toward outsiders with their past reserve or silence when they were married.

Higher-caste Muslims (or those aspiring to higher status) often observe stricter purdah than lower-caste Muslims, and the ability to seclude one's female relatives has traditionally been an indicator of status among both Muslims and Hindus. Purdah observation among embroiderers followed this principle up to a point: embroiderers belonging to lower-status occupational castes veil and limit their movement outside the house to a lesser extent than women claiming Ashraf affiliations. But caste is by no means the only determining factor in the decision to veil and with what degree of strictness. Where high status confronts education, wealth, and thus superior *class* position, purdah may actually be relaxed to accommodate new ideas about the social roles of women. Lateef (1990:134–35) further cautions that purdah reflects "regional and class differentials and the need for symbolic Islamic differentiation." A *burqa* is one of the most expressive, visible, and powerful symbols of Islamic identity and difference. However differences in veiling are to be explained, it is impossible to discount the influence of purdah on job opportunities, social relationships, and mobility, even when its restrictions are light (see Lateef 1990:148; Weiss 1991).

Access to the Household

An important measure of purdah constraints among Muslim women is the degree of access strangers (particularly unrelated men) have to the household, and the ease with which women can enter a home where men are present. It is difficult for me to be definitive about purdah observation inside Muslim homes in Lucknow, because, as a woman, my own access to the innermost parts of the house was unquestioned. Unless an unrelated man presented himself at the house in the course of an interview, I was unable to tell how he was likely to be received. However, if a man of the family was present during the conversation, it was easy to notice how his presence circumscribed the normal coming and going of women to and from the house. A woman might be glimpsed at the door or window, or peeping around the curtain shielding the entry-way, but she would just as quickly disappear, pulling her scarf around her face if she was not in a *burqa*. If she did not leave altogether, a terse communication would be conducted between the women on each side of the curtain. Once when I was visiting a skilled embroiderer and her nephew, a female friend of the embroiderer passed by the window, peering inside to see who was there. Catching sight of the young man, she sped on. When the embroiderer saw this, she called out, "It's alright, he's just a child," but her friend did not turn around.

Because their presence interrupts the flow of women in and out of the house, men cannot help but affect the activities and working habits of women, even when they do not take an active interest in their womenfolk's waged work. This is especially the case in small houses where it is impossible to designate a completely separate area for women. However, when there are no grown men to act as gatekeepers of the flow of personnel (and, inevitably, work), different kinds of problems arise.

All-female households, or female-headed households, face the difficult task of managing family honor at the same time as getting work that is necessary for the family's survival. Forced to take on responsibilities normally assumed by a man, women find they must shed their seclusion proportionately. The care and concern of brothers was especially important in preserving the modesty of divorced or unmarried women. Alternatively, women may find themselves "policed" by brothers or brothers-in-law, often indirectly through the vigilance of these relatives' wives. Widows who lack the protection and benefits of a constant male presence but who must maintain purdah constraints because of the irresistible, if intermittent, attention of relatives, are forced to strike a cautious balance between boldness and *sharam*.

For example, one skilled embroiderer, despite having attended many chikan sales exhibitions outside Lucknow, had resigned herself to not being able to do this in Lucknow, since her family would not allow it. Mindful of the deference she owed them, she could raise no objections. "When I'm in front of my elders, even now I don't look them in the eye." Given the fierce competition for exhibition slots and the dividends they are expected to yield, this was a serious concession indeed.

Women who can build on their own skills and attract some prestige, like my teacher, might venture out into the public realm in a way unimaginable when they were living under the supervision of an adult male. Communication with men becomes inevitable, and in my teacher's case, she had gradually become more comfortable in their presence. While purdah may be relaxed inside a home, dealings with business associates, *mahajans*, government officials, and so on can be managed more adroitly by women who can use purdah rules to limit their own accessibility. For example, entrance to the house may be denied if interaction with a man is not wanted at any given time, particularly if he is an agent or representative of a *mahajan* who is eager to get his *mal*! I also noticed that modified access was used in one house, so that a man who was on warmer terms with the family was admitted into the back room of the house (indicating that he was regarded with affection and was in the family's confidence), while a man who was less well known was hosted in a front room (indicating aloofness from the family, thus superiority, but also distance).

Wearing a Burqa

Virtually all married (as well as divorced and widowed) Muslim women are swathed in a *burqa* when they go "outside."[3] *Burqas* are not simply oppressive extensions of protective walls but often reflect relative wealth and personal style. Most *burqas* today are of the kind described over a decade ago by Papanek (1982:10) as "expensive and elegant." They are black, of cotton or synthetic material, and comprise a coat and cape that covers the head. The old-style, white-cotton *burqas*, made of one piece of cloth from the head down with eyeholes and a gauze "visor," are no longer used even by poor urban women. Depending upon the wearer's wealth, though, black *burqas* may be new and crisp, or threadbare and moth-eaten. Brown and deep blue variants of the black *burqa* can be seen occasionally, although the most dramatic designs (including tiger-stripes) are monopolized by wealthier, nonworking women.

One of the most interesting aspects of the *burqa* is that its use does not conform completely to the rules of interaction. Instead, wearing the *burqa* is situationally variable (Vatuk 1982:68; Jeffery 1979). Theoretically, a woman should be completely covered before unrelated men, anywhere she may encounter such men. But very few embroiderers that I met would put on their *burqas* to go into the lane just outside their house, or even to visit friends in an adjoining *gali*. In these eventualities, a shawl or a *dupatta* to cover the upper body and the head sufficed. If they expected to go beyond the vicinity of their homes, most women (excepting the very young, the very old, and some unmarried, youthful women) studiously donned their *burqas*. Again, once outside the city of Lucknow, and depending upon who accompanied them, women might remove the *burqa* altogether, some as soon as they reached the main railway station at Charbagh. The cape of a *burqa* has an attached veil that can be lowered over the face. Some women go about with the veil down, some do not. To some extent, this depends upon where the woman is. If she is close to home, she is more likely to wear the veil down, pushing it up as she enters territory where she will be unrecognized, and thus not judged. A few women, though, take care to veil themselves as soon as they step out of the door. Others told me that use of the face veil was a matter of personal choice. Brides and young daughters-in-law are expected to veil their faces more conscientiously.

There are subtle differences in the tailoring of some black *burqas*. Most coats, for example, have full, long sleeves. Others are sleeveless, the cape comprising the sole outer covering for the arms. Others have small details like scalloping on the cuffs or edge of the cape. I have never seen *burqas* being acquired, only being used, and so I am unable to comment further on the expression and implementation of women's choices in this most critical of garments. However, differences in *burqa* styling and embellishment, combined with the distinct stature and gait of the wearer, and the likelihood that one might glimpse some shaded features, together mean that the image of absolute anonymity under the *burqa* is mistaken.

The *burqa* is worn over a woman's ordinary clothes and wearers get very hot, especially in the summer months. But women did not speak of the *burqa* as a terrible burden. Because it allows a woman to go outside while taking the protection of her house with her—"portable seclusion" in Papanek's phrase—*burqas* are regarded as liberating. One woman even claimed a practical advantage for the *burqa*, "there's so much dust in the street, it [the *burqa*] keeps my clothes clean when I go outside."

The *burqa* was especially valued for the way it was thought to avert the attentions of unrelated men—and men in Lucknow were emphatically denounced as "*badma'āsh*," (scoundrels, bad types). "Men might want to ruin us," said one woman, "but this *burqa* conceals us and keeps our honor." The *burqa* (to paraphrase Papanek) symbolically shelters the wearer and confers respectability. I was not expected by my informants to wear a *burqa*, although I tried to ensure I was modestly (if not always very well!) dressed. However, it still came as no surprise to anyone that I should attract the verbal assaults and impudent gaze of men. But in the company of a respectably attired woman, it was a completely different story. Once, when riding in a cycle rickshaw with a completely veiled woman, I was struck by the fact that not a single man glanced even in *my* direction. This experience clearly demonstrated the chilling impact of the sight of a *burqa* on men's behavior and illustrated that men, as well as women, are responsible for concealing and mastering their natures. Staring at women was, in the view of the embroiderers, simply in the nature of men. Staring at a woman in a *burqa* (or anyone close to her), though, would be a grievous violation of etiquette, not to speak of an immense insult to the honor of the woman's family.

On another occasion, I was walking with my *burqa*-clad teacher through her neighborhood to the main road. She remarked at our destination, "See, nobody bothered you when you were with me, did they?" This might have been simply because being with my teacher, instantly recognizable even in her *burqa* since she did not veil her face, legitimized my presence in the neighborhood in a way that my solitary travels to and from the *galis* (neighborhood lanes) did not. In turn, this depended upon her adhering to certain standards of decent behavior, which included fit and respectable dress outside her house.

Vatuk's (1982:39) explanation of some of the situational variability in *burqa* wearing, specifically why *burqas* are often discarded among complete strangers, alludes to similar themes. The veil is intended to conceal a woman not from the outsider, to whom she is utterly unknown, but instead neighbors, distant kin, or acquaintances of the family. As she writes, "[o]ne observes purdah with reference to the social approval of persons whose opinions about one's respectability matter. Beyond this group, where one is completely anonymous, the veil becomes unnecessary."

As a general rule, purdah restrictions in the city today are more relaxed for women than in the past and no longer reflect rigid separations in the social worlds and roles of the sexes (Lateef 1990:145). Younger women can move about more freely and are more likely to be literate and even moderately educated. Expectations of when a girl should begin wearing a *burqa* have altered, in some families in the space of single generation. Where the older women in a household may have put on the *burqa* as children, certainly by the time they attained puberty, daughters of the house may not begin wearing a *burqa* until they are married. Deferring the use of a *burqa* until marriage is a trend among Muslims all over India. But it does not apply to all Muslim women, and varying degrees of veiling at successive stages of life may reflect different political and personal circumstances. Purdah among Shias in the old city is said by them, and by some Sunnis, to be observed with exceptional rigor, even by young girls. Divorced women, whose unenviable state has fundamentally compromised their own and their family's honor, tended to be more fastidious about the use of the *burqa* than their married or widowed counterparts.

No one expects *burqas* to be abandoned completely. For one thing, there is the strong influence of "*'ādat*" (habit, custom). *Adat* is roughly similar to what Jeffery (1979) terms more simply the "internalization" of purdah, but its meaning includes more than simply acceptance of, and commitment to, ideas and norms of behavior between the sexes. *Adat* is commonly used to describe both personal and community attachments. It is *adat* to wear a *burqa*, to wear a *sari*, to consume *pan*, to enjoy the taste of hot food ("*zubān par mirć kā zaikā hamārī 'ādat heh*"), and to eat with the fingers. Citing *adat* defines, in ascending order, the habits of a lifetime, the practices of the local Muslim community, and sometimes the customs of Indians. *Adat* cannot simply be abandoned, since it is ideologically intertwined with personal comfort and security *and* group integrity. In this sense, chikan embroiderers' wearing of the *burqa* indeed reflects "symbolic Islamic differentiation."

I labor this point because it is the *burqa*, more than anything else, that defines the embroidery worker in Lucknow. The *burqa*-clad woman hard at work on her embroidery appears in promotional literature and magazine articles as a sign of Lucknow chikan, although the chance that a woman might actually be embroidering while clothed in her *burqa* (since she only wears the *burqa* outside and she works inside her home) is practically nil. The only such occasions in my experience were when women gathered together in the semipublic spaces of the Uttar Pradesh Export Corporation (UPEC) production centers. Most advertisements and articles include drawings of veiled women, since it is clearly not possible in the normal course of events to photograph a woman embroidering in her *burqa*. The only photographic image of this type that I have seen is in a tourist brochure for Lucknow, and shows an elderly woman in her *burqa* with veil drawn back, seated indoors, apparently embroidering. Close examination reveals that she is in fact "embroidering" a piece of finished chikan and is sitting inside a chikan store. The impossible illusions of chikan advertisements allow the viewer to see what is normally unseen and signal the embroiderer's Muslim identity and exoticism in a nation where most women do not wear *burqas*.

The *burqa* has produced ambiguous effects in the lives of women. On one hand, its power to give shelter and respectability has allowed women to go out of the house where otherwise they could not. However, it cannot alter the fact that women may not enter comfortably, if at all, into face-to-face relations with unrelated men. Moreover, the need, time after time, to put on the *burqa* every time a woman goes outside—however brief a trip it may be—requires an effort that women are not always prepared to make. In short, while going outside holds neither fears nor surprises for the women I met (for contrast, see Jeffery's [1979] description of the trepidation of *burqa*-clad women going outside in her study of Pirzade women in Delhi), at the same time it is not the occasion for unmitigated pleasure.

Schildkrout (1983) observed that children in West Africa are used by their older female relatives as social and economic proxies, permitting craftswomen confined to the house access to markets. Children perform a comparable role for women in chikan embroidering neighborhoods. Girls fetch and carry chikan work to and from their mothers. Small boys run messages and buy provisions. But unlike the women in Schildkrout's study, chikan embroiderers are rarely so confined that they cannot go outside themselves if they need to. Using children to run errands also reflects the fact that women have other, pressing domestic tasks to perform, and that they are happy to use children as an additional resource. Women often said that having to go out to collect work was a time-consuming, burdensome job. In fact, to get work delivered to their homes was a stated preference.

Even if purdah were to be removed, women would not be presented with a host of employment or lifestyle options. Men, for example, are free to pursue a much wider range of occupations and move freely in public—and yet they too may be unable to get a secure and regular income. As for Hindu embroiderers, they do not experience the constraints of purdah in quite the same way as Muslim women, nor are they required to wear a *burqa*, but the dispersal of Hindu embroiderers in the countryside (whence most are now drawn) and their distance from the city has a negative impact on their lives and options comparable to the effects of stricter seclusion on Muslim women.

EMBROIDERY AND THE LIFE CYCLE

The majority of embroiderers are young women. Married embroiderers are often the mothers of young families, with no children of working age. Ayub Khan remarked to me that marriage was often the occasion upon which women gave up making chikan. When I repeated this idea to my teacher, she only grudgingly agreed. The glaring fact that *she* made chikan, and that so many of her married relatives and neighbors made chikan, and did so because income from men fell short, was obvious.

Marriage as a means to cement or improve status is well documented in the anthropology of Indian Muslims as well as Hindus (e.g., Ahmad 1978b). For the parents of a young embroiderer, a future in which she no longer has to work for wages, where any such activity would be regarded as both unnecessary and demeaning, must seem very attractive. Successful marriages (defined in this context as ones in which the bride's family makes its claims of status well enough to attract an entirely self-sufficient groom) do occur—although not as often as my male informant seemed to imply. Giving up embroidery at marriage depends upon whether a woman's new family is sufficiently socially differentiated from the mass of chikan-embroidering families; in other words, when the husband's income, or that of his family, is enough to preclude her working for wages.

On the whole, though, the frequency with which newly married women were required to *learn* chikan in order to start earning money more than offset those cases where brides had suddenly and unalterably stopped embroidering. Moreover, marriage presents more challenges and difficulties to a family than opportunities for social elevation (see Jeffery 1979 and Abu-Lughod 1988 for more observations on the ambiguous attitude toward daughters and marriages in Muslim society). The marriage of a girl is the measure of the respectability of a family and a test of whether it can properly discharge its most fundamental responsibility to its daughters (Jeffery 1979; Mandelbaum 1988). For the girl, marriage is among the most important events in her life. Her adulthood will be spent in the house of her husband and his family, and her happiness there depends on many factors: the compatability of their statuses; her ability to produce children, specifically sons; her competence in household tasks; her own personal qualities that may endear her to her new family and enable her to withstand the trials and abuse that a cruel family might heap upon her. Marriage between parallel cousins (the children of two brothers, two sisters, or two cousins of the same sex) is common among Muslims, and helps ease the transition for the bride, as well as requiring less adjustment on the part of her immediate family, because the family to which she is going is obviously well known. Several of my informants had married their patrilateral or matrilateral parallel first cousin. For those who had not, problems in the marriage were not infrequently blamed on the fact that the union was not between cousins.

Marriage is also a time of separation for the women in the household. Daughters can assist in household work while they live at home, or work on chikan themselves. Mothers and daughters work closely in the home, preparing food, cleaning, and working on embroidery. Their relationship comes to resemble friendship as the daughters grow older, although the older woman retains her fundamental authority. Upon marriage, a girl is lost as both income-earner and companion.

In the effort to broadcast their claims to status, and to ensure a daughter's future well-being in her new family, parents try to organize as lavish a wedding as possible. The marriage ceremony itself, and all its various accoutrements, as well as many expensive presents for the *susral* (in-laws), require a show of generosity that, while considered essential to the bride's standing in her new family, is financially crippling for her parents. A young, unmarried girl in a chikan training scheme told me. "I'm waiting for my marriage now. But in-laws want so much, refrigerators, scooters . . . it's too much money. How can you get it?"

Much of the cost of a wedding is borne through obtaining loans at heavy rates of interest from *mahajans*. One woman, known to me as "Ayah" because of having worked for my assistant as a nanny, had taken out such a loan to fund the marriage of her eldest daughter, which included expensive invitations and gifts, as well as the obligatory feast. The woman was still paying off the loan, in installments of Rs. 20, when I visited, two years after the marriage had taken place. The heavy cost that families feel compelled to incur for their daughter's weddings takes on an added urgency when they fear their child will suffer abuse, or worse, murder. And yet despite her efforts, and in circumstances of almost unbelievable horror, this woman's daughter had been burnt to death by her husband and father-in-law less than a year after her wedding, while in the advanced stages of pregnancy.

Occupational Diversification

If a wife is to give up making chikan later on in her married life, she must depend entirely upon the actions of her male affines or male children to make this possible, for no effort on her part (including doing chikan embroidery) will be sufficient to make any major difference in the economic fortunes of the household. Several women had husbands, sons, or nephews who were beginning to differentiate themselves socially from their neighbors with skills that were in demand in the Gulf states (referred to collectively as "*Saudi 'Arab*"). Decorative welding, jewelry-making, and watch-making/repairing were among these skills, dubbed "Muslim crafts" by non-Muslims. In my experience, all practitioners of these crafts with prospects abroad were young men. In one case, two brothers from a family of Nais (barbers) had recently learnt to make and repair watches and were preparing to go abroad during the time of my fieldwork. They were attempting to persuade their brothers, brothers-in-law, and cousins, most of whom no longer did barbering but had switched to a range of low-skilled manufacturing jobs, to join them. In particular, they hoped that by bringing the men into the watch business, the women would stop doing their sewing and embroidery. A lingering family dispute, whose details were not revealed, was given as the reason why the remaining male relatives had not yet gone along with this plan. Meanwhile, the women continued doing sewing work, and, on occasion, chikan work.

Women in families where these shifts in employment had already solidified did not make chikan. A cousin of one embroiderer was married to a man who made bicycles. She had six children, four of them adult, working sons. Two sons had learned decorative gold jewellery work and had jobs in the Gulf states. I do not know about the monetary rewards of making bicycles, but the family was sufficiently well-off for the sister-in-law to go on *hajj* (pilgrimage to Mecca). She could not even tell the right side from the wrong side of a piece of chikan work, despite her own mother's having done the craft.

In the absence of dependable institutions for the relief of poverty in India, ties to kin, neighbors, and patrons are essential for families without husbands and fathers, and nurturing those relationships is as time-consuming and as critical as earning wages (Sharma 1986:5). The fewer children, or brothers and sisters that women have, and secondarily, the fewer relatives living nearby, the less practical and financial help they can draw upon. Giving help, for example taking in less fortunate relatives, represents an additional burden to already strained family resources. Often, the threat of incurring such a burden is enough for people to rebuff their needy relatives, especially those related not by blood, but through marriage. Distance makes estrangements from family easier both to countenance and to achieve. Leaving Lucknow for work is to some a step toward a better living for the entire family and to others an opportunity to jettison family responsibilities. These are the occasions when husbands desert wives, brothers lose touch with sisters, or sons sever ties to their parents. An embroiderer with an uncle in the United States said the family never heard from, and certainly did not get any money, from him. However, the urban tendency to more dispersed and atomized households, particularly with the search for work pressuring more men to settle away from their parents upon marriage, means that simply moving to another part of the city may be sufficient to lose touch with the natal home.

The Developmental Cycle

As a woman grows older, her status in the household tends to grow, and many household tasks and wage labor are taken up by her children and her daughters-in-law. Older women are less represented among chikan embroiderers, but this does not mean that most women can look forward to giving up embroidery for money as they become seniors within the household. The prevalence of younger women reflects recent expansion of the industry and worsening poverty among the urban and rural poor.

True "retirement" for embroiderers depends not upon the vagaries of the developmental cycle of the domestic group so much as the group's overall economic status. A friend of my teacher's who had taken up chikan when her husband died gave it up once her seven children (including three sons) were almost all grown up. What had made the difference was that each child (including one daughter) had been educated and at least three were pursuing, or planning, professional careers. In short, she had only needed chikan for a short period of financial stress, shifting then to teaching Holy Koran before finally "taking rest" (*"ārām kar rahīṅ haiṅ"*). For this woman, being compelled to make chikan did not seem to hurt the pursuit of lofty educational and vocational goals on the part of her family. However, the longer duration of most chikan careers indicates more chronic economic problems.

A particularly pathetic category of embroiderers is wives of elderly men faced with having to secure an income once their husbands have simply stopped working, or even searching for work. On the other hand, women do not "retire" unless financial stringency ends or if they become physically incapable of doing embroidery. Between the poor evening light, the darkness of indoor rooms or the shaded courtyard, the low contrast of white thread on light colored cloth, and the fine detail of needlework, almost every women I met complained of eye strain, headaches, and back problems. Most feared was a degeneration in eyesight to the point of blindness. "Chikan destroys the eyes, and eyes are the most important thing in life," said one. Irreparable damage to the eyes had caused many old women to halt their chikan work, although how they were to sustain themselves in this eventuality was not explained. In fact, many women with quite severe eye problems probably work in spite of them for as long as they can. Some are forced to continue doing embroidery into extreme old age, in spite of obvious ill-health and declining strength.

Currently, the practice of embroidery is spreading as much throughout caste and status groups as it is between them, driven by the need for money and facilitated by marriages that bring women from "non-embroidering" *mohallas* and villages into "embroidering" ones (or vice versa). While the most prevalent form of skill transmission is from mother to daughter, a third of the women I met had learnt from their mothers-in-law or sisters-in-law, and had been working for wages all of their married life. Doing chikan or not doing chikan is, in these cases, a reasonably reliable indicator of socioeconomic differentiation.

CHAPTER 4

Work and Wages

Because there is no narrowly defined, hereditary group that makes chikan, there is no single name that is attached to its makers. This was even true in the past when men were making chikan on a more formal basis. Chikan embroiderers often refer to themselves, and are referred to as "*kārīgars*" (workers).[1] But *karigar* is not a consistent and exclusive label. Often embroiderers are simply called "*voh chikan banātīn hain*" ("*those who make chikan*") or "*chikan/kārhāi banānīwālīn*" (makers of chikan/embroidery).

With no name to distinguish them as a specific set of producers, do women regard themselves as professionals or wage laborers? Embroidery is commonly described by government officials, development workers, the Lucknow public, and especially *mahajans*, as work for "housewives," to be done in their free time (*fursat*), that gives them a little extra money to supplement the main income from men. As one *mahajan* put it, "*Ghar baiṭhe kām mil jātā hai, paisā mil jātā hai. Khālī time men*." (They just sit at home and they get work, and they get money. In their spare time!) Is this oft-cited description of them as "part-time" or "free-time" workers reflected in either their opinions or their practices?

In general, women look to men financial support and are disappointed if this support fails. Viewing men as the breadwinners assumes that the women are not, a perception that diminishes their significance as income earners.[2] Again, the fact that women do give up chikan in rare circumstances implies that women do not see their identities primarily constituted in wage labor and production. But the situation is not quite so clear-cut. First, the option to give up work is not a real one for many women, and it is in this context that we must examine their orientation toward work. Second, there are the highly skilled, who may not even state a desire to give up chikan work.

EMBROIDERY WAGES

No one in Lucknow, consumer, embroiderer, government official, or *mahajan*, disagrees that the wages for chikan embroidery are meager. Even the highest piece wages are low relative to the earnings of many others in the chikan production process or those involved in other craft activities. "If men can make Rs. 77 a day doing *zardozi*, why should they make chikan?" said Ayub Khan. "You only can make Rs. 10–12 a day for chikan." But while women could state readily how much they were to receive for a given piece, it was more difficult for them to say how much more money they would like to get, how many items they could make in a day, or to give weekly or monthly estimates of earnings, because "*kām mustaqil nahīn hai*" (the work isn't constant). The amount of work varies so much from week to week, and productivity with it, that earnings averages on their own are of debatable value.

Female agents, on the other hand, were usually able to say how much they made per week, or per month, or the most they could make in these time periods. Even the most skilled agents insisted that it was impossible to earn over a certain amount in a given week or month, however hard one worked. Smaller agents said they made around Rs. 100 a week. Rs. 400 a month was a consistent upper limit for them. The most successful agents, who had effectively entered into private enterprise on their own account, and numbered less than ten individuals, might make as much as Rs. 1,000 to Rs. 2,500 a month from making chikan and getting it made. For a simple embroiderer, Rs. 100 to Rs. 150 per month is the upper limit. Some may make as little as Rs. 10–12 a week, less than Rs. 50 a month. While wages from the *mahajan* are universally acknowledged to be very low, (even by the admission of several *mahajans*) the relative dependability of work makes the *mahajan* a preferred source—often the *only* source—of employment, compared to the various government and cooperative organizations.

Embroidery tools are relatively cheap. Women are not expected to supply the kacca (permeable, unfinished—"weak") thread required for most chikan embroidery.[3] *Pakka* thread (impermeable, fast—"strong"), which is used in all *jali* work and is similar to thread used in garment sewing, can either be supplied by the agent or *mahajan*, or, if the work is from the government or SEWA Lucknow, the woman may buy it herself. Reels of *pakka* thread come from the same shop as the *kacca tāgā* (thread) and in 1989 cost between Rs. 1 and Rs. 1.25 each, depending upon quality. A reel may last for a month or a week, according to the amount of work a woman does. Needles are bought by the embroiderer and cost ten paise each, although *jali* needles are a little bigger and cost a little more. A packet of needles will last some time, although embroiderers lose a lot of them.

In the commercial world, better wages are usually paid for more skilled work. Thus, the lowest wages are paid for *bakhya* and the highest for *murri* (although the wages for each become roughly equal if the *bakhya* is of an exceptionally fine quality). *Jali* is regarded by many as well-paid work that also demands a high degree of skill. *Jali* is the most demanding and difficult work, and the most draining on energy and eyesight. Rates of pay for *jali* are calculated on the basis of the number and size of *phūls* (flowers) on the garment, and discrete regions for the application of *hatkattī*. Wages are always stated in terms of paise per unit, not rupees.

The most common article for embroidering, in both the city and the village, is a *kurta*. Since the amount of work on a *kurta* is small, wages are usually under Rs. 10 per piece. The larger the piece, and the greater the amount of work, the higher the wages usually are. On the other hand, the embroiderer must work for a longer time before she receives her wages, and once she exceeds the average time for completing such an item, the lower her wage relative to what she might have received for a day or two's work. A continuous supply of simple *kurtas* results in a cash flow (or trickle) that outweighs the deferred, albeit larger, rewards of embroidering large items. However, few embroiderers are able to exert any influence over the kind of work they get.

There are many domestic jobs that a woman is expected to complete before she can turn to chikan. Therefore, the less work an item requires, the quicker it can be done—because the work is scant obviously, but also because women are more likely to finish it in less than a week, maybe even a day or two. Anything that takes longer is more likely to fall prey to additional household or social responsibilities, or the vagaries of the *tabīyat* (disposition, temperament) of the embroiderer—best described in this case as boredom, with an accompanying inclination to be distracted. In the midst of finishing an article, or several articles, women's guesses as to how long it would actually take to complete were always too ambitious, and on a return visit a few days, or even a week or two later, the same piece might be there, still unfinished. As time goes on, embroiderers are likely to sit on (sometimes literally) unfinished pieces, particularly if some quicker work comes their way.

Even very poor women admitted to not working if the mood did not seize them. To *mahajans*, this practice confirms the lack of seriousness of their female workers. But it does tally more or less with the common artisanal pattern of working (Kumar 1988), although the activities that "replace" wage labor, and the emphasis placed upon them, differ. The kind of embroidery work being done, irregularity in the supply of work, and any additional requirements of quality or speed (particularly speed) make different demands upon embroiderers' time. Women are also engaged in other daily activities with which chikan embroidery must be coordinated. The degree of control that a woman has over how she organizes tasks and spends her time affects her productivity in embroidery, as well as her capacity to exploit opportunities to make specially commissioned work, or be an agent. In my experience, widowed embroiderers and their families had more freedom than others to allocate their own time because there was no senior male in the household to make such decisions for them, or to set their schedules according to his demands. Agents of all skill levels enjoyed more freedom in allocating their time than mere embroiderers did. This was due to their relative freedom to make decisions apart from their spouses—if they had them—and the fact that they made use of younger relatives to do the bulk of the household work.

Individual earnings from chikan work vary according to several factors; the kind of work an embroiderer does, whether it is made to contract for quality or speed, and fluctuations in the supply of work. Some of these factors influence the actual piece-rate a woman gets. Others affect the extent of under- or unemployment she must endure.

Specializing in Forms of Work

Most women can be regarded as formal specialists in either *bakhya* work, *murri* work, or *jali* work. In general, a woman does not choose what type of work she will do, but simply does what she has learnt from others to make. With villages being the source of most new chikan labor, the familiar equation expressed by all manner of people connected with chikan of village: *bakhya (phanda)* versus town:*jali (murri)* is borne out in fact, largely because no traditions of *murri* and *jali*, associated with a specifically Muslim and *urban* population, seem to have taken root in rural areas. Conversely, urban women less often do *bakhya*, although *bakhya* is the most commonly encountered stitch in contemporary chikan. Thinking I had come into the neighborhood to have work made, a Khaddra woman once told me that I would not find *bakhya* being made around there, "it's village work."

Urban embroiderers seem to think that the differences in the kind of work that villagers and city-dwellers do reflects a qualitative difference between villagers' natures and their own. City and village production are simply distinguished by *mahajans* and embroiderers alike as the difference between *mahin* (fine) and *calu* (commonplace) work. Village women's *ṭāṅkās* (stitches) are all said to be thick (*mota*) and crude. Town women especially disparage *dehāt* (country/rural) work, no matter whether they are talking in reference to somewhere a hundred kilometers away or eight. An urban embroiderer gave me her impression of a village woman at work. She set her face in a tight-lipped scowl, grabbed some cloth in a huge wad in her hand, dug in an imaginary needle, and roughly yanked it out. A common joke is that villagers are so stupid they will embroider the mill-stamp on the edge of the cloth, as well as the printed pattern they are supposed to use.

Rural embroiderers are frequently regarded as simply incapable of more difficult kinds of work. Urban embroiderers repeatedly told me that village women cannot do *jali* and have no interest in learning. *Mahajans* seem to share this view. Several argued that *jali* was difficult work and beyond the capacity of village women. This observation is also echoed by other Lakhnawis uninvolved in chikan, who articulate, but cannot explain, the fact that rural women are either unfitted or unable to do more elaborate work.

In their disparaging statements about rural embroiderers, city-dwellers make no distinction between the inhabitants of nearby settlements and embroiderers in more far-flung settlements. Yet in villages a short distance from Lucknow, like Bijnor, Talkatora, Kakori, and Malyabad, women have stitch repertoires essentially similar to those living in Daliganj and Khaddra. There are not only women who profess to know "all the stitches" ("*sab kām,*" "*sab ṭāṅke,*") but stories of resident male artisans (now dead) who had been trained in an elaborate chikan repertoire. One of these men was Subhan Khan, master embroiderer of the village of Usalganj some twenty years ago. Subhan Khan was a skilled chikan embroiderer and agent, a follower of the great Fyaz Khan. Yet Usalganj is not a famous site for fine work today. Instead, Subhan Khan, and others like him, seem to have been more interested in acting as subcontractors, streaming cheap work to women rather than training them in refined embroidery skills. Village embroiderers today are usually called upon to make one or two forms of work exclusively—neither of which is *murri* work. But with up to two generations of family members involved in making chikan, embroiderers of the nearby villagers are clearly not the same as the neophyte *bakhya* embroiderers inducted into the industry in the last decade.

It is possible to find *bakhya* being made in the city, although of a higher quality than that which comes from the village. Urban makers of *bakhya* have shorter family histories in embroidery than women from nearby rural settlements. As well as learning *bakhya* from their families or neighbors as children, at least a third of my interviewees had acquired their skills after marriage. At the same time, women with *murri* and *jali* skills do marry into villages, and village daughters-in-law are time and again cited as the source of spreading chikan knowledge in villages. So why do *murri* and *jali* not appear in the villages, and instead only *bakhya* or *phanda*? Kamrunissa, a skilled embroiderer of Daliganj, challenged the idea that new brides can teach their families new embroidery skills: "Daughters-in-law can't teach anybody anything. They look down all the time. Everyone tells *them* what to do." There is no reason, though, why they cannot teach their children, or younger sisters-in-law.

An even more important factor may be the fact that the conventional divisions of labor in the embroidery phase, associated with the recent expansion of a mass-market industry, are so well established that there is no effort to transform them. With his limited control over production, the *mahajan* is an unlikely figure to urge the application of new skills in the village. The inability of village embroiderers to acquire, or sometimes to sustain, a more complex repertoire shows how the trend toward cheap, simpler work has created the village/city distinction, and not just built upon it.

The coarse qualities of village women and their inability to make "fine" things are frequently cited as the reason for their low wages. But not all urban embroiderers subscribe unreflectingly to these views. On the contrary, many offer astute commentaries into how the *mahajans'* interests drive changes that affect them and their rural counterparts. They will argue, for example, that it is the ignorance of rural embroiderers—an outcome of their simplicity and their physical confinement— that makes them ripe for the exploitation of *mahajans* and agents. While this version still relies upon a characterization of the "country bumpkin," it also recognizes that rural embroiderers are sought out for the advantages they offer the *mahajan*. Since low-skilled or unskilled village embroiderers are low-paid and plentiful, they threaten urban embroiderers' continued employment and higher wages. For the most part, urban embroiderers stick closely to their own specialities of *jali* and *murri*, specialties that become more threatened as *bakhya* becomes more entrenched.

Adjusting Wages for Quality and Speed

It is widely acknowledged that varying qualities of work attract different wage rates. As one agent put it, *"waisā kām, waise paise"* (as the work, so the money). While higher wages for quality may be built into the piece wage, I heard agents offering the incentive of a few extra paise or a rupee to elicit better-quality items. In fact, many embroiderers deliberately adjust the quality of their work according to the wage they expect to receive and the time they have to do it. For example, a common "mistake" in embroidery is fashioning a single leaf on top of two printed ones. *Mahajans* and agents regard this as a surreptitious and deceitful practice. However, in viewing it in this way, they effectively contradict the widespread assumption that village women are stupid (in which case, the flaw ought to be attributed to simple ineptitude).

Even urban women may be unconcerned about how their work reflects upon them. One day, a Madeganj embroiderer who worked for the SEWA Lucknow organization was tugging at some overtight *hatkatti* to ensure it would appear unpuckered. Predictably, it ripped, but she did not appear worried. "By the time they notice it, I will have been paid," she said. This woman was well aware of what distinguished good from bad work. In fact, she specifically criticized the stupidity and clumsiness of village embroiderers. She was quite capable of pointing out to me, as I tried some *bakhya* embroidery, what effects and appearances I was supposed to achieve in order for it to be "*aćchā kām*" (good work). But botching some *hatkatti* did not seem to bother her at all. Instead, she was thoroughly cynical about the worth of chikan as wage work, and gave it up without a second thought when she got some sewing work. "I haven't taken a vow not to make chikan again, but there's no reason for me to do it now."

Even the finest embroiderers habitually adjust the quality of their work, although they never stoop to making the very cheapest kind of embroidery. My teacher, for example, spent more of her time doing good, but not excellent work on commercial pieces instead of exercising her full powers upon her own or commissioned articles. But she bowed to no one in her fundamentally superior skills. "If I do some work [on a piece of chikan] and someone else finishes it, you'll notice the difference," she insisted. In a similar vein, another agent and skilled embroiderer said that if she were given something by the *mahajan* that required superior work, she would not give it to anyone else, but would embroider it all herself. She thus treated it like commissioned work and, of course, collected the entire piece wage for it.

Less-skilled embroiderers frequently referred to the fact that if work was "*ćālū kām*" (commonplace work) it could be done quickly, albeit for less wages than fine work. A *kurta* in "*ćālū kām*" might be finished in a single day, for example, but if finer work were required, an embroiderer might take up to eight days over it. An embroiderer from Madeganj said that fine *bakhya*, executed well, brought her Rs. 4. But if put on notice that it was not to be so neatly done, she might finish it faster and make Rs. 2. In some cases, the discrepancy was even greater, a commissioned (and thus well-embroidered) *kurta* commanding wages from Rs. 5 to Rs. 10 compared to Rs. 2 for run-of-the-mill work.

Opportunities for better-rewarded, commissioned work do not arise for the highly skilled very often, perhaps only once a month at most. For this reason, women were not clear as to which kind of work they preferred—in other words, whether they liked to finish work and get paid quickly or were happier taking more time over the work and getting paid more. They constantly stressed that they did "whatever work we can get," giving no evidence that they were ever in a situation when they might be forced to choose.

For urban embroiderers, at least, the conscious decision to make *calu kam* indicates that an obvious decline in skill in chikan embroidery represents in part the deliberately downgraded product of women who are as capable of doing good-quality work when the occasion demands. This does not, mean, however, that women can do different *kinds* of work. The more accustomed a woman is to a particular form of work, the faster she becomes in making it. Even if a woman claims to know several stitches, she will admit that one comes to her more easily than others. An accomplished maker of *jali* prefers to do *jali* rather than *murri* that will force her to pause and proceed more slowly. Thus, the requirement that a woman produce an average set of products in a given time also tends to strengthen specializations. The difference, then, is in quality *within* categories of work.

Better wages are also given for urgent work. Skilled embroiderers would often say they were given such assignments, and liked to emphasize that *mahajans* put great faith in their ability to get the job done. Embroiderers who were also agents might do more of a consignment of embroidery personally if it was needed in a hurry. That agents and the highly skilled take on the burden of doing most of the urgent work implies they have more flexibility than ordinary embroiderers, and thus a greater capacity to benefit from better-paid work assignments.

Piece-Rate Deductions

The opposite of additions to wages for quality and speed are deductions for shoddy work and excessive delay in turning it in. Female agents readily acknowledged that they exacted penalties on women for poor work. But no one specifically said that *mahajans* made deductions in either eventuality—at least the older, established companies. In fact, from several women's perspective, it was the one point in manufacturers' favor that they did not make deductions, whereas government-sponsored production centers were prone to making deductions for late or badly executed work. On the other hand, most literature insists upon a system of deductions functioning in the private sector (Mathur 1975; Lucknow City Magazine 1988).

It is quite feasible that *mahajans* might negotiate a lower rate with their agents based on the quality of the finished work. Just because *mahajans* can sell poor-quality chikan does not mean that they would not prefer, on balance, better work for the same outlay of cash. In addition, penalties may indeed encourage more timely returns of work, but no one seems to think they can outweigh the counterpressures of an informal production system in which delays and production bottlenecks, particularly among household workers, are endemic. However, *mahajans* and agents alike are notorious for *delaying* payment of wages to embroiderers. The *mahajans*, for their part, talk only of delaying payment when the entire consignment of goods has not been returned to them, although one long-established shopkeeper made explicit reference to the fact that he paid his workers promptly, "not like these new businesses." Either way, deductions and delays reflect problems of cash flow in the industry. Their exaction is also an opportunity for depressing the piece-wages of embroiderers even lower.

Fluctuations in the Supply of Work

There is no time of year when there is no work for the embroiderer, although the workload intensifies and diminishes throughout the annual cycle. Most work is available just before and during the summer months, when demand is at its peak. Work is hardest to do at this time of year, when most people have no recourse from the stifling temperatures besides retiring to a darkened room or under a crude thatch in the courtyard to escape the sun. In the winter, sales in South India and stockpiling for the summer keep embroiderers employed. The only slack time is the rainy season, when the washing stage is so difficult that it causes the entire production process to back up.

Un- and underemployment are less tied to fluctuations in the yearly cycle of work than they are to irregularities of the work supply from day to day. Most women depend upon agents to supply them with work. For those women with a degree of mobility, particularly urban embroiderers, much of their time is spent visiting the agent in pursuit of work. A common complaint among embroiderers from the town and the nearby villages was that while wages had improved over the past five years, the amount of work had declined. In dire need of cash, however little, women made it clear that they wanted more work than was available.

Work Alternatives

There are very few work alternatives to chikan. One embroiderer from Khushalganj told me her sisters prepared coconut for sweet-making. Older women sometimes teach girls to read scripture. Another craft alternative, found in, but not restricted to the Khaddra area, is *mukesh* work (known also as *badlā* or *fardi*), in which women make shiny stitches amid chikan embroidery using a needle and long, thin strips of metal. This work is also given out to women by agents. A *fardi* worker told me she got Rs. 6.50 per item and that she could make two items per day. However, like embroidery, the work was not in constant supply.

Sewing is the most common alternative for urban dwellers. The number of women who can sew is necessarily restricted by access to sewing machines, which are either the woman's own or borrowed from relatives. Those who can sew prefer it to embroidery, saying it is less tiring to the eyes, easier and quicker to do, and better paid. As many as five to eight items can be stitched in a day, but only about two *kurtas* can be embroidered. On a day-to-day basis, underemployment in sewing may be as marked as it is in embroidery, but the return to labor is much better. Most sewing work involves stitching *kurtas*, blouses, and *salwar-qamizes* for chikan embroidery. A sewing machine also opens up other, petty productive opportunities. Ayah's daughter had her own job from agents across the street stitching caps. She got Rs. 1 per cap, and could make twelve caps a day. But in a week, she might only have two or three days work. She also received occasional jobs sewing festive hair ornaments.

A seamstress in the village of Mirzaganj got sewing work from a male agent. She did not employ women outside her household but did some work herself and distributed the remainder among her daughters, two of whom two were living and actively working at home. The third had married her cousin and lived in the house next door. The agent's affinal relatives were heavily involved in subcontracting chikan. "I am smarter than the others," said the agent, "and my husband is basically useless. He doesn't drive trucks now, he doesn't earn money. Embroidery came into this family because of me. I taught everyone else in the home that knows it."

The woman had at least three machines, all with a foot treadle. Altogether, her own little "unit" could turn out up to twenty-four *kurtas* a day when each person was working at full stretch. At this rate, and if the work were constant (which it probably was not), at Rs. 2.50 a *kurta*, this seamstress could be getting as much as Rs. 1,000 a month. Ayah told me that many tailors starting to work for a *mahajan* might go for several months without any pay at all in order to establish their "trustworthiness," a phenomenon also reported among female *zari* (gold thread) embroiderers in Lucknow (Jalees 1989). She did not say it had happened to her, though, nor was purposive withholding of wages over a trial period reported by chikan embroiderers.

Most of these embroidery alternatives share all the same problems as chikan work—low wages, irregular supply of work—and only sewing is looked upon as a truly preferable source of cash, from which women without sewing machines are necessarily excluded. Chikan, even in spite of its difficulties, is still the most likely and dependable source of income for most women.

WORK HABITS

Women often talked of spending four or five hours per day on embroidery. Work on chikan was only begun when other household responsibilities had been discharged. After a scant breakfast, beds and bedding are put away, water is fetched, there are *bartan* (utensils) to wash, maybe clothes to launder and sweeping to be done. By mid-morning, an embroiderer and her daughters may still be cleaning up plates, bathing themselves or younger children, or may have gone out on an errand. Then there was the food to be prepared for the midday meal, if there was to be one.

These daily tasks seemed to be regarded as primary, since no embroiderer spoke of doing chikan before they were done. In the country, women may have other kinds of tasks to do—for example, tending to animals—that precede any work on chikan. Some jobs must be done frequently, even daily, but cause minimal interruption of embroidery work. A good example is the continual stocking of the *pān* box (*pān dān*), the indispensable feature of every house and the centerpiece of women's sociality. Betel nuts must be cracked, and supplies of lime (*ćūnā*), *katthā*, and cardomam (*ilāćhī*) kept up. Other responsibilities may intrude more on chikan embroidery. Caring for children lies at the heart of women's identities as mothers, although much of the burden of childcare can be borne by other women and girls in the household.

In ordinary circumstances, women do embroidery in the afternoon until they must sort rice and pulses, grind spices, and make *roti* for the evening meal. Women will mention working in the evening or even all night, but of course they must have an artificial source of light. Most urban dwellings have at least one bare electric light bulb, the better-off having two or three. However, the electric supply is unreliable. In poor areas, power station "load-shedding" (brown-outs) occurs far more frequently, and for longer periods of time, than it does in wealthier ones. Electricity may be out for hours, or even days at a time.

Chikan work may be interrupted or stopped entirely when embroiderers are obligated to care for relatives, tend to guests (whether expected or not), and observe religious holidays. While I was in Lucknow, the major religious celebrations were Shab-barat (noncolloquially, Shab-e-barat), the night Muslims believe the fate of all individuals is inscribed in heaven, and Id ul-fitr, the festival that ends Ramadan, the month of fasting. Shab-barat is observed with nightlong prayer and recitation (in the mosque for men, and at home for the women). Food, especially *halwa* (a traditional sweet), is prepared in memory of the dead and prayers are offered on their behalf. On the day following Shab-barat, embroiderers were extremely tired from the effort of cooking special food and having to stay awake all night. Around a day and a half to two days were given up entirely to preparing for, or recovering from, the festival.

Id-ul-fitr's beginning is signaled by the sighting of the moon, which people await eagerly. Since Id-ul-fitr is an official holiday throughout

India, its start has little to do with whether anyone in Lucknow sees the moon or not. Instead, the pronouncement is handed down from the capital. But this fact did not hinder the crowds from gathering on the rooftops to catch a glimpse of the moon, nor did it in any way diminish the evident excitement in Muslim neighborhoods.

Id is a time of great activity for women, making the special, select foods that are distributed and enjoyed on this festival. "On Id, we eat food—*biryanī* (goat meat and rice), *siwāī* (vermicelli and milk pudding), meat. There are new clothes, we greet people in the street, we feed guests." In houses where such things can be afforded, visitors are treated to *phulkī dahī* (a dish of yogurt and *besan* [ground chick-pea] dumplings), as well as *biryani* and *siwai*. Before Id, new clothes are tailored, often by the women themselves. The duty to provide the customary foods and gifts for Id is, however, a burden. No embroidery was done on the days on which Id fell, and I heard Id cited as the cause of a temporary lull in embroidery contracts.

Observing Ramadan should mean more rest and less household work, as devout Muslims fast during the waking hours. However, not all women observed *roza* (fasting) conscientiously, and they seemed to be doing as much work as they did when no religious observances were prescribed. Eating very little or even nothing during the hours of daylight is, moreover, a common experience of poor women like embroiderers.

Women must, though, set aside time to make the special dishes for breaking the fast in the evening. This meal is more than usually tasty and plentiful, including many foods coated in *besan* and deep-fried. A portion of what has been prepared is sent off with a child to be shared with neighbors, and is reciprocated with more platefuls of food. Activity intensifies in neighborhoods at dusk, with women working in the kitchens, and children ferrying food from house to house. To make the foods, and to participate in food exchanges, is no small expense for embroiderers and their families, but it is borne with enjoyment and some pride. "The food is special for Ramadan," said my teacher. "We eat better things now . . . milk in the morning . . . this food in the evening."

Muharram, the festival whose rich communal and political history in Lucknow has been widely discussed (Oldenburg 1984; Cole 1989; Freitag 1990), occurred before I arrived in Lucknow, and it was to my great regret that I was unable to observe preparations for that festival. Given its great importance in the life of Lucknow's Muslims, this is an important area for further study. Although Sunnis have well defined Muharram practices, it is a quintessentially Shia observation. At Muharram Shias allegedly give up their work for as long as two weeks.

Tending Social Relationships

Cultivating ties in the neighborhood ensures access to work and to workers, as well as mutual help and emotional support in the shared experiences of hardship and tragedy. The misfortunes of family and neighbors absorb much of the women's attentions in close-knit *mohallas*. A death in the family of a neighbor or relative causes many women to temporarily suspend all chikan work. Marriages, relations with distant family, and the patronage of status superiors also depend upon a woman taking her social responsibilities seriously and carrying them out well. These activities are rarely acknowledged in literature on chikan, but they help reproduce social relationships that are more than simply sources of entertainment and company (see Jeffrey 1979).

Casual visiting is a fundamental part of all day-to-day social life and affects both men and women. Obviously, the obligation to play host interferes with the embroiderer's ability to get work finished. But the dictates of mood are important also—for while an embroiderer may feel comfortable continuing her work in the presence of a close female friend, she might as likely choose not to do it at all.

Hospitality toward guests is not measured in a narrow economic sense, but it is an obligation that every household takes seriously. Sociability also yields distinct pleasures—the company of one's relatives, their conversation, seeing them enjoy food. Women's embroidery work is less likely to be interrupted by the visits of close friends and female relatives than by the comings and goings of senior relatives, particularly men of the household, who require attention, food, or both whenever they appear. Embroidery was also always set aside without demur if more distant or senior relatives, particularly male relatives, came to visit.

Skilled embroiderers with important patrons invariably suspended their work when one of these patrons visited. After all, the fortunes and future of the family depend upon the embroiderer's being a willing and proper host. Frequent visits by government officials, individuals commissioning work, journalists, and so on meant that women such as these were often torn between doing embroidery and nurturing relationships that might (but might not) lead to lucrative opportunities.

Lengthy family visits might be extraordinarily disruptive of normal work schedules. My teacher was visited by her cousin and her family and for the last few days of their stay, her daughter's new in-laws. During this time (as I heard her telling a visitor later), "There was hardly any space at all, no space even to sit down." While her cousin assisted in meal preparation, and her niece, who had already been staying with the family for a protracted period, had worked alongside the other women cooking and embroidering, the demands of the visitors still outstripped their contribution. Male visitors did little if anything to assist during the day, stopping in only to eat and talk, then departing for several hours.

The greatest expenditure of time, money, and effort was reserved for the most important of guests. At a meal for the in-laws (in which I was urged to participate, seated with the honored guests instead of with the cousin and her family, who remained in the courtyard), special dishes were served, of *bakrī* (goat meat), rice, *rotī*, fresh lemons for the water, and a sweet dessert.

Once freed from the duty of hosting visitors, the family shifted into high gear for two or three days to finish incomplete work. Daily chores and periodic tasks like mending sat a little longer, and the girls usually responsible for them concentrated on chikan.

Patterns of Cooperation

Most household tasks can be done by any girl or woman in that household, and they are done as they become available by whoever happens to be around to do them, or whoever is ordered to do them by a senior relative. Simple chikan work can also be done by any minimally proficient person in the household. A piece of work that is started by one person can be finished by another. The notion of a single, autonomous craftswoman, working by herself on a piece of chikan, is belied by actual practice. Only a few embroiderers regard their own work as exceptional, thus distinct, and share work in carefully controlled circumstances (in other words, doing work of a lesser standard and sharing it only with relatives who have been taught by them).

Women may sometimes work together on the same item, usually a *sari* or some other piece large enough to allow two women to work on different portions simultaneously. Because most articles are small, and because there are recurrent household tasks that demand immediate attention, opportunities for women to work simultaneously on the same piece of embroidery are few. More commonly, women in a single household work serially upon the same item, whatever it may be. Again, a large piece like a *sari* may be worked on both simultaneously and serially at different times, as was the case with a privately commissioned *sari* I saw being made. Over several months, at least four women worked on the *sari*, sometimes together, sometimes consecutively.

Sharing work is an important means by which young girls gain experience as embroiderers. Girls are said to learn chikan by embroidering playfully upon a piece that her mother has set down in order to do some other household task. The implication is that a new embroiderer can pick up embroidery in midstream, the moment the previous embroiderer is called away to do some other job. However, work sharing also follows some rules. For example, women adhere to the conventional distinctions between forms of work, so if a piece requires both *murri* and *jali*, one woman in a household of skilled embroiderers might do the *murri*, and another the *jali*. Another common arrangement is for one woman to embroider the placket of a *kurta*, and another member of the household to work additional designs on the shoulder (using the same form of work). A further possibility in a more complex piece of work is for each embroiderer to work on a single repetitive motif, or stitch, at a time. Thus, all *gol murri* stitches (a particular chikan stitch type, see next chapter) might be embroidered by one woman, and all fine *bakhya* stitches done by another. Embroiderers are aware of the fact that the work of individuals with different abilities varies, and these kinds of divisions may help mitigate any glaring inconsistencies in the size and evenness of stitches in the final piece.

Whenever a single stitch occurred in any profusion, however, different women might consecutively embroider the stitch. *Tepci* work might be done in this way, as well as the scalloped borders of table linens (edged entirely with a stitch known as *kat*). According to my teacher, what was important was whether the different women had well-matched skills, in which case few or no irregularities should appear. With border stitching, though, I noticed that abrupt changes in the size and formation of stitches were fairly common.

Sharing work is also the germ of an agent system among women. A small girl probably does not expect to get a wage for the portion of a garment she embroiders and a single fee for a piece that represents the collective labor of a larger household will likely not be split up. When work is given to women outside the household, the wage will be broken up. For example, in the case of the *sari* made by my teacher and her family, the one close neighbor who fashioned much of the *jali* work received Rs. 12. for what she did. Sharing work in this small-scale way is a response to the availability of work. If work is scarce, an item of embroidery is kept within the household. When work is more plentiful, giving some out to others benefits the distributor by allowing her to take on more work and getting it done (and getting her wage) in the same amount of time.

AGENTS AND EMBROIDERERS

As I worked in Lucknow, I became aware of the importance of female agents in the production of chikan. However, it was extremely difficult for me to uncover the variety and extent of their activities in the city. It was not a subject upon which women were inclined to be candid, and the examples I encountered were partial and highly specific. What I have to say is pieced together primarily from comments of embroiderers at different points in the productive network and *mahajans*. Because of the sensitivity of the issue, I have concealed the identities of specific agents I discuss in the following pages.

Marx (1976:695) describes two kinds of subcontracting systems in which piece wages prevail, or what he calls "hierarchically organized systems of exploitation and oppression." In one system, an agent comes between capitalist and laborer, which is what happens when men act as the intermediaries in chikan production. In the other system, a worker is contracted to supply work to the others, as it is with female agents. As Marx (ibid.) writes, "Here, the exploitation of the worker by capital takes place through the medium of the exploitation of one worker by another."

Forms of Subcontracting

Collecting work from its source, whether the manufacturer, the government, or SEWA Lucknow, can involve women in more or less complex contracting activities. The simplest form that I observed was when a woman gave out a piece or two from a small bundle of *mal* to someone outside her household. A woman in this position represents only the smallest agent in a system of agents. Whether she charges for giving out work, and if so, how much, is not immediately apparent. Embroiderers involved in this kind of petty subcontracting gave no hint that they took anything for themselves for giving work to other women. An embroiderer from Alamnagar, a settlement on the edge of Lucknow, had a *sari* she said came from the *mahajan*.[4] The *sari* had both *phanda* work and *jali* work. She expected to get Rs. 70 for the *phanda* and Rs. 20 for the *jali*, which her daughter would do. She had too little work for herself to give out this *sari* for another woman to embroider, but if she did, she said she would pay them the Rs. 70 she expected to receive.

The points of interest in this account are, first, the woman's attempts to emphasize the cooperative nature of petty subcontracting, rather than its exploitative dimension. Yet it was clear that she would pocket the entire Rs. 90 for the *sari*, her daughter's contribution notwithstanding. The anonymous neighbor would benefit from getting the assignment to do the *phanda*. She would, of course, be denied the opportunity to complete the whole thing; the *jali* was reserved for the agent's family. Moreover, she would only get the work if the first woman felt she had enough for herself. The would-be agent's apparent generosity was quite calculated. Besides, getting other people to help out on a piece of chikan considerably shortened the time needed to finish it.

"If I do it myself, it's two month's work. If four people work on it, it's only five days."

The petty subcontractor of the kind just described may be taking a portion of the wages in return for the "favor" she is doing her neighbor. Between the assurances of government sources that subcontractors even at this level do this, and the contrary insistence of women that they do not, I cannot make a definitive statement either way. Perhaps these divergent opinions reflect a truly complex and variable situation.

In order to make a lasting arrangement with a *mahajan*, a woman must be prepared to take a large quantity of work on a regular basis that she then gives out to a wider circle of workers. "One or two [items] a day won't do. You must take one hundred or five hundred in a month." This statement is, I believe, true of the work that is most in demand, including *bakhya* work, sewing, and *jali* work. All these kinds of work are fetched directly from the *mahajan* in large quantities, from fifty to one hundred pieces at a time. Larger items like *saris* and elaborate *murri* work are collected in smaller amounts, perhaps as few as twenty pieces at a time.

It is difficult to estimate how many female agents of this type exist, not least because they have largely gone unrecognized in the literature. The only exception is a reference in an unpublished Uttar Pradesh Niryat Nigam report to "*uch koṭī kārīgar*" (higher-class embroiderers), who, alongside male middlemen, supply work to other women. Subcontracting is widely regarded in government circles and among the middle classes in Lucknow to be the source of much of the poverty and oppression of women embroiderers. Ironically, the most active female agents are the very same people who are the objects of other forms of government assistance, and as a result perhaps, there is little detailed description of them in official literature. Shopkeepers, however, freely admitted that much of their city work, that is, *jali*-work, is conveyed by female embroiderers, although a handful of the shopkeepers I talked to said they dealt only with male agents.

My teacher believed relatively few women, "*khālī ek hazār*" (only a thousand), collected work from the *mahajan*. But she went on to distinguish between these women and the "*das, bārah*" (ten or twelve) whose operations were different in character and in scale. Among the "thousand," my teacher was probably counting the female agents that were small-time operators, giving work out to less than ten women at a time and usually dealing with only one *mahajan* (although even these small production circles can turn out a hundred or so finished items in a week or two). These small, urban agents included women giving out *jali*, and to a lesser extent, fine *bakhya*, *murri*, and sewing work, and they made up the majority of agents dealing directly and regularly with *mahajans*.

In contrast, a few agents make their living from constantly getting large amounts of better-quality *murri*-work from several *mahajans*, which they give out to dozens of local women. Some even claimed to get work from the government in bulk, although state organizations vigorously denied they made any such arrangements. There were several women like this in the Daliganj area. Other women who were agents on a large scale took cheaper work from several *mahajans* and gave it out to women in villages. Some agents in Daliganj distributed embroidery in villages along the Sitapur Road north to Barabanki District. One embroiderer who lived in the old city told me she traveled to a village called Gumta, in Barabanki District, to get *bakhya* work done on *kurtas*. When asked about how she started in the business of subcontracting, she gave vague answers, saying only that it was at the suggestion of her younger sister and people in the neighborhood. It was they who told her whom to see, and which houses to go to. Every Sunday she would take *mal* to workers at Gumta, and two weeks later, that batch would be ready.

There were several differences between the big agents and the smaller ones, apart from the variation in the numbers of *mahajans* and embroiderers they deal with. The first was that the bigger agents usually had exceptional skills themselves (Saliha Khatun's figure of ten or twelve women quoted above was only a little higher than the number of women she believed knew the entire repertoire of chikan stitches). They invariably have had dealings with government chikan development schemes and had received government patronage. Small agents were unlikely to be as skilled, although they were almost always capable of doing some embroidery themselves. The more highly skilled the agent, the more likely she had shifted to supervisory or quality-control functions. Most small agents did at least some of the work they received from the *mahajan*.

Embroiderers looking for work usually hear of agents through word of mouth. "*Kārīgar jab suntā hai, ek banātā hai, aur do sunte hain, to do phir khūd māngte hain*" (When one hears about it, she does it. When two more hear, so those two ask for work themselves). The amount of work moved by female agents, per head and in total, is generally less than that processed by men. For the manufacturer, using female agents is an efficient way of getting work directly to embroiderers in the city. Unlike most male agents, female agents can send items through both *bakhya/murri* and *jali* circuits consecutively. These women may either be big agents or small ones. A large agent might give out large consignments of *murri* or *bakhya* to be made, and later contract the *jali* out too. A small agent might do the *jali* on garments that she got embroidered in fine *bakhya* by her neighbors.

It presumably saves the *mahajan* time and money to have a single agent handle both embroidery stages for him. But I am unable to state conclusively that *all murri* articles made in the city pass along this path. For example, one *mahajan* said he got what he termed *"pakkī murrī"* (i.e, *murrī*) done in Daliganj. At a separate point in the conversation, he said he got all his *jali* done in Hussainabad. Interestingly, his agents were all men. An intriguing question, which at this point I am unable to answer, is whether the splitting of the stages of embroidery between different agent categories and different city locations in any way corresponds to the gender of the agents.

Agents collecting work on a regular basis from *mahajans* hold an opinion of themselves and their work that comes as close to being professional as is possible among women whose primary identification is as wives and mothers. Their livelihoods have become very much bound up with chikan. They are in regular contact with *mahajans*, they know more about the market, and they spend more of their time engaged in embroidery-related work, collecting, distributing, returning, and doing chikan.

The difference in income between agents and workers, while measurable, is not sufficient to make the former rich by comparison to the latter, unless the agent is functioning on a very large scale. Most agents operate on a small scale, however, and while better off than the women to whom they give work, they aren't enormously so (see also Mies 1984:88). They extract a smaller portion of the piece-wage than male agents, who do not do any of the work, have scant familiarity with the techniques of embroidery, and whose greater earnings are based on comparatively little effort.

Among the social factors that do differentiate small agents and their clients is age, since there are few, if any, young agents as far as I could determine (unless they had been propelled into a position of greater influence through receiving a government award for their work, or were under a greater compulsion after being left by a husband early on in their marriages). Almost all women talked of starting agent activities by their forties at the earliest. The ability of a woman to exert authority over other women probably only comes with maturity and at least several years of marriage.

Agents are often less constrained by purdah, a fact other women allude to when describing the kinds of women who become agents. Since purdah is observed less stringently in the city than the village, more female agents are town-dwellers. The older one gets, the lighter the constraints of purdah, and so age and less seclusion are factors that, over time, coincide. A woman's personal qualities are also considered significant. Ayah said that very few women were agents because only the smart ones could do it. One embroiderer freely admitted agents intimidated her. "You can't argue with them. They're sharp, slick characters" (*tez, ṭerhe dimāg wālī*).

But it takes more than force of character to become an agent. Certain women have advantages that other women, no matter how determined, find hard to match. For example, a woman may "inherit" a relationship with a *mahajan* from a male relative (her father or husband). These female agents come from a social stratum already slightly differentiated from that to which their clients belong. At the very least, a would-be agent must provide another female agent's reference to the *mahajan*. A woman need not hand over a deposit, although several women were under the impression that they had to, and said that it was for this reason that they had not taken up agent activities themselves.

Agent Income

Female agents who deal directly with *mahajans* admit to taking an amount for themselves for getting work made, but are not always forthcoming about how much this amount is. Eager to stress their own poverty and the importance of their "business" to their own survival, female agents did not go out of their way to conceal their activities but at the same time were evidently uncomfortable telling me the exact nature of their financial arrangements with other women. Many discussions between agents and embroiderers were deliberately held out of my hearing. Even when transactions were carried out in front of me, it was difficult to grasp their full meaning.

Agents going directly to the *mahajan* and operating on the scale just described get a very small amount from him specifically for doing this job—a matter of a few paise, maybe a rupee or two—no more. They also get the cost of the thread. (A village embroiderer said that her mother, who had collected work for others in the community, used to make a few rupees by buying thread for less than the amount apportioned for it in the amount given to her by the *mahajan*.) But female agents' principal income from this activity, as with male agents, comes from taking a cut from the piece wage for providing the work to the embroiderers.

While the manufacturer was apt to refer to the agent's fee as separable from the total wage bundle, this fee is in actual fact included in the rate per piece that the two parties negotiate. What the agent subsequently extracts is this "fee" and then a further cut from what is left of the piece-rate. The "double" nature of the agent's income is noted by *mahajans* and government officials, since agents, they say, regard themselves as doing both the manufacturer and the embroiderer a favor. Yet agents all spoke about their "earnings" without making these distinctions, referring to their share as a simple, indivisible sum. One agent explained it this way: "Say I get something to do from the *mahajan* for Rs. 5. Then I might get it done for Rs. 4 and I'll get Rs. 1 for my trouble."[5]

Shopkeepers most often quote a wage rate of Rs. 2 to Rs. 8 for *kurtas*, but a skilled embroiderer who subcontracted out to villages said she got only Rs. 1 from the *mahajan* for *bakhya kurtas* made in the village, from which she had to take wages for *bakhya* and *jali*, and her own cut.[6] She obviously could not be taking as much as Rs. 1 from each piece wage. In town, embroidery workers usually spoke of receiving from just under Rs. 1 to Rs. 5 per piece. Female agents circulating *murri* and fine *bakhya* work in town are more likely to be getting at least a Rs. 1 cut. *Jali* is something of a special case, since it is priced in paise per *phul*. The amount of *jali* can vary considerably from item to item. Thus wages to the embroiderer vary from a few paise to Rs. 1 or Rs. 1.50 per piece just on *kurtas* and *salwar-qamizes*, and the agent cut will fluctuate accordingly.

Female agents getting work made in the village take a cut that represents a greater financial gulf between them and their workers than is the case among agents and workers in the city. They do none of the village work themselves, acting as agents only (and are thus more like male *thekedars*). The case of women getting *murri* done in the city environs is more difficult to assess. These agents are more likely to be doing some of the work themselves, thus beefing up their own share of the wage bundle. But the *murri* agent will have to wait longer to get her share than the woman getting cheap work made in the country.

There is a strong likelihood that the agent's absolute share of the wages goes up as the wage per item goes up—as opposed to remaining around Rs. 1 per piece. This is certainly true with the very highly priced items, which take weeks or even months to complete and are given out as single orders. In these cases, the agent takes, and admits to taking, a substantial portion of the wage at the outset, up to 25 percent of the total, which may be hundreds of rupees.

It is extremely difficult to be definitive about the mark-up for intermediate items, partly because the wage rates are so variable. For example, shopkeepers quoted between Rs. 8 to Rs. 15 (even occasionally as much as Rs. 20) in wages for *salwar-qamiz*.[7] Embroiderers reported getting Rs. 4 to Rs. 15 for *bakhya* work on *salwar-qamiz*, sometimes even Rs. 20 for *murri*. What is the agent getting in this case? Curiously, agents repeatedly said they got Rs. 15 for *salwar-qamiz* from the *mahajan*. Given the range of wage rates quoted by manufacturers, this would mean that agents were making either as much as Rs. 10 per piece or practically nothing.

Once one gets away from the standard *kurta* range, even into the low to mid-range *salwar-qamiz* ranges, wages begin to vary as the difference in the possible amount of work per piece begins to fluctuate between batches. (The amount of work on a *kurta*, while itself variable, is more spatially restricted than that on a *salwar-qamiz*, and therefore more consistent.) As they give out work, manufacturers assess the total wages on a bundle-to-bundle basis. My conclusion, then, is that the agent's profit in each case is not predictable. The agent may try to extract Rs. 1 at least, but as the wage approaches and surpasses Rs. 10 per piece, she is likely to determine afresh how much she should take for herself on each occasion, and in effect, take more like Rs. 3 to Rs. 5 per piece.

Making a good living from the agent business necessitates operating on as large as a scale as possible and employing many dozens of women, whatever the kind of work being made. Of the large agents I met, most were involved in some form of village subcontracting, indicating the extent to which the countryside is the site of the greatest profitability, for *mahajan* and agent alike. A cut of a few paise per piece is not much at all, but if the scale of operations is large enough, this amount rapidly converts into hundreds of rupees per month, especially as the work gets finished at such a quick rate. Like the *mahajan*, the big agent protects herself by operating on a shifting scale all the time, able to stoke up her labor network when the work requires it, and restricting work to an inner circle when supplies are thin. Some big agents were giving work to a lot of women in one phase of labor (i.e., the *bakhya* phase) and to just a few in another (i.e., the *jali* phase).

Specializing in *murri* means that one cannot make money on the scale of other large agents. Yet the *murri* subcontractor can set herself apart from small agents getting any kind of work done simply through her capacity to process a lot of work, and employ a lot of women, albeit for short periods of time.

Subcontracting Sewing

Subcontracting in the sewing phase provides an interesting contrast to embroidery. I never heard of sewing piece-wages from the *mahajan* dipping below Rs. 2 per *kurta*. The agent can easily take out Rs. 1 per piece and, using manual sewing machines, get the work finished very quickly. Ten women can sometimes make as many as ten *kurtas* each in two days, at a rate of five per day. A bundle of 100 *kurtas* can be finished in one week. However, work rates are inconsistent and it is hard for any agent (or worker) to function at this level of intensity. Depending upon how much she takes per *kurta*, and how many women she gives the work to, an agent can make 25 percent more money than her workers, or up to seven times as much. If she contributes some of her own labor, her income goes up markedly. Giving out the work that remains after her own labor to the same five or ten other women, she can get a large share of the wage bundle, get the work done faster than if she did it all herself, and establish an even greater gulf between her and her workers, making up to ten times as much as them.

Agent and Worker

Agents supplying their neighbors and relatives with work share many of their clients' experiences. Like them, they are wives and mothers. They inhabit the same neighborhoods and they too struggle with economic disadvantage. But neighborliness masks relations of dependence. Regarding entrepreneurs and embroiderers in San Santiago, Spain, Lever (1988a, 1988b) writes that bonds of trust and intimacy between women animate as well as disguise unequal relations. Close neighbors interact with agents on many occasions and in many ways that do not directly relate to embroidery. They help each other, exchange food on festivals, endure familial, marital, and financial crises together, and spend time in each other's company. Agents often professed to allocate work on the basis of relative need.

But formal antagonism between agent and worker lies not far beneath the surface, even if they seem to be friends. If an agent does not have the cash to pay a worker, or if the flow of work is interrupted, ties become strained. Arguments may break out if an agent offers an incentive of a higher piece-wage for high-quality work and then refuses to give it. Even favored workers express annoyance with the agent when a dispute erupts over wages. The scarcity of work and poor wages also mean that the worker balances loyalty to one agent with a desire to seek out work from any source.

A particularly potent source of disagreement is over the attempts of workers to return fewer finished *kurtas* than the number given out initially. The most innocent explanation for this would be that the missing item had simply been mislaid. Or the embroiderer simply finishes as many *kurtas* as she can in a day or two of work. Finding some obstacle to completing the last item, she simply brings, or has delivered, the ones she has done, hoping to finish the last item at some indeterminate future time. However, why should there be only one left undone, in bundles of as few as six to as many as twenty items? This is where agents suspect some mischief. Perhaps the embroiderer thinks the pile of finished clothes will not be counted, and they will get the wage for, say, six items, when they only completed five. What then, is happening to the mysterious "lost" garment? The possibilities include, as I see it: diversion to use or sale; loss or damage (this excuse is most cited, even by *mahajans* talking about the business risks they have to deal with); the piece is merely forgotten; or it is embroidered later and tossed in with a completely different bundle of clothes.

It is difficult to see how an embroiderer can hope to get away with any conscious withholding of items, since careful counting of garments before and after embroidering is standard practice among female agents, and I expect male agents do the same. But counting does not seem to forestall arguments, and certainly does not prevent chikan pieces from getting "lost." How agents explain themselves to *mahajans* if the lost pieces never turn up, I do not know, although stringing the shopkeeper along for as long as possible before all the *mal* is complete is a practice much lamented by *mahajans*, since it adds to the overall time a garment is out of their control, unavailable for sale and profit-taking.

How many chikan garments get diverted from the path from fabric to finished article is hard to determine. There is decidedly some leakage in the system that is the result of the unorganized nature of the handicraft industry and strategies to stretch wages and lighten workloads.

Case Studies

A small agent. My first case is a woman in her late fifties from Madeganj. She had been employed for eighteen years collecting work from *mahajans* and distributing it to local women. Her husband was living and worked as a painter and whitewasher. She was taking work from one of the largest stores in Lucknow. She collected about fifty pieces at a time and gave out work to about five or six women directly, and four other women took work from her to give out to other embroiderers themselves. The agent herself did *jali*, but the work she subcontracted was *bakhya*.

The agent took finished work back to the shop as it became ready, requiring anything from two visits per week to the store, to one visit in a month. About two to four times a month, she received specially commissioned work from the store that needed to be of a higher standard. This work might even have been brought directly to her.

She would not tell me outright how much she gave the women who worked for her. But one of her workers making a *bakhya* blouse told me she would receive Rs. 4 for it. The agent said she got Rs. 15 for fine *bakhya* on a *qamiz* (woman's blouse). Altogether, she reckoned that she made about Rs. 100 a week from her work.

Some of the agent's neighbors directly contradicted her on some of her statements about chikan. When she said that wages had not gone up in the last ten years, she was roundly criticized. The three other women in attendance during the agent's interview agreed that wages had indeed gone up in the last ten years, although not as much as they would have liked. The agent also believed there was a shortage of workers—a remarkable echoing of what several *mahajans* had told me—but this remark was greeted with derision by her listeners. While they were prepared to concede that *jali* workers were fewer, *bakhya* workers were abundant. Outside her hearing, women who knew her said that the agent collected a lot more work than she let on—up to one or two hundred pieces at a time—and that she made more money than Rs. 100 a week.

A large agent. This agent was a highly skilled embroiderer, in her forties, living to the southwest of the Chowk area. She came from a family of skilled embroiderers, including her *nana* (mother's father), who was a well-known embroiderer of the early decades of this century. This agent had had a checkered personal history. Her husband had taken a second wife after marrying her, and she now lived apart from him with her mother's family. Since her separation, she had had to provide for herself and a young child. She had received a state award in recognition of her skill in chikan work and had led some training schemes on behalf of the government, but had not attended any exhibitions. Her living came primarily from subcontracting chikan embroidery to workers in the village and her immediate neighborhood: "*Paisā kam hai lekin yah hai ki naqd hai*" (It's less money [than from government patronage] but it's cash just the same). She worked for several branches of Chhangamal, Raza Hussein, and other shops. She had been getting work made in this way for about fifteen years, and before that time, she had stayed "inside" and done chikan for her agent father.

Most of the work she got made was mere *mota* (coarse) or *calu kam*. "Of course, it is coarse work," she admitted, "but it provides for us." She subcontracted work to women in Kakori and Malyabad, where her paternal grandfather's family resided. At least fifty women worked for her there, either directly or through other intermediaries. Some work she conveyed herself for distribution, particularly when there was a lot of it. Otherwise, male agents, numbering around ten altogether, come to collect it. These men she described as distant relatives, "*dūr ke rishte ke haiṅ*," that she felt she could rely upon. "If you have a responsibility from the *mahajan*, you can't trust strangers. You give your trust to your relatives." She would not say exactly how much work she got done in the village personally, but estimated that on the whole, as many as five hundred *kurtas* might enter and leave the village daily. She quoted a low wage rate from the *mahajan* for *bakhya kurtas*, only Rs. 1, from which her *āmdānī* (income) and the piece wage to the worker had to come. She gave out different wages according to the kind of work, giving out more for *hatkatti* than for *bakhya*, for example.

In her own neighborhood ("*is 'ilāqe meṅ*"), she got *jali, murri, katao* and *mukesh* work done, as it was needed. She received Rs. 3.50 for *murri kurtas* from the *mahajan*, and she gave the work to about ten women. She admitted to taking deductions from work that was not up to standard. Her monthly income, she figured, was Rs. 600–700.

She only did this work because of necessity. If she were living with her in-laws in the usual way, and experienced no scarcity or difficulty in her life, she simply would not do chikan. Yet other remarks seemed to suggest a sense of pride in her status as a professional embroiderer. For example, she noted that the Chhangamal store might send a *čaprāsī* (servant, peon) with work to be made specially by her. Whereas other embroiderers would not or could not do the work to a high standard and on time, a *mahajan* could rely on her to put everything else aside to finish a piece in one day, and to do it well. For work of this kind, she said, she could be paid whatever she asked.

A businesswoman. This agent was a woman in her early fifties, a skilled embroiderer who had elevated herself beyond mere agent to small-time manufacturer. She had worked for *mahajans* until the late 1970s, when her efforts to do work on her own behalf started. Her husband was living and was a water surveyor. She had been involved in, and was currently the head of a so-called "cooperative society," a phrase that, in another context, Marglin (1991) describes as a euphemism for "putting-out enterprise." The genesis of this society was never clearly explained, but it had been formed in 1980–81, a few years after the end of an abortive society in which she was involved in the 1970s.

She controlled every stage of the production process. She had taken out loans to buy cloth, which she then had tailored in Chowpattiyah. Male agents came to collect work from her and take it back to the village, where it was distributed to about seventy-five women. She had easy *bakhya* work done in the village and fine work was given to about two dozen women to distribute to embroiderers in close-by areas like Takkurganj, Nakhas, and Chowk itself, where she lived.

Her current position had been made possible largely through generous and ongoing government patronage, giving her access to donations and low-interest loans. She said she sold finished products to the Uttar Pradesh Handloom Board (but she stated emphatically that she had no connection with the Uttar Pradesh Export Corporation [UPEC]) and also to a female client in Delhi, who tended to request unusual and fine-quality designs and was prepared to pay well for them.

In addition to the women she employed via her agents, she had five daughters who worked for her, including two who were married.[8] Because she owned the materials in the production process, and because of the larger scale of her operations, she made more money than the large agent described above. She reckoned her monthly income at around Rs. 2,500, and this was before exhibitions, training schemes, and other income-generating activities in which she had been involved. Even if she was given to exaggeration, she was obviously a rare being in the world of chikan.

A *murri* agent. This agent was a highly skilled embroiderer, but did not make a living on a scale with the previous businesswoman's agent and business activities. However, she had been able to eke out a living for herself and her family through a combination of getting work made for *mahajans* (her main source of income), doing and contracting out her own products on an occasional basis, making commissioned articles, as well as seeking government patronage of various kinds.

She was a widow in her late forties with two daughters and two sons. The daughters were fine embroiderers in their own right, although the elder daughter had a wider range of skills than the younger. One son was chronically sick and the other was quite young. Her husband became an agent when ill-health prevented him from doing other work. Before his death, he had been as active in chikan embroidering and training as his wife. When she was widowed, she was forced to draw on her own achievements as well as any knowledge of subcontracting she had received from her husband in order to support her family. The job was especially onerous since the family had been thrust into desperate straits by the expenses of her husband's illness.

She lived in Daliganj, known both for its fine work and for the number of female agents who live there. Daliganj agents give work out to embroiderers in their *mohallas*, to embroiderers living in nearby neighborhoods like Madeganj, and even as far away as Barabanki. She began learning about being an agent about twenty-five years before, when her husband was the *thekedar* and she the principal embroiderer, and she learnt the techniques of successful subcontracting from him. In 1989–90, she was taking work from several *mahajans* whenever she could (even when she had other current sources of income) and distributing it to her neighbors, "up this *gali*, up that *gali*." She did not get work made in the village. Indeed, all work she subcontracted out was either *murri* and *jali* on *kurtas* or *salwar-qamiz*.

She regarded the work she got made as superior, the kind that could only be bought at the better sort of shop *(ūṅci dūkān meṅ)*, such as Lal Behari Tandon and the Chhangamal stores. She had worked for a range of shops, most of them in the Chowk area. Besides the work from *maha-jans*, at the time of my visit she had two pieces of work that had been privately commissioned: a *sari* that took five months to finish, and a collection of table linens, napkins, and a *ćunnī* (large scarf) that were ordered in February. The latter collection was still unfinished when I left. Work on the *sari* was kept in-house, for two reasons that I can surmise. One was that its quality and design were best suited to the superior talents of her family. And second, given that the *sari* passed through different hands even within the household on its way to completion, to have channeled it through different women outside the home would have made it almost impossible to keep to schedule. The table linens, by contrast, were contracted out to other women.

From what I observed, work proceeded in fits and starts. The agent said that she could not anticipate when, or even how often, work would be brought by the *mahajan* (or his representative) to the house. Relatives were favored when giving out work. The family also professed to help women suffering particularly from *pareshani* (troubles, need). One woman, who lived just across the street, was both a relative and a woman with troubles. She would even sit inside the agent's house to do her work from time to time. At times, the house would be a scene of feverish activity as the family worked on embroidery, and received and checked a flood of work from outside. Work might be going out to as many as two hundred women (a very high figure I was unable to confirm independently). After a period like this was over, there might be little or no work for a few days, or even over a week. A trickle of women would come by each day to ask for work, only to be turned away.

Kurtas and *salwar-qamiz* were given out in bundles, usually of five or six pieces tied together by the sleeves. *Jali* work was massed in stacks of five, ten, or fifteen *kurtas*. Women usually, but did not always, take the complete bundle. When collecting work, women would often take several minutes looking over the work, deciding whether to do it, and if so, how many pieces to take. In many instances, a young girl was sent to pick up work on her mother's behalf.

Once, a child left with a batch of *kurtas* for *murri* work, only to return ten minutes later with the same batch, asking for something with a smaller "*bel*" (in other words, less work). This request was honored good-humoredly. The girl was given a pile of *kurtas* that required a small amount of work around the collar. She was told the wage would be Rs. 5, "Rs. 5.50 if it is good." "Give Rs. 5.50 then," said the girl with a sly smile as she went out. It took a long time before wage negotiations were carried out in front of me, and I am unable to say whether the exchange I have just presented was typical. On another occasion, a woman returning work asked for more money, and was flatly turned down.

In tracking the flow of work to and from the house, I was impeded by my own ignorance of which pieces (of those being returned) belonged to which batches I had observed being given out. The family had its own means of keeping track, which never involved any written account-keeping at any time I was present. However, judging from the time embroiderers told me it took to finish work, and the perception of the interval between embroideries going out and being brought back that began to occur to me, I would estimate that a bundle of five or six *kurtas* would in most circumstances be brought back after a week to ten days at the least.

The first intense episode of work that I observed came at the end of February, when women were taking *murri kurtas*. (The previous consignment of *chikan* had been completed around February 21.) This work was being returned throughout the first week of March, and by March 9, it was being sent out again for *jali* embroidery. Just after Shab-barat on March 12, the family resumed work on the privately commissioned *sari*, which already had three months' worth of work on it.

From about March 15 to March 19, finished *kurtas* were being returned. As women brought their completed work, they were told there was no more work for them to take at this time. I could not be certain that these *kurtas* were from the batch given out at the end of February, or whether they came from a more recent consignment. I now suspect the latter to have been true, especially since I did not visit the house for four days from March 4 to 8, when it is likely such a consignment may have been given out. While a week would normally be enough time for the bulk of the work to be done, the intervening festival of Shab-barat would have been sufficient cause for the *mal* to be away for longer than seven days.

On March 20, a new, large consignment of *kurtas* was distributed. These *kurtas* were being returned at the end of March and beginning of April. In the interim, there was no work at all. Yet, for reasons unknown to me, two girls who came on March 24 did get bundles of *murri kurtas* for their mothers. Every other woman who came by for work was turned away, up until March 29.

On March 29, the first day of Ramadan, a new batch of *murri salwar-qamiz* was ready to go out. The next day, the already finished *kurtas* (from the March 20 batch) were being given out for *jali*. By the second of April, there were both *kurtas* and *saris* ready for embroidery. Work was coming and going in large quantities in this period at the end of March and beginning of April. The pace and pressure was most intense at this time. The first week of April was taken up with finishing the commissioned *sari*. At the end of the week, some of the mats that had been commissioned in February were trickling back. Also at this time, *hatkatti* work was started on embroidered *kurtas*. These may have been the *kurtas* from the March 20 batch, or from a more recent job. I base this assumption on the fact that no other women seemed to be taking the *hatkatti*, and therefore it may have been a last-ditch effort by the immediate family to finish an overdue job. Virtually no work was done between April 9 and April 12, during which time the agent was alternately away and sick. "I always get sick when there's so much hard work," she explained. There was then another lull until the last week of April, when a *mahajan* delivered four large packages of chikan to be embroidered. Because government-sponsored activities intervened around April 18, I could not tell the fate of these bundles.

On two occasions women came with single pieces of finished work, one a *murri sari*, the other a large *kurta* of an unusual cut, completely covered in *bakhya*. The maker of the *sari* got Rs. 200, which was handed to her as a wad of notes. She was invited to count the money, but did not. The embroiderer of the *kurta* made at least two further visits to get the Rs. 50 she said she was owed. There were other occasions when embroiderers came demanding their wages. Although I eventually witnessed several instances in which wages were paid directly upon return of the articles, it was clear that this was not always what happened.

Mahajans probably kept back some of what they owed until all the goods were returned. Certainly *mahajans* informed me that this was their usual practice. How agents manage to keep current with their payments to workers is then their problem. Juggling various expenditures meant that there were many occasions when debts could not be settled.

When *jali/hatkatti* work was distributed, there was no thread to go with them, something that seemed to irritate the embroiderers. The only wages I heard quoted for *jali* work concerned the batch being given out on March 29, and these were Rs. 1.50 per piece (an exception to the rule that *jali* wages are expressed as *paise* per *phul*). The wage for the *salwar-kamiz* being given out at the same time was Rs. 15, and for *kurtas* in the third week of March, Rs. 5 to Rs. 5.50 (as mentioned above). The impression these figures give, sparse as they are, is that the work was better rewarded than average. Of course, this was relatively high-quality work, and the wages were set accordingly.

As for the specially commissioned work, the *sari* was probably started with enthusiasm, but was put aside as work flowed in periodically from the *mahajan*. I first saw the *sari* in the middle of March, when I was told that there was only ten days worth of work remaining on it. Mother and daughter both took turns working alone on the *sari*. But the greatest number of hours were spent by one daughter and a visiting second cousin on embroidering it together. As the agreed date of completion, April 5, drew closer, attention turned again to the *sari*, and not a day went by when someone was not working on it. At the beginning of April, the agent took over the work for two days on her own, doing the more complex *murri* elements throughout. The final stage was the completion of the *jali*, for which the neighbor was brought in. A daughter was responsible for finishing the *bakhya* on the *sari*.

Twice I saw the agent chiding her daughter for not working on the *sari*. The first time, she was taking a break and relaxing. The second time, she was working on a *kurta* from the batch that arrived on March 29. For the last few days before the *sari* was taken to the Dhobi, neighbor and daughter worked side by side, the latter finishing the *bakhya* and the former the *jali* in *phuls* scattered about the cloth. I asked for whom this was being made, and what their fee would be. I was told it was for a local dignitary's wife, and that the family would receive several hundred rupees for it. There was no mention of how (or even if) the fee would be divided among family members. The table linens commissioned at the end of February did not receive much attention until April, as noted above.

Because of the relatively short period of observation, and because of intervening visits of relatives and preparations for leading a state-sponsored training scheme at the end of April, it is hard to know how much embroidery the agent would have done were circumstances different. Of course, it is entirely possible that what I observed was quite "typical." As a senior member of the household, the agent was freed from many of the most basic household responsibilities by having her daughter do the cooking and cleaning. But she was also the one who went outside to go shopping, and was responsible for fetching and carrying the *mal*. She also had to handle the social interactions and hosting that were so critical to her family's well-being, foremost among them marriage negotiations for her daughters. And on top of all this, she had to spend time humoring me. She did not do much embroidery, specifically the top-quality work of which she is capable. The *sari* was the only piece on which I saw her do much work, and while of good quality, the embroidery was not as delicate and intricate as that on the pieces she has entered into award competition. When I asked if she was currently doing her best work on anything, she replied that she had neither the time nor the strength to make such a piece.

One day, one daughter turned a tearful embroiderer away, saying there was no work available. I then asked her whether there was enough work for her own family to make. "*Kāfī rahatā*" (There's enough) was her terse reply. In all, the income from getting their own work done (i.e., when the cloth was their own property), accounted for only a small proportion of the family's yearly income, and work from the *mahajan* was the staple. Other sources of income, like training schemes and exhibitions from the government, were highly desirable but only occasionally available.

To become more independent of the *mahajans*, the agent had even figured how much she would like to have to start her own business. She said that Rs. 37, 000 would cover her costs, "and two percent of that would be for the bribes!" She complained that she did not have enough money to protect herself against a slump in business, or to sustain her during periods of ill-health when she can neither work herself nor get much work done by others.

The family had committed itself wholly and without question to the business of chikan. They did not seek out sewing work, even though they had a sewing machine and the kinds of contacts with *mahajans* to get access to this type of work. The agent's status as a professional, skilled artisan benefited from, as well as reinforced, her "investment" in chikan. She was pleased with what she had achieved, especially since the death of her husband. When asked if more women embroiderers might get into business like her, she said she hoped they would, since "that's the only way there'll be progress."

SUMMARY

Female agents are involved in petty, as well as large-scale, economic arrangements linking embroiderers and *mahajans*. The large-scale agents possess high skills in chikan and are likely to have male relatives who were agents before them. Large agents also appear to exercise the most control over their use of time and the allocation of domestic tasks. They also enjoy more freedom to choose what work they will do, when they will do it, and how to divide up the rewards.

Female agents differ from male agents in important ways. For example, they have a background in embroidery and continue to make chikan, in a limited fashion, even when they are heavily committed to agent activities. Many, though not all, of the embroiderers who work for them are consociates, and together embroiderers and agents may reproduce the social life of the *mohalla*. Between agents and the women to whom they are close, and who they favor in dispensing work, there are strong bonds of kinship and neighborliness. They also share experiences like the constraints of female modesty, and the trials of marriage, family, and financial crisis.

But cooperation and empathy disguise formal antagonism. The disagreements between agents and workers that arise over how much agents make, how much work they give out, and how much they ought to pay their workers reveal conflicts of interest that dispel any illusion that agents and embroiderers, by virtue of their common gender, are a solidary group. I would therefore question any attempt to replace the analytic category *class* (defined in terms of relationship to the means of production) with a community bound by the collective efforts and "relatedness" of women (e.g., Sacks 1989). Conflicts of interest are most pronounced between agents and the embroiderers who live outside their immediate locality, who in turn see agents as formidable and distant figures. I have no doubt that village embroiderers routinely receive only a few paise for their work, even when the rate from the *mahajan* is higher. The agent can exploit the village women's isolation from, and ignorance of, the market to inflate their own "profit." But even within neighborhoods, agents do not have identical interests with the women they give work to.

Female agents cannot and do not bring to bear upon their workers the kinds of pressures that male agents, as figures of authority inside their homes and even outside their homes, can. But they can manipulate access to work and wages so as to maintain their position vis-à-vis the women who depend upon them. Toward these workers, agents act as judges and petty, somewhat unreliable patrons, evaluating and perhaps penalizing their embroidery, giving out extra work, or capriciously withholding it, extending loans or stalling on payments. Toward the *mahajan*, though, agents may assume the stance of the worker. After all, they do work as embroiderers as well as agents, and in that role they battle for more money and more work.

Embroiderers look either favorably or neutrally upon the existence of female agents, appreciating the fact that female agents provide work close to home, and free women from the time-consuming and socially difficult task of going out to get work for themselves. In return for convenience, however, women at the bottom of the agent-worker ladder find themselves utterly dependent upon female agents for work, and they are the most vulnerable to fluctuations in its supply.

IS CHIKAN EMBROIDERY "FREE-TIME" WORK?

Chikan work is an occupation open to almost any woman as a means to alleviate a dire need for cash. Wages are variable but generally low. Irregularity in the supply of work means there is forced underemployment, which is worse for those on the lowest rungs of the *mahajan*-agent-embroiderer ladder, farthest away from, and thus less able to influence, the sources of work. The combination of low wages and insufficient work tend to exacerbate poverty among embroiderers.

By their own admission, most women subordinate chikan to other domestic activities, in accordance with the prevailing ideology of female identity and duty. Their willingness to do this, even when embroidering is of primary importance in the production of chikan and for the reproduction of their families (and is the foundation of the employment of many thousands of *men* in the other stages of production), perpetuates female embroiderers' inferior status as producers.

But the prevalent description of chikan embroidery as "free-time" (*khālī-time*) labor distorts the true circumstances of embroiderers' lives. The implication is that they have empty, leisure time in which to do some extra work and that filling these hours with work for wages is a matter of simple, personal choice. But women do not have much time in which they have nothing better to do, and it is not out of choice but from necessity that they do chikan. If they seem to "sit around waiting for work," it is because of forced unemployment. Almost all embroiderers say they would like more work than they receive.

Construing womens' work as a pastime means that its real significance in their lives, and in the industry, is perpetually hidden, even from the women themselves. Their wages can be dismissed as a "favor" for work that is a "natural" emanation of domestic work (Mies 1982:54, 147). For most girls, training in the craft is itself part of their training as housewives for which the *mahajan* need not pay (see also Lever 1990) .

These generalizations aside, it is important to remember that embroiderers are also socially differentiated, distinguished in terms of the work they do, and their relationships with *mahajans* and other embroiderers. The kind of work an embroiderer does marks her as an urban or a rural embroiderer. Urban women, with a better knowledge of the market and armed with superior skills, get better wages, but they are now in competition for work with low-paid, low-skilled rural women who produce the dominant *bakhya* work.

Increasingly important in mediating between *mahajan* and embroiderer are female agents who have been able to transform their own manner of insertion into the production process. Female agents devote a lot of time to chikan and to their own business lives, and the most highly skilled resemble the professional male chikan workers of old. It is among the largest and most skilled embroiderer/agents that social differentation is most obvious.

Embroidery workers are not necessarily unaware of their exploitation. A chikan embroiderer in Madeganj commented that even if women worked all day on chikan, they still would not make enough from it. Complaints were rife about the low wages, the dearth of work, and the richness of the traders compared to the poverty of the embroiderers. Unlike Mies's lacemakers (see Mies 1982), many in the city population, at least, were fully aware of their situation, although the details of the degree of their exploitation are obscure to them.

In spite of the image projected in the literature and the rhetoric of businessmen and social workers of secluded and ignorant women, direct observation reveals that many are, in contrast, resilient and resourceful. Understandably, it is the agents who stand out in this regard, who are able to approach *mahajans* in person, and who must chart a course between "part-time" laborer and professional embroiderer.

Ironically, perhaps, to people unfamiliar with societies in which women are secluded, purdah and strength of character are not contradictory phenomena (see Abu-Lughod 1986). Life inside the household, and relationships inside the *mohalla*, are far from inconsequential or sunnily cooperative. These experiences are part of an ongoing education in the uses of petty power. While women are at a distinct disadvantage in the commercial world, it does not mean that they do not at least attempt to exert what pressure they can to improve their economic position and that they do not cultivate interpersonal relationships that may enhance their wages and access to work. Still, they recognize that the most effective means are beyond them. One embroiderer told me that she and others talked about forming a union to demand higher wages, but it did not seem as though plans had gone beyond the discussion stage, since everyone knew that there were always other women prepared to do the work if they refused. Meanwhile, agents said candidly that they had dared ask *mahajans* for better wages, and that the reactions had ranged from laughter and refusals, to threats.

With limited opportunity and virtually nonexistent leverage over *mahajans* or, indeed, over the agents above them in the production process, women face singularly difficult and lonely responsibilities. "*Itnī choṭī-sī jān, itne sāre gam uṭhāī*" (So tiny is my soul, so great is the misery I bear).

CHAPTER 5

Skill and Knowledge in Fine Chikan Embroidery

In the midst of an industry in which simple, coarse work prevails, a few still learn the complex skills of an accomplished embroiderer. Skilled embroiderers are defined by their control of a much larger repertoire of stitches and their ability to embroider an entire article by themselves. Despite complaints about the overall decline of quality in embroidery, present-day masters can make work as stunning as that of their predecessors. All embroiderers, no matter what kind of work they do and what level of skill they acquire, learn in what is known as an "informal" manner. But this one term cannot possibly describe the different processes and results that learning in various categories of embroidery involves. There are many ways of learning "informally." The economic conditions of the industry can be as important as psychological/educational perspectives to understanding the patterns and acquisition of skill, if not more so (Buechler 1989). On this point, discourse among embroiderers about the motivations that lie behind the acquisition of embroidery skills, expressed in their use of the words *shauq* (love, interest) and *pareshani* (troubles, need), is especially illuminating.

DISTINGUISHING THE WORK OF A SKILLED EMBROIDERER

Highly skilled embroiderers distinguish their best work from the mass of work on the market. "My embroidery," commented Akhtar Jahan, "is not for riff-raff." For work to be considered high quality, several conditions must be fulfilled. First, an embroiderer must use good cloth and good thread. Superior cloth is thin but dense; the larger the number of threads per square inch, the better the cloth. Several shopkeepers assured me that the finest muslin (*mulmul*) was unavailable today, a comment that by itself condemned all embroidery of the present day to the second-rate. Embroiderers did not say this, although they agreed that fine materials were hard to obtain. In general, superfine cotton and lawn (a form of gauzy, soft cotton) must suffice for the better-quality work, and embroiderers did not make any complaints about it. More and more commercial work is being done on synthetic cloth. However, shopkeepers and highly skilled embroiderers generally agree that pure cotton is the "authentic" base material. My teacher criticized the contemporary use of silks, either as the base cloth or in thread. But this preference may not always have prevailed, since silk thread (*tasar*) was used in old chikan articles of the highest quality. Today, however, chikan is quintessentially a "cotton" product, although there are no ideological dimensions to this fact.[1]

All skilled embroiderers insisted that *aṣlī* (real) chikan is made with white thread on white cloth. They disapproved of the use of color, either in the base material or in the thread. Colored base cloth is very popular in the market and while colored thread is more unusual, it is commonly found in the *ulṭī* or "*bharam*" *salwar-qamiz* ranges, where the *bakhya* is done on the front side.[2] As for the embroidery itself, three criteria for judging its quality were consistently invoked; minuteness, number of stitches, and clarity. Minute stitches contribute substantially to the achievement of evenness and regularity in a piece of embroidery. When doing a few *bakhya* stitches on a child's *kurta* under the supervision of a moderately skilled embroiderer, I was chided for making long stitches. The woman pointed to the stitches and showed how they had become uneven. Making short stitches means making a lot of them and embroiderers intensify the effect by making each needle stroke close to the others. A piece of exquisitely embroidered *bakhya*, densely packed with tiny stitches, is technically related to the apparently haphazard, randomly distributed embroidery of the cheapest child's *bakhya* work *kurta*, to which it bears no outward resemblance. Even commercial work is subject to the discriminations of stitch number. One manufacturer described one or two surface "stitches"[3] in a *bakhya patti* (leaf) as "not good." "Good" can range from ten per *patti* to up to thirty. *Jali* is another case where sheer number of needle strokes is important, less for the number of stitches produced than for the apparent absence of them—in holes. Another *mahajan*, Chandra Prakash Garg, from one of the oldest stores in the city, was especially proud of the fact that each *phul* in his *jali* work contained as many as one hundred holes, whereas the work in other shops contained no more than twenty. The highly skilled drew a strong association between the requirement for so many and such small stitches and the onset of reduced vision, even blindness.

Added to minuteness, number, and control, and in some ways encompassing them, is the attribute *ṣāf* (lit., clean, clear). The most common use was in phrases like "her [the embroiderer's] hand is *saf*," making an explicit connection between the embroiderer's control of her hands and the quality of her work.[4] Embroidery was time and again judged *saf* by approving embroiderers, and *mahajans* used the word, or used an English equivalent ("neat," "clean," and "crystal-clear"), to describe superior embroidery.

Quality of workmanship is directly related to the minuteness, number, and clarity of stitches. Encountered together, these attributes define a piece of work as *mahin* or *barik* (fine, thin) as opposed to *mota* (thick, coarse). *Mota* is widely recognized by embroiderers at all levels to mean both crude stitch-craft and the category of work that includes such stitches. Thus, *bakhya*-work is quintessentially *mota*, and *murri*-work is *mahin*. Even the use of the term "shadow-work" in the language of the highly skilled seemed to suggest a deliberate attempt to segregate *mota* work from *mahin* work in which the *bakhya* stitch has a respectable place. It is true that a piece of shoddily made *murri* may well be dismissed as *mota*, but it would not be termed an example of *mota kam*— a class in which *bakhya* work, but not *murri* work, belongs.

A well-executed stitch may, however, be termed *mota tanka* if it is meant to contrast with a stitch that is *patlā* (thin). In this context, *mota* refers to a solidity in the stitch that is a legitimate element of its construction. Observing the appropriate contrast of *mota* and *patla* in one's choice of stitches, and a heightened sensitivity to the visual and textural interplay of different stitches, distinguishes the fine embroiderer from the merely competent.

The quantity of embroidery is also an important indicator of quality. Teeming stitches, thickly massed embroidery, and profuse *jali* recur often in old pieces from 20 to 100 years old. Chikan work, the visual subtleties of white thread on a white ground aside, is not always marked by sparseness and understatement. Similar aesthetic preferences are evident in the dense stitching and appliqué of *zardozi* work. My teacher once expressed this taste when she showed me two sets of satin *pan* box covers (for the inside pots, inner liner, and a massive outer cover) being made for her daughters. They had been embroidered in *zardozi* by a relative, from design suggestions by Saliha. Both girls had requested the outer covers be reworked, since they felt the covers looked "too empty" (*khālī*) and wanted fish motifs in the areas presently unembroidered.

Minimally "good" work invariably contains some *jali*, which by extension means that it must have been worked on by city embroiderers. A middle-class consumer of chikan once insisted to me that chikan simply is not chikan—even if it is simple *bakhya* work—unless it has *jali*. Since *bakhya* without *jali is* marketed successfully as chikan, this opinion cannot be shared by all. Yet many people ask for good "network" and proceed to examine the *jali* carefully, so it may well be an expected and important element of chikan for a large number of customers.

Rare but prized details on chikan garments are the many varieties of *turpai* (hand-stitched seams) and *daraz/katao* (appliqué). There are a small number of women who specialize in *katao* work. One of them is Kanis Usgar. She considered her work distinct from chikan embroidery, although *katao* usually appears together with chikan. Both *katao* and, to a greater extent, hand-seaming and stitching are hard to find in the commercial sector, but both have been revived in the SEWA Lucknow collections.

KNOWLEDGE OF CHIKAN

According to the highly skilled, knowing chikan is knowing stitches. Knowing a stitch means knowing how to name it and how to make it. This knowledge has never been set down in any authoritative text, or even an oral canon. It is not even universally shared, since what women claim to know is highly variable from neighborhood to neighborhood, and woman to woman. Yet certain characteristics of naming and embroidery practice set those who genuinely "know" chikan apart from those who merely claim to know it.

Even sparsely educated, lower-class women in Lucknow who do not make embroidery for money may say they know how to do "this embroidery." Middle-class and convent-educated women claim a knowledge of chikan because they were taught how to do embroidery at school in the English style. While these women can create similar stitches with names like "lazy daisy," "chain stitch," and so on, they do not know the names used by women who make chikan for a living, and do not know chikan as a specific art form. Most, moreover, would make the embroidery freehand without aid of a print, something quite alien to the working habits of a professional embroiderer, for whom the inter-play of print and stitch is integral to their creativity. They never embroider without some preexistent pattern, whether this is printed or simply drawn on. In a similar vein, blockmakers do not carve a design without its being sketched on the wood to start with.

The most accomplished say they know at least 12 different stitches, frequently as many as twenty and even up to seventy-five, compared to the 4 or 5 in the repertoire of a moderately skilled *murri* worker. Among the highly skilled, there was disagreement over the number of similarly skilled craftspeople in Lucknow, phrased as those people who "know all the stitches." Ayub Khan said there were only fifty people who could do proper chikan today. Anwar Jahan said there were twenty to twenty-five while Saliha Khatun said there were only eight or ten.

Some embroiderers perhaps have more complex repertoires than others. Embroiderers also play a kind of "stitch-upmanship" in which knowledge of more stitches is taken to mean more knowledge—thus greater skill—in general. But differences more often reflect alternate approaches to naming. For example, Akhtar Jahan's statement that there were around seventy-five stitches was at variance with her sister Rehana's equally emphatic view that there were and have always been thirty-six. My teacher insisted that there were thirty-two stitches in chikan. Government officials usually said there were fifty-two stitches, corresponding to the figure given to me by Sultana Begum. (How often other embroiderers quote that figure is unknown.)

In response to claims that there are many dozens of stitches, several embroiderers object that this involves counting *motifs* as discrete stitches, instead of recognizing that a motif is made up of two or more stitches. Ayub Khan was a strong proponent of this view, arguing that some apparently distinct stitches, like *kīl* and *kangan*, are in fact compounds formed out of more fundamental elements, and that therefore they were not to be counted separately.

Almost all embroiderers were hard pressed to give names to all the stitches they claimed to know. Chikan knowledge is highly contextual and difficult to talk about in the abstract. Confessed Sultana Begum, "I can't remember all of the stitches. I wasn't ready for a question like this." "There are so many *tankas*," remarked Nur Jahan. "I forget them. When I see the piece in front of me, it comes back." Her comment was true of other embroiderers, who might start promisingly enough with the four or five common stitches of *murri* work, but then had to look at a piece of actual embroidery, or, as in my teacher's case, a sample book of the kind often produced by students in government-sponsored training schemes, in order to go further. If a stitch was recalled that did not appear on any work the embroiderer had available, embroiderers were unable to explain the stitch, or draw it, and were reluctant to make it in the absence of a print.

I expect that the embroiderer's knowledge of stitches is elicited in practice by the print and the possibilities it suggests. Because stitch lists do not directly relate to the way in which embroiderers use stitches, their analysis has obvious limitations in the absence of data about the way decisions and choices in embroidery actually unfold. It is also possible that numbering and listing stitches is fairly recent practice, stimulated by government patronage and the research efforts of scholars (myself included).

The work of highly skilled embroiderers is categorized as *murri* work, but *murri* also takes its place as a specific stitch in their repertoire. Only Anwar Jahan Khan's list of stitches sounded very much like a grouping of categories. Listing *murri* with *bakhya, phanda, jali, hatkatti, tepci, hul,* and cutting (the edging stitch for table linens), she argued that "*kīl, kangan, bijlī, kaurī . . . murrī men ke andar men sab* makeup *ā jātā haiṅ.* Total *ek nām hamne batāyā"* *(Kil, kangam, bijli, kauri* . . . in makeup they all come under *murri.* We call them all by one name). Most embroiderers, however, regard *kil, kangan,* and so forth as separate stitches. They also make a clear distinction between *gol/mundī murrī* (round/millet *murri*) or *lambī/nukilī murrī* (elongated, pointed *murri*).[5]

Many stitches that are part of skilled embroiderers' repertoires only rarely show up in the work of less skilled women. Some are used infrequently even in the best work. One of the more striking features of knowledge of many stitches is the vast increase in the repertoire of *jali* work an embroiderer can execute. For example, *jali* of most commercial work is specifically named in more extensive repertoires as *sidhaur jāli,* where it takes its place among several other types of *jali,* including but not restricted to *makrā, bul-bul čashm, tāj mahāl,* and *mandarāzī jālī*— the *jalis* acknowledged by my teacher. These other *jalis* look different from sidhaur and are considerably more complicated. Variation in the naming and numbering of *jali* types is among the most pointed areas of disagreement among skilled embroiderers. To cite a few: Anwar's list of *jalis* omitted *taj mahal* and *bul-bul cashm,* but included one called *malhaur.* Nur Jahan distinguished only two types; *čatā'ī jālī* and *jali* (presumably *sidhaur*). Ayub Khan's list was similar to Saliha's, with the addition of *chattāiyā, sherkhānī* and *singhārā kī jālī. Satkhānī mor jāli* made an appearance in Akhtar Jahan's stitch descriptions, and is mentioned in chikan literature (e.g. Pande 1968). Most embroiderers seemed to agree that there is only one kind of *hatkattī.* However, Anwar Jahan spoke of *sādī hatkattī* and *madrāsi hatkattī* and Akhtar Jahan said there were many *hatkattis,* listing merely a few—*sīdī dar hatkattī, tilkadī, sabudānā, dohrī* and *teherī hatkattī.* Embroiderers also named the standard *hatkatti* in slightly different ways, Kanis Fatma referring to it as *kīnārī kī jālī* (border *jali*) and Sultana as *bhāg par kī hatkattī.*

A key difference in embroiderers' recitation and description of stitches, besides the different stitch totals, was whether they gave brief classificatory names, or extended, discursive descriptions of different stitches. Sultana Begum's example of *bhag par kī hatkattī* above is an example of the latter, but Akhtar Jahan was the most outstanding in this respect, describing the stitches in her work in vivid and elaborate terms. For example, the *dhānīyā pattī* of other lists became, in Akhtar's account, *čikan kā sukhā dhānīyā.*

Akhtar Jahan gave distinct names to embroidery elements that others would probably regard as compounds of two or more stitches. For example, she called a *kangan* with an interspersed double row of *hatkatti,* "*banārsī kā kaṅgan.*" Where Saliha described *karan* as simply a version of *kherkī,* Akhtar reeled off at least three different varieties of *karan.* Indeed, in two meetings with her, Akhtar came nowhere near accounting for all seventy-five stitches she knows (and she admits that the figure of seventy-five is not certain, there may be one or two fewer stitches, or one or two more). Her expansiveness and descriptive detail may explain why she claims there are so many stitches, the highest number anyone quoted to me.

Akhtar Jahan expounded upon the appearance of certain stitches (for example, of *nukili murri* she said: *"jūhī kī k͟hīlā k͟hiltī lage"*—"a jasmine bud about to bloom"), but other embroiderers offered no commentary of this kind at all. It is difficult to say whether Akhtar is idiosyncratic in this respect, or whether other embroiderers were simply more diffident, and would be prepared to offer such commentary upon closer acquaintance. But even the embroiderer I knew best, my teacher, did not expand much upon either the names or visual effects of different stitches.

There is a possibility that commonalities and differences in stitch naming correspond to distinct neighborhood traditions. This was most apparent in the case of the *phanda* stitch. My teacher distinguished *phanda*, which she used to describe *phanda* work exclusively, from *cikan*, a specific stitch that was ostensibly made the same way. She distinguished two kinds of *cikan*, *gol* (round) and *lambi* (long) *cikan* (the latter she also referred to as *dhaniya* [coriander] *patti*). She described the *cikan* stitch as being like a round, smooth (*ciknā*) grain. Daliganj embroiderers used *"cikan"* to refer to a discrete stitch but embroiderers from the old city did not, preferring to use *phanda*, or a subdivision of *phanda* and *murri* (*kaccā phandā, kaccī murrī*) or *dhaniya patti* to describe what Saliha called *lambi cikan*.

The *phanda/cikan* instance hints at possibilities definitely worth further research. Paine's (1987) stitch names most closely resemble the partial listing given to me by Akhtar Jahan, now resident in Takkurganj, but who learned from her father when living in Muftiganj. While a precise mapping of patterns in stitch naming would be extremely valuable, it would not account for all the present-day variability in stitch naming, as the discrepancy between Akhtar Jahan's and Rehana Begam's statements regarding the total number of stitches indicates. These kinds of differences are more difficult to explain, but may be related to the more informal structure of learning and practice established within the household compared to the *karkhana*.

The names given to chikan stitches, in those areas where there is consistency, show a disposition towards items of female adornment and plant terms. In the first category fall *bijli, kangan, kil, karan, zanzīrā, and jhūmar*.[6] In the second category, there are *ghās kī pattī, cānā kī pattī, dhānīyā pattī, bājrā pattī, and khājūrī pattī*. There are also some of the varieties of *hatkatti* quoted by Akhtar Jahan.[7] The association between a stitch and a particular plant is not merely fanciful or metaphorical. One day, when my teacher was preparing a lunch, she put out some *cana* pulses and said spontaneously that there was a stitch in chikan called *cana*. She picked up a *sari*, found a stitch she wanted me to look at, and said, "Look, this *ghas patti* could be *cana ki patti*." She picked up some leaves from a bunch of green fodder for her rabbits. "The difference is," she continued, "that *cana ki patti* in chikan has a spine up the middle, like the real leaf." And with that she pointed to the "spine" on the leaf with her finger. Some stitch names refer directly to the kind of effect they create, or the manner in which they are made. Thus, *rauzan* is a hole, *jorā* (a joint) is a roughly symmetrical alignment of contiguous stitches, and *pencnī* (lit. "twisted") is a wrapping, twisting stitch.

I have been unable to avoid using some western terms to describe the embroidery stitches I learned from my teacher, partly because they do convey a good impression of the appearance of the stitch, and partly because I find them easy to use, owing to my own cultural background. In other words, English "equivalents" are presented as though they were really chikan. Because of the differences in embroidery technique, as well as the different systems of naming and organization in chikan compared to European embroidery, it must be borne in mind that they are not.

LEARNING CHIKAN

Few embroiderers employed in the commercial sector confessed to ever having received much instruction in the craft. To the question, "How did you learn the embroidery?" the common answer was, "I saw everyone doing it, so I did it," or "I learned by watching." Anwar Jahan talked of it as an inescapable children's activity, "I learnt it in play" (*khelne khūd men hī voh kām ā gāyā*). When asked when they learned the craft, women would usually hold their hands at below shoulder height and say, "when I was this high," or indicating a teenager present, say, "when I was smaller than him/her." *Bakhya*-embroiderer Safia said she had been embroidering "*jab se hosh sambhālā*" (for as long as I can remember). For these embroiderers, a recurrent scenario was of the child observing her mother work, then taking up the needle and embroidering on a garment when the mother was engaged in some other task. It was not usual to have started on scraps of cloth, although the early stages of my own instruction involved working in such a way. Instead, embroiderers usually launch directly on to a "real" piece of work. "I did it the first time," was the accompanying commentary to such a story. Superficially, it appeared that training began and ended with this experience.

Learning chikan is invariably what is known as "informal" learning, meaning that it happens outside a classroom, without a curriculum or tests, and without the formal structures of institutional education. The focus is on practical skills, not knowledge about those skills—although it would be wrong to assume that embroiderers are incapable of talking about chikan in the abstract. It is simply that talking about chikan plays a relatively insignificant role in the training of young embroiderers. Girls in embroidering households learn chikan in the course of learning other skills around the house. In Fortes's (1938) terms, learning is a "by-product" of the culture routine. As children become more proficient in a wider range of tasks, they move from the margins of social life to its center (Fortes 1938: ibid.; Lave and Wenger 1991). Lave and Wenger even have a term for this kind of learning: "legitimate peripheral participation." Children and adults live overlapping lives, with few of the ruptures experienced in the western world. Women and their daughters, in particular, become close as the girls grow up, their relationship maturing into a warm and mutually supportive one, even though it is never quite equal. Whether acquiring the lowliest skills or the most profound, girls are involved in social relationships that structure the learning process. They do not learn in a linear fashion nor are they mere receptacles for their teacher's "knowledge." Instead, context is everything; simpler tasks are worked into the production of goods for specific marketplaces. Gradually, responsibility and skill increase, until one day a girl can make critical creative decisions herself, and control her own income (Lave and Wenger 1991). Watching is an enormous component in learning, so even the moderately skilled women who say they "learnt by watching" are not necessarily describing a wholly casual or ineffective method by which skills are reproduced generation to generation. Whatever its benefits, the problem with learning having become almost indistinguishable from other everyday activities is that it contributes to the image of embroidery as a form of "nonwork" that has already been shown to be so damaging.

On the other hand, the tale of "taking up the needle one day after seeing it done" conceals the fact that transmission of some embroidery knowledge, specifically the knowledge of the highly skilled, must be more systematic. Because the *karkhanas* no longer exist does not mean that learning today lacks rigor and discipline. *Daraz* artisan Kanis Usgar seemed to refute the very idea that learning was seamlessly integrated into daily life. "When I was small, my mother said, 'You take this and make it. All you do now is play.'" For skilled embroiderers, there is always an inherent order to the stitches a young woman learns and how she learns it. Novices are also subjected to critical appraisal, for being able to construct stitches is simply the preamble to being able to make them well. Akhtar Jahan specifically rejected the notion that really fine skills could be developed by merely watching another embroiderer work. She had learned from her father, Hasan Mirza. Instruction in chikan for Akhtar Jahan consisted of her father watching *her*, making her unpick and remake her stitches, telling her how to use the needle and how to refine her work. She recalled exactly the order in which she learned her first stitches: First she did *tepci*, then *pencni* over the *tepci*, then *ultī bakhyā* (i.e., *bakhya*), *rehat* (possibly what other my teacher and other embroiderers referred to as *sīdhī bakhyā*),[8] then *murri* (she meant, specifically, *nukili murri*), *gol murri*, and *baldā*.

Others repeated the familiar formula of taking up their mother's work in her absence, but cast doubt on it by their later comments. For example, my teacher's daughter Asiya said she had learned in the conventional way, but later said she had learned from her father (who had learned in his own turn from Saliha), in an apparently more formalized atmosphere. Sultana Begum, when reciting the familiar story of learning by seeing, qualified this by saying she learned first, in order, the stitches *bakhya*, *phanda*, *murri*. Slipped into the formula is crucial evidence that what Sultana saw, or watched, was her mother working systematically with the goal of getting her daughter to master specific stitches.

Although learning chikan is talked about in terms of acquiring knowledge of stitches, what one learns is at once this much and more. The novice must learn what needles and thread to use, how to prepare the thread, how to hold the cloth and needle, and how to adjust each as the work proceeds. Doing one's first stitches is a complex challenge, because one must not only try to embroider a complete motif, but struggle to manipulate the cloth, needle, and thread acceptably as well as structure the specific stitch involved. With time and practice, the rudiments of technique are internalized, and the student advances to more complex, demanding—and better-paid—forms, and takes on more responsibility for choosing which stitches to use (see Lave 1982).

SHAUQ AND PARESHANI

An indispensable ingredient for the acquisition of superior skills is the *shauq* of the pupil. *Shauq* (love, interest) and *pareshani* (troubles, hardship) are used to describe the twin motivations in learning and doing chikan. *Shauq* is what stimulates the novice to hunger for knowledge, to find a master and to devote herself to learning the intricacies of chikan. *Shauq* is equally indispensable to learning and doing other artistic pursuits (see Kippen 1988:133 on *shauq* among musicians). On the other hand, *pareshani* lies behind the entry of most embroiderers into the contemporary chikan industry—the desperate search for money.

For Banaras artisans, *shauq* is an ingredient of their leisure activities (Kumar 1986). While I did hear women use *shauq* in reference to pursuits of pure pleasure, the connotation of right performance contained in its use with reference to work was noticeable. Teachers are pleased to observe *shauq* in a pupil. They say they are prepared to teach an interested pupil for nothing. *Shauq* need not be restricted to any group or person—some Hindu girls have shown *shauq* in training schemes, and I displayed *shauq* in my desire to learn chikan. Several skilled embroiderers made it clear that "it is *shauq* that matters, not religion." *Shauq* can appear unpredictably. In an earlier chapter, I introduced Ahmad Ali, a member of a chikan-embroidering family whose *shauq* was for print blocks. In response, he apprenticed himself to a master blockmaker and established a new family handicraft tradition.

Only pure *shauq* can stimulate learning and only *shauq* can explain facility in the craft. My teacher became fond of telling her guests that I, with my *shauq*, could do stitches her own daughters had no interest in doing, that "you tell her once, then immediately she will do it" ("*ek bār batāie, phir banāiengīň*"). If visitors were surprised that I was not there to get work made, the explanation that I had *shauq* was usually sufficient to explain why I was spending so much time in the neighborhood and why I was learning the craft.

By contrast, *pareshani* stimulates learning only in highly constrained circumstances and for the sole goal of getting money. Thus, Kanis Fatma argued that while Shias had originated the craft, Sunnis took it up when they realized they could make some needed money doing it, as also had Hindus in recent years. Nur Jahan ventured that *shauq* might grow as people realized how there was money to be made. But Saliha was adamant that *shauq* had no association with the pursuit of gain in the craft. Instead, Saliha regarded *shauq* as something that grew apart from the need to make money.

Yet, by Saliha's own admission, *shauq* and *pareshani* can alternately occupy the motivations of even the best chikan embroiderers throughout their lives. Thus, a woman may have begun the craft out of *shauq* but may practice it through much of her adult life because of the rigors of *pareshani*. When Kanis Fatma said that she had learned chikan in childhood out of *shauq* but *pareshani* had forced her to do it for money as she got older, she affirmed what Saliha had said about money having very little to do with *shauq*. Saliha's own ancestors experienced a succession of changing circumstances, with *shauq* and *pareshani* alternately dominating their activities generation by generation. Thus, her great-grandmother, the first to learn chikan, did it because of *pareshani*. Her daughter, Saliha's grandmother, learned out of *shauq*. Interestingly enough, this was the woman who taught Saliha. *Pareshani* compelled Saliha's own mother to do chikan, when her husband died leaving her with young children. As for Saliha, she began out of *shauq*, but fell captive to *pareshani* with the sickness and death of her husband.

Learning seems to be intimately associated with *shauq*. *Shauq* stimulates the experience of embroidery as an unfolding process, unconstrained and unbound by troubles. Kippen's (1988:133) explanation of a tabla-player's view of *shauq* is worth quoting at length:

> [T]he delight a man takes in contemplating himself is proportionate to the scale of his powers of imagination. The more vivid his imagination, the more joy he feels in his (imagined) unique powers. This self-contemplation is really self-deception, but without it man could not survive. . . . A bad tutor will only stifle the pupil's *shauq*, or channel it in the wrong direction. Alternatively, a good tutor will expand the capacity of the pupil's mind, thus increasing his powers of imagination and understanding. A good tutor therefore encourages the pupil's *shauq*, which, in turn, leads to greater fulfilment.[9]

This intimate connection of *shauq* and the imagination explains the repeated claim among embroiderers that designs came *man se* (from the mind), and that a person with great shauq could exercise their creative powers unassisted, and untrammeled, by the printed design.

This process of learning through the expansion of mental abilities, as well as the honing of physical powers, is frustrated by *pareshani*. Without other resources, even if the woman has no interest in embroidery, there is no alternative to doing it if she needs the money. When a woman must regard chikan as a sole means of support, or a source of money to supplement a husband's meager income, *pareshani* forces her to apply her creative powers in the absence of passionate interest. However, if *shauq* is great, it is not clear that pareshani can destroy it utterly. There were very few skilled women who continued to work, as opposed to those who "retired" to supervisory or entrepreneurial activities, that did not live with some degree of *pareshani*. But none admitted to any diminution of their *shauq* for the embroidery.

Even *shauq* is not without its hazards, as a conversation with a retired chikan embroiderer, a friend of my teacher, illustrated:

Friend: Why is she learning? Does she have to?

Saliha: It's interest. [Turning to me] You tell her, are you doing this for employment or from interest?

CWW: From interest.

Friend: Ah! When you do it because of troubles (*pareshani se*), that is one thing, but from interest (*shauq se*), that is something else. Don't your eyes ache?

CWW: My back hurts.

Friend: Yes. If you have interest, you work more, and your eyes go bad. So even out of interest (*shauq se*) come troubles (*pareshani*).

Embroiderers invoke *shauq* and *pareshani* to explain chikan's decline. My teacher and other highly skilled embroiderers complained frequently about the lack of *shauq* for the craft among young girls. Even among those women who did *murri* work, absence of *shauq* explained why they did not know more stitches, or did not develop their skills further. Saliha, quite convinced of the opposition between *shauq* and the need for money, argued that if wages were to increase, there might be more women who would be prepared to learn just a few stitches required for average *murri* work. These women might want to work as much as possible, but such women would not be interested in learning more stitches. For most women today, their only interest was in what kind of money they could make.

Women with high skills and abundant *shauq* might continue embroidering, even if it were unnecessary for them to do so. I asked my teacher's daughter if she would give up chikan if there were no need to do it for money, and she answered, no. But I also knew of cases where women with *shauq* and skills were expected to give up embroidering if they made an auspicious marriage. Continuing to make chikan in the absence of *pareshani* must presumably be at the discretion of a woman's affinal family, and depends upon whether they take an interest in her skills. Only a very tenacious woman would continue making chikan when her family sees no pressing need for her to do so. Nobody I met ever talked of having fought to do chikan in the absence of need, although in all practicality, few had any illusions of ever being in a position where they might be faced with such an option. In other words, while *shauq* is deemed fundamental to chikan embroidery by all who know it well, continuing to do it depends, to some degree, on continuing *pareshani*. Anwar Jahan said she would not do this if she lived in comfort (referring to both agent activity and embroidering). And yet her ability to do fine work depended upon her having *shauq*.

The present-day prevalence of *pareshani* had blighted *shauq*, and embroiderers thought that *shauq* was scarcely to be found in a city so debased from its days of glory. However, it does not seem that the very finest skills are diminishing or disappearing, as the number of young faces in the government brochures of handicraft award winners—and my own encounters with several highly skilled women in their twenties—imply. But there are few opportunities to display high skills in the marketplace, and were it not for highly specific outlets provided by the state (see next chapter), *shauq* would have practically no avenue for expression.

PROCESSES OF LEARNING

Although I cannot claim to have learnt in the same circumstances as the majority of Lakhnawi embroiderers, I was exposed to the fundamental procedures one must master in order to be a highly skilled embroiderer (some of which must also be mastered by even the minimally skilled worker). For ease of presentation, I have described these procedures in the order in which they are done by an accomplished embroiderer. However, a girl does not learn all the steps of making chikan in strictly linear order. For example, preparation of the thread, which must be done by a skilled embroiderer before any embroidery commences, is not learned by the novice until after some basic skill in forming stitches has been acquired. As Lave (1982) noted in her study of Moroccan tailors, it is only after some time that an apprentice can begin to undertake all the tasks involved in making a garment from start to finish. Typically, training begins with giving the apprentice discrete jobs that follow later on in the labor process.

Two kinds of thread are used in chikan, *pakka* (i.e., cauterized) thread for *jali* and *hatkatti* work, and *kacca* (soft, breakable) thread for everything else. *Kacca* thread comes in large bundles several inches thick and is uneven and lumpy. Poorer-quality *pakka* thread costs less than Rs. 1 and good-quality varieties cost Rs. 1.50 a reel.

To prepare *kacca* thread for embroidery, a smaller hank is pulled from the original one, creating clouds of cotton dust. The embroiderer wraps one end of the smaller hank around her big toe, straightens her leg, and pulls the hank taut. Holding the hank tightly, she teases strands from it. Since there are irregularities in the density of the strands in the hank, and different stitches are supposed to vary in thickness, the embroiderer separates out anywhere from five to seven strands to make a composite thread. She places this thread to the side, and repeats the process until she has about five or six threads arranged like spokes on a wheel. She will then spit on her hands and twist each thread between her palms, unwrap the hank from her toe, wrap the ends of the threads in turn around the toe, and pull their other ends out from where they remain attached.[10] The threads are then ready to use.

Every embroiderer must learn to prepare thread for herself, no matter her level of skill. When I began learning, threads were prepared for me, but after a few weeks, I was told to prepare the thread myself. At this point, I had seen the procedure done many times, but still needed help to finally tease out the threads. When an embroiderer prepares her own thread, she must know how many strands to pull out for different kinds of stitches, since some are made with as few as four (for example, *tepci*) and others are made with as many as nine (*bakhya*). The reason for this variation is that stitches are classified as *patla* or *mota*, where *mota* refers to the solidity and mass of the stitch, not that it is badly made. Given the irregularities of *kacca* thread, the embroiderer must also learn to vary the number of strands she puts in her threads for embroidering. Rather than there being a fixed number of strands for a given stitch, therefore, there are only approximations, subject to change if the strands are thicker or thinner than normal. Thus, the embroiderer must learn to literally "size up" her thread in the preparatory stages in order to make a satisfactory stitch.

Kacca thread, unlike *pakka* thread which comes on a reel, has a predetermined length. Laila Tyabji, SEWA Lucknow's chief designer, observed that part of an embroiderer's skill is a tacit calculation of how to complete a stitch motif with a single thread, without running out of thread at the midpoint. This ability shows once again how important it is for the embroiderer to work creatively with the print. She must adhere to it but also be able to graze it, find the shortest distance around curves, if she is to finish a section and not find herself in need of more thread in the middle. My teacher did not repeat this requirement to me explicitly but I did notice that she only ran out of thread once she reached an appropriate point to conclude a section of embroidery.

For most embroiderers, starting work means putting a frame on the area to be embroidered. Highly skilled embroiderers, however, disapprove of using a frame. My teacher never used one, but her daughters did, saying that it was useful for doing the center of a large, thick piece of cloth, when the amount of cloth wadded in the palm would be uncomfortable. But when one of them suggested I use a frame as I learned, my teacher rebuked her, saying that the use of a frame was "*dehat*" (rural, backward). Most frames were made of wood, and bought at the market. A few had made custom frames out of tin wrapped in rags (see figure 5.1).

From the moment she begins to learn, a girl who is expected to be a skilled embroiderer must hold the cloth in a particular way, known as *ćuṭkī* (lit., a pinch). *Cutki* refers to the embroiderer clasping the cloth tightly around the index finger, holding it firmly between index and middle fingers and allowing it to fall over the rest of the hand. A neat crease between the fingers is a sign of good *cutki* (see figure 5.2). The proper way to hold the cloth is emphasized from the very beginning of training, for it is the foundation that delicate, and difficult stitches are built upon. For my part, if my embroidery was found wanting, my teachers' first response would be that I must have lapsed from good *cutki*.

Grasping the cloth in this way produces a tautness in the cloth that is deemed essential to the results. As Saliha expressed it, the tighter the cloth is held, the firmer and better the stitch. A *mahajan* once told me that a sure sign that the *cutki* method had been used (as opposed to either a frame, or slack holding of the fabric) was, ironically, slight imperfections in the work. "When you use *cutki*, the needle is pulled tight and the threads break. That leaves a hole." As work progresses, the cloth is continually readjusted so that the design to be worked is directly over the outer side of the first knuckle. This was pointed out to me after a week or so of instruction. By doing this, one ensures that the part of the cloth being stitched is stretched over a firm base, and that the work is kept in tight focus, since the knuckle is less than an inch square. Embroiderers who use *chutki* have characteristically thickened skin around the index knuckle where it is rubbed by the cloth and pricked by the needle.

The work must also be done close to the body. While she showed me how to adjust the cloth as I worked, Saliha drew an imaginary line

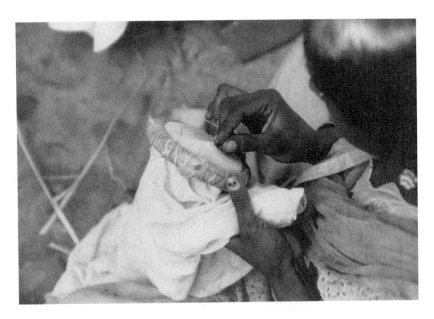

FIG. 5.1. Embroidering with a frame.

from the work to the *nāk* (nose). This technique seemed to increase control and meant that the gaze of the embroiderer on her work was consistent. Using a frame probably makes it easier to stray from this ideal, although Saliha did not specifically say so.

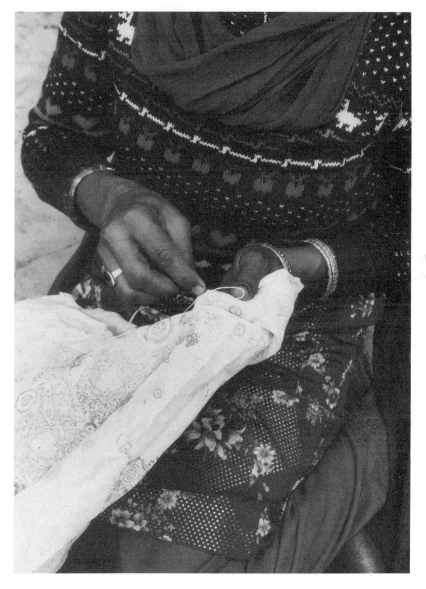

FIG. 5.2. Embroidering using cutki.

Using the Needle

A fundamental difference in European and South Asian embroidery technique has been repeated by authors since Watt (1903:370) made the following comment: "There is a peculiarity of all Indian needlework that may in passing be mentioned in this place since it doubtless has something to say to the styles of work produced, namely the fact that the needle is pulled away from, not drawn toward, the operator." The "peculiarity" of European and North American embroidery is to pull the thread *toward* the embroiderer. This mode of handling the needle is taught simultaneously with specific stitches in Europe and America, and needle technique and stitches are also taught together in South Asia. Watt rightly remarks that this way of using the needle affects the styles produced, but does not explore the implications of this, continuing: "The persistence with which the inhabitants of Eastern countries work in this so-called 'opposite direction' seems due to the lesser development of the extensor muscles of the body and not a perversity in character." Watt dismisses one "Orientalist"[11] explanation of difference—the possibility of moral failing—only, it seems, to suggest another, this time based on physical difference. Naqvi's (1971) response to Watt is to point out that Indian floral motifs are consistently worked "as the flower grows," or from the base of the stem to the petals. This choice has nothing to do with muscle development or anything else, and Naqvi rightly states that it is a "reasonable practice." As a rule, chikan embroiderers do tend to direct the needle away from the body and embroider motifs from bottom to top instead of from top to bottom. However, some idiosyncracy in the way in which the needle is manipulated seems to be tolerated. This became evident in the different ways in which sisters Sajda and Asiya Khatun made *kaj*, or the edging stitch used on table linens. Whereas Sajda consistently inserted the needle into the cloth vertically, Asiya directed it sideways. There was no tangible difference in results as far as I could determine, nor did I ever hear any negative commentary on their technique.

Learners pay careful attention to the demonstration of a stitch by the teacher, and then make their own approximation of the same stitch on the remainder of the motif, in silence (see Lave 1982; Lave and Wenger 1991). Demonstrations of a stitch were almost invariably conducted in silence with no commentary by my teacher other than mention of the stitch name. These demonstrations might last as long as several minutes. On being handed the work, I would be encouraged to ask for help if needed. If I did ask for help, the response would invariably include a fresh demonstration of the stitch, again held in silence.

Sometimes, explication and commentary are offered at the time the student is trying her own hand at the stitch. Observation by my teacher of my first efforts at doing a stitch was often close and intense. There were three different instances of commentary that I was offered. The first was advice given in the very first lessons of where to direct the needle, and which *patti* (leaf) or stem to do next. The second concerned adherence to the print, and came up when I was trying to do the stitch *ghas patti*. Seeing me stick closely to the print, Sajda commented that since the stitch requires a sharp inward angle, it was not possible to do this while following the lines of a rounded leaf pattern. Besides, she said, the stitch length must be even both sides of the imagined center line, however the print may appear. Saliha later seemed to contradict this advice, for observing me going outside the print, she cautioned me to stick to it. Indeed, evidence of her greater skill was her ability to graze the pattern with her stitches, yet retain evenness and symmetry in the motif. Subtle adjustments of needle strokes to pattern are done by the embroiderer routinely. Doing the stitch effectively meant placing each stitch extremely close, even touching, the previous one.

The third, and most frequent occasion of commentary was to point out errors of technique and style. Preferred uses of the fingers, needle and thread were pointed out while I was working under my teacher's or her daughters' eye. The most memorable of these was the admonition not to let go of the needle and pull the thread through the cloth with my fingers, but to continue drawing it through with the needle until the thread formed a loop over my left thumb, with whose aid I could ease the stitch into its precise place. This dictum also appears in some written sources (e.g., Rastogi 1988:67;[12] Pande 1968:45). Using the left thumb in this way makes a dramatic difference to control and the attainment of minuteness, evenness, and clarity. On another occasion I was making *lambi murri*, and Saliha pointed out how some stitches needed to be a little tighter, and some a little looser, to keep the motif smooth and *saf*.

Errors might also be pointed out after I had completed hours' worth of work on a stitch without anyone having observed me at all. For example, I was told that the *kils* I had made were unsatisfactory, and had to have a large and raised knot at the center. I also learned after several hours of making *sidhaur jali* perpendicular to the base of the *phul* that it was supposed to be made at a 45 degree angle. Most (perhaps all) other forms of *jali* are made perpendicular to the base. *Sidhaur*, the most popular *jali*, is the exception. *Sidhaur* on commercial chikan work is often perpendicular to the base but all highly skilled embroiderers insisted that this is incorrect.

These kinds of commentary suggest that there is no systematic body of knowledge that the teacher is concerned to pass on, particularly one that is expounded in association with showing a student a new stitch, or methods of preparing or using materials. There is, however, a loose body of conventions governing technique and stitch styling that are expressed in relation to concrete examples of error or deviation from these conventions on the part of the student. This approach to learning may help explain some of the idiosyncratic differences in the work of embroiderers, for example, the difference between holding the needle sideways or vertically in *kaj*, or knotting *jali* thread, or using a double thread. After observing the teacher construct a stitch, the pupil attempts her own approximation of what the teacher did, in the best way she can. So long as any variations in the way the student tries to copy the stitch do not materially affect results, they are unlikely to be corrected. In my own case, I found that making the stitch *dhūm* became much easier and more successful when I worked one part of it with the cloth oriented one way, and the rest of it with the cloth turned another way. I have no idea whether my strategy for the doing the stitch was like anyone else's, but it produced passable results and was never remarked upon or criticized.

Repetition is the key to mastering a stitch (see Lave 1982; Lave and Wenger 1991). This is why many hours of continuous working may go on without interference by the teacher—and these are the times when any stylistic and technical idiosyncrasies are likely to appear. Critiques of the final product, though, can be sharp. In my own unusual position, I escaped the harshest forms of rebuke, but my work was often only grudgingly accepted, or disdained as *mota*, the word embroiderers used most to describe work that they did not find pleasing. I was never asked to unpick work and do it again, although some say that government and commercial employers require shoddy work to be redone, or at least corrected by finishers. On the other hand, it seems unlikely that all errors are corrected, since quite a bit of obviously flawed work makes its way to the shelves of chikan stores. The situation is different among the highly skilled. Akhtar Jahan said she continually had to remake stitches under the tutelage of her father, working and working until the stitch was satisfactory. Reworking embroidery may well be an important device in the training of skilled embroiderers.

Making Stitches

Descriptions of how stitches are made appear in several texts about chikan (Paine 1986; Pande 1968; Naqvi 1971). Some notes of my own are presented in the appendix. Here, I shall confine myself to remarks about how learning stitches is patterned.

The first stitches learned by highly skilled embroiderers are always some version of a sequence including *bakhya, tepci, pencni* or *urmā*, and the different forms of *murri*. They are some of the most commonly found stitches in chikan work and form the basic repertoire of the moderately skilled *murri* worker. All of these stitches are made with *kacca* thread. *Pencni* is similar in construction to *urma*, featuring a wrapped stitch over short running stitches called *pasūj*. According to Saliha, the difference between *pencni* and *urma* was that *urma* was the essential *bel* (creeper, the curvilinear patterns from which leaves and phuls issue), a consistent feature of chikan (see Paine 1987:9). If an embroidered *bel* appeared without *pattis*, it was called *pencni*. Subsequently, however, I heard the word *pencni* referred to more often than *urma*, even at times when according to Saliha's own definition *urma* was the appropriate term.

Further stitches are added to the repertoire of the student in a variable sequence. In part this must reflect the fact that some stitches only appear infrequently in commercial work and so there are fewer opportunities to practice and perfect one's technique. A special piece of printed cloth must now be made available for practicing these more complex and rare stitches.

Jali work can be started after instruction in the basic stitches, but not necessarily after all stitches made with *kacca* thread are mastered. *Jali* specialists probably do learn and know some other stitches in the chikan repertoire, but quickly turn to the exclusive and repetitive production of *sidhaur jali*. Highly skilled embroiderers, on the other hand, are expected to master several different *jalis*, none of which appear in commercial work.

Whereas other stitches must conform to the shapes and solid lines of the printed pattern, in *jali* the print only defines the space in which it must appear. This is the only case in which each needle stroke is made essentially freehand. The skill of the embroiderer is manifest in the small size and large number of "holes" she is able to open up in the space, and the extent to which the tight stitches that hold the network open recede into invisibility.

Jali is not pulled or drawn-thread work. Only one *jali* that I was taught required a thread to be removed from the cloth, and that was *bank jali*. Whether other embroiderers follow the same procedure as my teacher in making *bank jali*, I do not know. But most were emphatic that the common description of *jali* as drawn-thread work is wrong. Instead, most *jalis* depend entirely upon the precision of the needle strokes and firm tension in the stitches to "open" the cloth. All *jalis* in *phuls* start with the definition of a center line. Then, the embroiderer adds a new line, parallel to the first. The *jali* holes are opened as a pair of lines are completed. The embroiderer goes on like this until one side of the *phul* is finished. Turning the cloth around, she returns to the center line, and makes parallel lines on the other side until the motif is complete. *Hatkatti* is made using the same technique and is linear in construction. An embroiderer can be more flexible in her use of *hatkatti*, highlighting any number of other stitches by circling, skirting, or interlacing them with *hatkatti*.

The holes in *jali* are made by pushing the threads of the cloth aside with the point of the needle, and then drawing the needle through quite forcibly, pulling the *pakka* thread tight. *Hatkatti* is done with even more vigor. In the less accomplished, the base cloth can appear puckered and warped after fervent *hatkatti* or *jali* embroidering. If the embroiderer's work is slack, the holes are irregular, the *pakka* thread is visible, and there is more cloth than hole. In the highly skilled, by contrast, each hole is perfectly shaped, the space is transformed into a delicate lattice, and there is no pinching and puckering. Variable methods of ensuring good results in *jali* are widely tolerated. For example, while some never knot their thread, some do, and Sultana Begum even used a double, knotted thread for *hatkatti*, to increase its strength.

Complex *jalis* require a firm grasp of spatial relationships and complex stitching. Two lines are worked on at once, only one of which is being completed as the other is half-defined. The final shape of the *jali* emerges not as a single line is finished, but as a new line is added. The embroiderer must anticipate, in her imagination, how the *jali* will appear upon completion. The more breathtaking examples include *jalis* in which a single thread from the base fabric transects the hole (*makra*), or two threads form a cross-hair suspended in each, or alternate holes (*bul-bul cashm* and *taj mahal* respectively).[13]

Working with the Print

There are four elements to the printed pattern that correspond to different kinds of embroidery, the *bels*, the *phuls* (the space for *jali* that appears on the print as bounded space shaped like a flower), the *pattis* (leaves, where *hatkatti* may be placed), and *būṭīs/būṭās* (circular motifs where round designs like *kil* and *kangan* go).[14] Embroiderers do not spell out these distinctions explicitly, but the terms correspond to "landmarks" on the printed design that embroiderers implicitly recognize.

The highly skilled expect more of the print they work with than do the less skilled, arguing that a good embroidered design depends upon a good printed one. They see the print as one element in the impression the finished, embroidered work creates. Embroiderers strive, at least rhetorically, to monopolize the entire creative process, claiming that even the block designs issue from *their* own minds, and the blockmaker and printer simply follow instructions. The printer and the blockmaker, on the other hand, are reluctant to acknowledge such an encroachment upon their own aesthetic and occupational territory, or, at the very least, to concede that their skills are of a purely technical and noncreative order.

The most extreme example of this contestation comes from those embroiderers who deny the significance of printers altogether, saying that with sufficient skill, designs from the mind can be placed on to the cloth to be embroidered without aid of printed guides. If this is true, then the blockmaker too is inessential, and his own claim that designs issue from his mind an empty boast. Embroidering without a print is considered a feat, perhaps the supreme mark of an embroiderer's *shauq*, but in practice is rarely, perhaps never encountered.

In practice, the three main ways in which the embroiderer actively engages the print are through choosing a stitch appropriate to the printed motif, modifying or adjusting a print to accommodate a desired stitch, and reprinting a section of cloth entirely to force a new selection and arrangement of stitch types.

Choice of stitches. In commercial work, the matching of stitch to print is a simple task. *Bakhya* work is made on a *bakhya* design, and the details of a *murri* print can easily be fleshed out by the average *murri* embroiderer. In actuality, only a few print motifs *dictate* a particular stitch to be used, like *kil*, *kangan*, and *jali*. On most areas of the print, more than one stitch can be used. However, not all stitches can be made on all kinds of print. For example, neither *gol* nor *lambi murri* can be done on a *bakhya* print, and vice versa. Because there is no fixed relationship between a particular stitch and a particular print, the embroiderer is constantly adapting her choice of stitch to the work in progress. The embroiderer enjoys a limited, but critical freedom to choose the stitches she wants, in the places she wants. Learning what possibilities exist and how to decide which stitches to use is an important element of the highly skilled embroiderer's training. For example, a motif suitable for *bakhya* might well be used for *balda* or *dhum*, whereas a motif for *gol murri* could be used for *lambi murri* or *tepci*, to name but two. Understanding the choices available means being able to distinguish *mota* (thick) and *patla* (thin) stitches. For example, *bakhya*, *dhum*, and *balda* are all *mota* stitches and are associated with specific leaf and petal forms. But the print does not invariably dictate whether a *mota* or *patla* stitch is required, and again it is up to the embroiderer to decide what kind of stitch she wishes to use.

The run-of-the-mill embroiderer is comfortable not having to make choices in the stitches she uses. I once saw Saliha's daughter grow impatient while suggesting stitch alternatives to an embroiderer making *kur-*

tas for her mother. The worker was clearly unwilling or unable to make choices among stitches, but there was also exasperation on the daughter's part that this kind of decision could not be left in the worker's hands. The woman making fine *murri* for the market may be the only commercial-sector worker who is consistently faced with the problem of choosing what stitch to use. To the extent that she can avoid it, she will. But for the highly skilled embroiderer, making these kinds of choices is at the heart of her special talent.

At what point, and how a student comes to make her own decisions about what stitches to use are questions that cannot be answered without further research. My teacher's daughter often ventured ideas as to what stitch to put in different areas of the piece I was working on, most of which were overruled by Saliha. In this way, Sajda's suggestions were continually put forward, heard, and contested, and her judgments refined.

Saliha denied that choice of stitches is an aspect of design. According to her, stitch choice simply arose out of the arrangement and appearance of the print. "What stitches you choose to use are just that—a choice." But this explanation does not seem to apply when we look at the aesthetic goals of an embroiderer like Sultana Begam, who does unusual things like use *kaj* on motifs in the middle of the cloth, instead of confining it to the outer edge of her embroideries. She could choose from a range of more conventional stitches, but she does not and is consciously innovating when she makes such an unusual decision. "New ideas keep coming to me," she said. "I try them when I feel like it. Sometimes I'll try something and then abandon it." A piece of fine work is, by definition, the exquisite working of a printed design. But while a perfectly acceptable design can be turned into something splendid with the use of only a few stitches—as in the examples of antique chikan displayed in museums—innovation in stitch choice now bears aesthetic weight, perhaps stimulated by government patronage.

Modifying the print. Most skilled embroiderers demonstrate their creativity, and assert their aesthetic centrality through the simple device of print modification and revision. In the process, they demonstrate that while a print of some kind is indispensable to their craft, they reserve ultimate control over its role in the finished piece of embroidery.

The highly skilled embroiderer, unlike the commercial or low-skilled embroiderer, feels free to make modifications in the print in order to achieve a visual effect or to do a stitch that the original print did not permit. Several examples came up in the course of my instruction, some involving mere use of the outer perimeter of a print motif as a guide, and some requiring redrawing on top of the print.

An example of the first kind of modification was when Saliha decided to make a stitch named *bijli* in a motif with a central *phul* surrounded by four *pattis*, two on each side, and three smaller *pattis* opening at its base. The three inner *pattis* were originally supposed to have been done in *bakhya*, but instead, Saliha placed the hole of the *bijli* at the root of the clustered leaves, and allowed the stitch to cover and extend slightly beyond them. Meanwhile, tiny printed floral sprigs that issued from the side of the *phul* were ignored completely (see figure 5.3). In a further example, Saliha decided to use *balda* to define a *phul*'s perimeter, instead of *bakhya* as she had previously intended. The adaptation required for this was to convert a double circumference to a single circle; the double line would have served as the edges between which the herringbones of the *bakhya* would have been suspended. Since *balda*, like *pencni* and *kaj*, is made in two stages—a running stitch (*pasuj*) followed by some kind of oversewing—Saliha was able to effect this transformation by literally "tacking" from one circle to the other with the *pasuj*. Once she began the second element of *balda*—a precise, closely clustered stitch that wraps around the *pasuj*—she made a perfect circle by carefully placing the needle around the base stitches, and at critical points pulling it gently into the desired shape.

Of the second kind of modification, one instance was when Saliha was looking for a place to put *kangan*, a large circular stitch. She decided to adapt a repetitive motif that encircled the inner flower and stem sequence. The motif was made up of an elongated heart shape, surrounded by rounded petal forms and with an internal triad of petals. She placed a fresh, circular guide for the *kangan* on top of the old design by using a *ćawannī* (a 25 paise or four *annā* coin) to draw a circle in the widest point of the pointed oval. The petal shapes were left untouched (figure 5.4).

Print modification shows the sense of freedom the embroiderer feels in working creatively with the print, and also shows that decisions about stitch choice and arrangement are not fixed at the inception of work. In fact, it seems that highly skilled embroiderers actively construct their works in the *process* of embroidering. This point emerges once again when we consider the decision to reprint designs.

Reprinting. Sometimes one sees, on a piece of unfinished chikan, print laid upon print, with the embroiderer picking and choosing what she wants of each. Reprinting takes place either to restore a faded design or to adjust a printed pattern that the embroiderer does not like. In the latter case, reprinting is done to accommodate a marked shift in the embroiderer's conception of the piece and illustrates the limits of stitch choice and print modification in satisfying the embroiderer's creative impulses. Perhaps she wishes to demonstrate a more bravura use of stitches—for example, a richer and more abundant use of *jali*. Or perhaps she simply wants to adjust the spatial distribution of design clusters. She may attempt to lighten (if not entirely remove) the unwanted print by rubbing it in water. In general, reprinting a design involves the use of blue dye, irrespective of the original dye color.

The embroiderer who was most forthcoming about the ways in which she tried to achieve certain aesthetic effects in her work was Sultana Begum, whose work bore several traces of reprinting. A *sari* being embroidered by my teacher's family also had areas of reprinting. The *sari* was high quality, with a dense application of embroidery. It took five to six months to make, and at an early point Saliha had made the

FIG. 5.3. Modifying the print.

FIG. 5.4. Modifying the print.

decision to alter an important element of its printed design. A series of diagonal panels with small flowers—some of which were retained and embroidered in the final version—had been replaced with strips featuring larger flowers later embroidered in *kauri* and *bakhya*, and waisted *phuls* filled with *sidhaur jali*. When I asked Saliha about this, she said that she had thought to herself (of the original design), "If I were to buy this, I wouldn't like it," and as a result had gone to the printer to make the changes.

Of course, Saliha had liked the original printed design well enough to start work on it. But it appears that as the embroiderer begins to choose the stitches she wants to use, and works each stitch in its assigned place, her impression of the unfolding design may alter. She may decide she wants to change the range of choices she will be faced with as she goes on to a new portion of the design. Each choice of stitch the embroiderer makes, therefore, has multiple ramifications for the piece as a whole, ultimately dictating whether reprinting is necessary.

THE EMBROIDERER'S "DESIGN": PLANNING AND EXECUTION

The overall design of a piece of chikan is not much discussed when talking about what constitutes "good" embroidery. Yet embroiderers like to emphasize that they are the "authors" of their designs, although it is only in specifically commissioned articles, or in pieces made for the government competitions, that imagination is given free rein. I experienced in some small measure the creative effort behind making an entire design in my own training on a piece of cloth that Saliha had specially printed for the purpose.

Asked about how she goes about making a design, specifically when she was free of the constraints of a customer's requirements, Saliha said she thought first of the blocks she wanted to use, and how to organize them to create an overall effect, and only later considered the types of embroidery to use. A visit to the printer was portrayed as a lengthy consultation, in which the embroiderer would review designs printed on paper, and then decide which ones should be transferred to the cloth. Sultana Begum said that she deliberately exploited the fact that different printers had different blocks, and consulted different printers in order to introduce variation into her designs, over which she still had considerable autonomy. Some embroiderers have their own collections of print blocks.

From the organization of the printed design Saliha had obtained for me, it was clear she intended to display stitches in the same way she had done in at least one previous award piece (now hanging in the Central

Design Centre in Lucknow). Arranged around a central, circular pattern were sixteen distinct stem and flower patterns. These were attached at their bases to a polygon around the center. My teacher turned her attention first to the stems and flowers, which were to bear the load of her main design objective. She wanted to display eight different embroidery stitches, and she intended to achieve this through designating floral motifs that stood opposite one another as a pair. The two flowers in a pair were embroidered the same way, and each pair was different from the others. The result of this process would not simply be the display of a cluster of stitches, but also an explicit demonstration that many different stitches can be applied to the same print (figure 5.5).

FIG. 5.5. A stem and flower design.

On the remainder of the design, eight similar stem and flower patterns turned inwards from the inner side of the polygon. There were *buti* prints arranged in the space between the compact area of the central portion and the more widely spaced print of the outer zone. The perimeter was filled with a sinuous *bel* print, and was bordered by the characteristic scallops that are almost always embroidered in *kaj*. I was asked again and again whether I liked the design, implying that it had value separate from its finished appearance as embroidery.

After looking at the cloth for some time, Saliha told me to take a pencil (since a pen would permanently mark the cloth) and write down the different stitches she would put on the first six stems. These were, in order, *bakhya, jhumar, tepci, cikan, ghas patti, jorā, kauri,* and *lambi murri.* But as the work proceeded, Saliha did not stick to these initial choices, and she did not make any further explicit attempts to plan where to put stitches. Nor did she require me to work through all the central motifs before going on to some other subproject on the piece. Instead, after several of the central motifs had been done, she directed me to start work on other stitches in other locations of the cloth (figure 5.6).

There is no set place where the embroiderer must start her work and the embroiderer often varies her routine by working on different parts of the cloth from day to day. This prevents boredom but I believe that it also allows the embroiderer to view the unfolding of her embroidered design in a complex, almost organic way. She does, of course, observe how stitches work together in closely clustered motifs and series of motifs. But in working different areas of the cloth, she observes the structure and relationships contained in the whole. As I was directed to return to an unembroidered central motif, Saliha would regard this portion of the design with fresh eyes, in the light not just of its neighboring motifs, but in terms of the other embroidery being built around it.

Of course, it is also possible that she had simply forgotten what she had intended to do in these central portions. After a few weeks, my written code faded, and she had no immediate cue as to what her original plans might have been. My own uncertainty on this point stems from the ambiguity of our relationship. I was acknowledged to be a research scholar who asked many things about embroiderers' lives and circumstances. But I was also a student of Saliha's, in a position where I could not easily question—or be seen to question—her decisions and actions regarding chikan. When I did draw her attention to the existence of a previous choice, she said nothing and simply continued with the stitch she had just chosen to employ.

What the embroiderer deems to be "good" is redefined as the work progresses, and each new stitch alters the way in which others, as yet unmade, may appear. This principle influenced the choice of stitches and also the mode of application of specific stitches. For example, when demonstrating *zanzira*, Saliha first made the stitches long, and worked them in the center of each *patti*. Then, she began to unpick them and replaced them with smaller *zanzira* stitches that followed the edges of

FIG. 5.6. Detail of embroidery in progress. This is the piece of embroidery I worked on as a student of Saliha Khatun.

the *pattis*. I asked if she had made a mistake. She shook her head, and, referring to her new stitches, said "*aćhā lag rahā hai*" (This looks good, that is, this looks better). She went through a similar process of revision when doing *pencni* as a leaf, as well as a stem design, substituting a more feathery, many-stitched effect for sparser, larger stitches.

Mota/Patla

As the embroidery began to fill the design, the distinction between mota and patla stitches became apparent. Sajda once offered *bakhya* as a possible choice for one of the central circle of motifs (Saliha's original choice having been forgotten). Saliha recommended *cikan* instead but both of them stressed that a *mota* stitch must be chosen, since *mota* and *patla* stitches were supposed to alternate throughout the circle.

In this context, *mota* refers to the solidity and higher relief of a stitch, not to its crudeness or poor execution. Outside the limited context of chikan, mass or bulk is often appropriate to the form and substance of some objects. For example, when she showed me the zardozi *pan* box covers I mentioned earlier in the chapter, Saliha asked if I liked the heavy crimson satin material they were made from. I said yes, and commented that it was "*mahin*," intending this to mean that I admired its good quality and sheen. But Saliha looked surprised, and objected that, far from being *mahin*, it was *mota*, and rubbed the material between her fingers for emphasis. She clearly did not mean that it was inferior, rough fabric, only that it possessed a substance and feel that could not be described as "fine," in the sense of airy or insubstantial.

The harmony of *mota* and *patla* elements was a critical element in making an article of chikan beautiful. It was so important to Saliha that she rendered what was usually a *mota* stitch as a *patla* one for the sake of maintaining symmetry in the *mota* and *patla* elements. For example, three of the alternating stitches, *zanzira*, *tepci*, and *pencni*, were unambiguously thin stitches. However, the fourth stitch in this alternating pattern was *lambi chikan*, which is clearly recognizable as a thick, substantial stitch from the presence of a *gol* at the end of each stem. Saliha made no further comment on this apparent discrepancy, but she did have me remove one strand from the thread intended for *lambi chikan*, to make it "thinner."

Creativity and the Exemplary Piece

In the end, I did not learn the entire thirty-two stitches my teacher claimed to know. All of the printed areas were accounted for with twenty-seven executed or planned stitches (one was even worked on the edge of the material without a print). To have interpolated all the remaining stitches at this point would have required more than simple print adjustment. Midway through my training, Saliha was clearly aware that it would not be possible to demonstrate all thirty-two stitches on the cloth. She offered—but I did not press her on the offer—to make samples of the missing stitches in a separate "binder."

This led me to wonder how Saliha could ensure, on a piece made for a government award competition, that all thirty-two stitches would be included, particularly given the spontaneous nature in which critical stitch choices are made. I concluded that when the stakes were much higher than they were for giving instruction to a foreigner, more time and thought would be exerted on all stages of creation of a piece of chikan. Blocks, printed design, initial plotting of stitch choices, and subsequent decisions to revise these choices, would all receive much more of the embroiderer's attention than they did in my case. There was also, of course, the possibility of reprinting.

WORKING FOR THE MARKET: CONCESSIONS IN SKILL

Chikan embroidery is not a dangerous job and it does not require strength. It is, however, demanding in other ways. Eye-strain, backache, and muscle cramps are common complaints. The embroiderer must maintain a high degree of precision and coordination in order to produce satisfactory embroidery. The thread is inclined to twist, and the increasing slipperiness of the needle as it is moistened by sweat is a nuisance. These difficulties, on top of the mental and physical concentration required to make acceptable stitches, made my own embroidery efforts proceed extremely slowly. Saliha often seemed surprised that I had not finished a portion of embroidery as rapidly as she had expected, and this based on the assumption that I had never done any kind of work like this before!

Concerned about my slow progress, she arranged at one point for some of the work (a *murri bel*) to be done by a neighbor. I was told to set aside Rs. 40 for this woman's contribution. After two days, in which the woman worked on my article in the mornings, the *bel* was finished. Not only had the woman finished the work many times faster than I could have done, she was able to achieve a consistently good (if not exceptional) standard of embroidery. Mastery of individual stitches is thus not the only accomplishment of the *murri* embroiderer. It is a further indication of craftsmanship to be able to work rapidly.

Of course, no embroiderer, whatever her level of skill, is immune from having to work quickly. In order to continue being employed, the embroiderer has to make an average set of goods in an average period of time, whether she is making *bakhya* work or *murri* work (see Marx 1976:694). Some women clearly do evade these requirements, but a few stray or late items here are there are perhaps to be expected in an informal productive system such as chikan's. As arbiters of the system, it is up to agents to discipline workers, not *mahajans*.

Being an agent is something that a young woman learning fine embroidery must aim for. Just as she observes and participates in her mother's embroidery, so the daughter of an agent watches her carry on her transactions with embroiderers and picks up the "tricks of the trade" of subcontracting. One thing she learns is how her own mastery of many stitches contrasts with the more limited knowledges of the women to whom she is giving work. Agents make no effort to alter the distribution of skills among the women who work for them. Skilled embroiderers usually do not teach girls outside their immediate families. As a result, no matter how much *shauq* some girls exhibit, not all can expect to learn much more than how to make the forms of work the market already demands. Embroiderers in rural areas or outside the family circles where high skills exist, cannot help but remain trapped within their specialties.

Fine work of all types is increasingly rare, but even more difficult to find are more esoteric examples of the embroiderer's craft. Among these is the specialty known as *chiriyāgar*, in which animals like elephants, horses, and birds dominate the design. A kind of chikan that has taken on almost legendary proportions is *anokhī* chikan, or embroidery that leaves no trace on the underside of the cloth. Rehana Begum said that *anokhī* chikan had not been made since the time of her father. But Saliha said she had made a piece of *anokhī* chikan.[15] It had been intended for an award, but Saliha sold it instead to a store-owner. She had never made another piece like it, so time-consuming had it been and so hurtful to her eyes.[16]

Whatever the kind of fine chikan, it will take many months, usually the best part of a year to make. The realization of the embroiderer's vision proceeds almost painfully slowly, as she works on first one section of her work, and then on another. A truly spectacular piece may linger in a woman's house for several years, taken up on occasion and worked, then put away again. No embroiderer either expects, or gets, to work in such a way for a commercial employer. What incentive exists then, besides her own *shauq*, to produce such articles? The answer lies in the provision of government patronage, to which I turn in the next chapter.

CHAPTER 6

Development Schemes
and State Patronage

Historically, the modern Indian state has played two roles with regard to chikan. It has employed embroiderers in its own production schemes, and it has patronized top-flight embroiderers. Each realm of activity has different objectives, and the result has been two distinct arenas of government activity that are sometimes at odds. There is one NGO (nongovernmental organization) involved with chikan in the city, called SEWA Lucknow. Its aims are slightly different from the state's and its influence is of a different kind. However, its challenges and contradictions overlap with those of the government.

The account in the pages that follow reflects the situation in 1989–90. Government support of chikan, it will become clear, has fluctuated over the years and continues to do so in the present. But the dilemmas and problems of development projects among embroiderers remain true no matter the scale of government or NGO operations.

GOVERNMENT HANDICRAFT POLICY

Chikan is classified as a handicraft by the government. What is called a handicraft today used to be categorized under "art manufactures" (Mukharji 1974) or "industrial arts" (Birdwood 1880) in the colonial period. In the post-Independence era, handicraft has been portrayed as any product made under so-called traditional patronage relations of the court or the village (e.g., Chattopadhyaya 1963), or as any object in which some work has been done by hand, particularly any purely decorative portions (see Fisher 1974). While broadly similar to any kind of production that is localized, informal, and small-scale, Benegal (1963) emphasizes that handicrafts are distinct from village or small-scale industries because handicraft products and processes differ widely from region to region, and handicraft producers differ in their organization, numbers, and ability to retain skills in the midst of social change. Handicraft commodities are strikingly diverse, ranging from brass utensils to ceramic horses, from embroidered *kurtas* to stone-inlaid coasters.

Official concern for handicrafts can be traced to the late nineteenth century and early twentieth century, and the ideals of *swādeshī* (self-reliance, home industry) put forward by nationalist intellectuals to counter the perceived demise of indigenous industry in the face of cheap European imported goods (Sarkar 1973). If only Indians would make, appreciate, and consume the goods they made at home, then dependence upon imported goods, particularly cloth, would wane—no matter that colonial terms of trade favored imports and made them cheaper. The *swadeshi* movement of 1905–1908 is regarded by many scholars as both a cultural and political watershed in the history of the Indian independence movement, for despite its shortcomings and failures, the movement awakened interest in handicrafts, folk art, and lifestyles opposite to those associated with industrialization and urbanity. The Congress Party adopted *swadeshi* principles and symbolism into its political platform throughout the 1920s and 1930s, with Mohandas K. Gandhi taking a leading role in these activities (Gandhi 1922; Bayly 1986; Bean 1988; Cohn 1988). *Swadeshi* came to represent national pride, independence, and a celebration of a distinctly Indian approach to the problems of social change. Gandhi, in particular, endorsed a model of India that would turn toward handicrafts in a revival of village life and a rejection of all manufactured forms, whether Indian or foreign. The Gandhian philosophy no doubt continues to color policy toward handicrafts today.

Government approaches to handicraft promotion also echo many of the sentiments and objectives of colonial arts and crafts critics, exemplified in the Delhi Exhibition of Art in 1903. This is hardly surprising, since the same critics added their voices to those of Indians disillusioned by the increasing prevalence of non-Indian commodities in Indians' lives. Europeans were already interested in acquiring Indian handicrafts by the end of the nineteenth century (Mukharji 1888). In 1903, Sir George Watt (1903:ix) wrote that some kinds of handicraft "hardly, if ever, met with in India at the present day," were being brought especially for the occasion from the South Kensington (now the Victoria and Albert) Museum "to be shown to the Indian people" (ibid.) The British founded training schools and museums of collectibles, the better to objectify India for middle-class Indian viewers and to initiate their own revival of disappearing craft traditions. *The Journal of Indian Industrial Art*, later renamed *MARG*, was first issued under British auspices.

In World Fairs outside India, in particular the Crystal Palace exhibition of 1851, India's massed articles of royal regalia and splendor presented a striking contrast to the unadorned products of mass machinofacture of nations such as the United States (Breckenridge 1987). Indian products selected for display were all "handicrafted," their "unmanufactured," that is, nonindustrial quality setting them apart from the goods made by England and its emergent industrial competitors. Other kinds of objects and products of India were kept from view. In this way, handicrafts were presented as essentially Indian and at the same time depicted India as "pre-industrial" and "underdeveloped."

What is surprising is the degree to which the manner of colonial patronage of indigenous crafts has continued. The Delhi exhibition was a landmark effort to categorize the plethora of "art manufactures," and for the first time, divisions and sections were organized in terms of common technique, origin, or character instead of geographical location. The exhibition was itself an inspiration of the then governor of India, George Curzon. "(O)ur object has been to encourage and revive good work, not to satisfy the requirements of the thinly-lined purse" (quoted in Gupta 1987:xiv). New official displeasure with innovations in craft production designed to satisfy European desires for cigarette cases, teapots, and so on—like the distaste expressed by Indian writers before and after Independence—fueled the determination to identify and reward authenticity, as well as quality.

A whole new set of critics and taste-makers, including heads of Indian schools of art, museum curators, customs officials, and other experts whose primary talent was for organizing and classifying helped select what would go to the exhibit.[1] The system of accession for the exhibition involved junior officers of the civil service "encouraging the craftsmen to undertake the work required of them, [of] supervising and checking the special preparations, and [of] fixing the prices" (p. ix). Such a system is strikingly similar to the functions of government officials in supervising government-sponsored production and preparing exhibitions today. Prizes were given out for work deemed to be exceptional, without regard to rewarding each and every type of manufacture, much as national and state awards for craft excellence are given out nowadays (see later in this chapter). The exhibition was both museological and trade-oriented, just like exhibition cum sales in the present, with "living artisans" practicing their specialty as visitors watched. Finally, the trader and manufacturer was accorded pride of place as an exhibitor, not at all out of keeping with what happens in contemporary handicraft promotion.

The ideological opposition of the "modern" and the "backward" affects policy in the present day. Only a few years after Independence, the new government took steps to "protect" handicrafts, with the goal of rescuing those moribund traditions that had been thwarted by colonialism or warped into the production of crude European-style goods (Benegal 1963). Promoting handicrafts was intended to breath life into an essentially Indian folk tradition, lodged in the village and the productive relations of village life. But nostalgia and an ideology of "culture" were not the only elements in this attempt at crafts revival. To this day, handicrafts development has clearly defined political objectives: to bolster the rural economy, to retard urban migration, and to employ (although with what rewards is not clear) many poorer and ill-educated Indians (All India Handicrafts Board 1963). In keeping with its *swadeshi* heritage, handicrafts promotion represents a form of "alternative development" to conventional massive investment and transformation in agriculture and machine-based industrial production. The problem with this is that handicrafts have been viewed as benign examples of "backward" forms of production and the relations of production that exist in them have received scant attention, or have simply been overlooked in the nostalgic yearning for a "simpler" age. Handicrafts policy is therefore conservative in many senses of the word. What is more, the intended recipients of government assistance have not always been the ones who most benefited from it.

Another reason why handicrafts have continued to get attention is that they have considerable potential as export commodities, reinforcing once again—for better or for worse—India's image as a land of simple artisan production. It is safe to say that handicrafts marketing, particularly to overseas destinations, has been, and remains, something of an obsession of both central and state governments, in spite of the acknowledged volatility and unpredictability of the overseas market for Indian commodities (see Swallow 1982).

Since Independence, states have set handicrafts policy, not the central government (Benegal 1960; Fisher 1974; Saraf 1984). The extent of the central government's influence on handicrafts development consists of providing consultation, funds, grants and loans, and, above all, furnishing marketing opportunities and settings to encourage the states to boost the production and sale of their handicrafts. In turn, the states' willingness to assist handicrafts producers and products depends upon the extent to which crafts represent a viable existing or potential export resource (inside, but preferably outside India), and the cultural prominence of those handicrafts throughout India (Fisher 1974). Cultural critics have complained that the focus on overseas export of handicrafts has come at the expense of thoughtful promotion of handicrafts within India (see Mitra 1969:60). They point to the failure to integrate handicrafts markets with Indian cultural and consumption patterns, and suggest that handicrafts demand, even within India, is based on shifting sands of appreciation and comprehension (Jain 1990; Tyabji 1990). In essence, *swadeshi* ideals are still being reinvented and debated, a hundred years after they were first proposed.

GOVERNMENT PROMOTION AND PATRONAGE

One role of government, in which state agencies predominate, involves promoting chikan production as a means of women's economic development, especially in rural areas. The government takes the place of the *mahajan*, and directs the production of chikan from cutting and tailoring to the final stages of finishing and marketing. While the services of all productive specialists in the chikan manufacturing process are required for this, the government employs only a few and it is not primarily interested in changing the livelihoods and activities of these other specialists. Rather it concentrates on distributing work to embroiderers, who get higher wages from government work than they do from the private sector. Embroidery is officially viewed as both the key creative stage of chikan manufacture (and thus most representative of an artistic heritage of India that deserves fostering) and the one with the largest number of producers in desperate economic straits (thus meriting government assistance).

The second role is to ensure the craft's survival through nurturing aesthetic excellence. Central and state government institutions extend patronage toward highly skilled artisans. Award competitions, exhibitions, and training schemes are intended to showcase and support the skills of acknowledged masters of the craft (alongside skilled practitioners of other crafts traditions in India), without explicit reference to any of the other specialists in chikan production, or to the commercial nexus in which most contemporary chikan is produced.

Government chikan production draws in embroiderers with a range of abilities, whereas awards, training, and exhibitions are oriented more to the highly skilled. The two arenas of activity are kept, for the most part, separate, but the objectives they represent are at times in conflict, and the highly skilled are affected by policy in both.

Central Government Institutions and Chikan

Office of the Development Commissioner (formerly the All India Handicrafts Board). The All India Handicrafts Board was set up in 1952 as an outgrowth of the All India Cottage Industries Board established shortly after Independence in 1948 (Benegal 1963). Its goals were to promote and to offer advice on crafts production and marketing throughout India. The Uttar Pradesh branch of the Office of the Development Commissioner (still referred to in everyday speech as the AIHB or All India Handicrafts Board) is located in Lucknow. Embroiderers usually referred to two AIHB offices, one in Golaganj, and one in Barabanki, a field office to the east of Lucknow.

Through its patronage of craftspeople, the AIHB has assisted enormously in raising the profile of handicrafts in India. A collection for a museum of handicrafts was put together in 1953, and a building provided by 1957. The Crafts Museum now occupies an area of Pragati Maidan in New Delhi, and includes buildings and open spaces for "living displays" of crafts and craftspeople. The museum supposedly hosts a chikan embroiderer every three months to demonstrate her work in the "crafts village." The museum also maintains a biographical and reference catalog of artisans of all kinds. A major AIHB marketing initiative has been the establishment of state emporia for the sale of handicrafts, and the number of emporia has mushroomed since the 1960s. By 1984, there were 250 state emporia all over India (Saraf 1984). The Central Cottage Industries Emporium in New Delhi, which is now over forty years old, is a thriving enterprise in which the products of many states are sold.

In its advisory capacity, the AIHB was to concern itself with the welfare and wages of craftspeople and with handicrafts promotion as factors in rural development. Overseas exports continue to be a major concern of the AIHB and seem to be as important and prestigious in the Uttar Pradesh (U.P.) handicrafts establishment. Many pages of the AIHB-sponsored *Handicrafts India* volumes are devoted to overseas export issues, as well as to listing the names of prominent exporters (see Handicrafts India 1989, 1990, and 1991). Because the central government is prevented from involving itself directly in handicrafts policy, the role of the AIHB is circumscribed and unclear (Fisher 1974). There is no way to assess the usefulness of its advice about obtaining credit and financing, and its impact on crafts wages is practically nil. AIHB effectiveness is more marked in those programs it can run itself, like award programs, exhibitions, and training initiatives (ibid.).

The Uttar Pradesh State Government

Uttar Pradesh is well known for its diverse industrial enterprises, including heavy and light manufacturing, workshop-based businesses, and a considerable range of cottage industries (Shankar 1987). Handicrafts flourish in the state's urban communities, particularly in Banaras, Agra, and Lucknow, and they are showcased in the chain of successful U.P. handicraft outlets called "GANGOTRI." There are few distinct "U.P." characteristics to handicrafts, unlike, say, the folk aspects, styling, and color of Gujarati and Rajasthani products. Instead, it is the sheer diversity of handicrafts in the state that is remarkable, including carpets, wood-carving, silk weaving, *zari* embroidering, *bidrī* and brass work, stone carving and setting.

Chikan has received special attention since incentives and programs for handicrafts were first launched by the new state governments of India. By 1947–48, the Directorate of Industries had started a program known as the Chikan Embroidery Scheme, employing 250 women. Its objectives were to provide regular employment and "fair" wages for work funneled through production centers, to improve the quality of work (through employing supervisors at the centers), and to expand the market for chikan (Mathur 1975). The numbers of women employed jumped to 630 by 1952 (Wealth of India 1953) and 1,000 in 1962 (All India Handicrafts Board 1963). Finished chikan goods were streamed to the CCIE (Central Cottage Industries Emporium) in Delhi, and Uttar Pradesh Handicrafts stores throughout India.

After a rapid expansion in the 1950s, during which the value of goods produced exceeded Rs. 200,000, a downturn in the Chikan Embroidery Scheme's fortunes followed. Production fell slightly from Rs. 258,377 worth of goods in 1961–62 to Rs. 237,822 in 1963–64.[2] Thereafter, financial stringency and private competition forced centers to close, although one soon reopened specifically to funnel finished goods to U.P. Handicrafts stores (Mathur 1975). The scheme disappears from the AIHB Annual Reports altogether until 1967–68, when it resurfaces as the Chikan Production Unit.[3] Production had picked up to Rs. 190,000 worth of goods when the unit was renamed the Chikan Production Centre in 1969–70.

In 1971, the Government of Uttar Pradesh Handicrafts Export Corporation (UPEC) was established and the chikan scheme of the Directorate of Industries suspended (although see the description of the Khanna Mill operation below). The corporation is better known by its acronym, UPEC, and is part of the Small Scale Industries Division of the Directorate of Industries. UPEC is a marketing and production organization. It operates the GANGOTRI stores, and sponsors fairs and exhibitions of handicrafts. It has also run a production scheme for chikan embroiderers since the early 1970s, with headquarters at Moti Mahal, a converted palace close to affluent Hazratganj. Although in 1990 women were collecting work from one of a handful of production centers opened during the 1970s and 1980s, many still referred to collecting work from Moti Mahal.

In 1977–78, two chikan production centers were opened by UPEC with a loan of Rs. 1,300,000 (its source unspecified). Two more centers were added in 1979–80. Figures from the late 1970s show that production fluctuated year to year, the value of goods produced increasing from Rs. 500,000 to Rs. 2,460,000 between 1978 and 1980 with the opening of new centers, and then falling back to only Rs. 302,000 in 1981–82 when centers were closed (for undisclosed reasons). Perhaps in reference to these later events, some embroiderers at one of the oldest centers commented on how previously arrogant staff members had been humbled when the center was closed some ten years before.

In 1986–87, two centers, Crown Gate (near City Station) and Koneshwar Temple (in Chowk) were again in operation and the staff rehired. In 1987 a third center was opened for rural workers in Kakori (16 km from Lucknow) and production leapt to Rs. 6,000,000 worth of goods. A fourth center in Malyabad (27 km from Lucknow) was started in 1988, and by 1989, Rs. 8,500,000 worth of goods were produced annually.[4] In 1989, the local director of the four centers said that the production goal for the UPEC chikan scheme was Rs. 12,500,000.

At the time of my visit, UPEC dominated government chikan production. There was a production center at Khanna Mill, in Daliganj (where it had been relocated from Turiaganj, in the old city), supervised by the District Industry Corporation (DIC). Complicated relationships between some of my principal informants and personnel at Khanna Mill, as well as an ill-starred visit there at the beginning of my research, led to my knowing relatively little about this center. An official at UPEC denounced the operation at Khanna Mill as useless, with an unmotivated staff and little or no productive activity. A more recent arrival in 1990 was MAHAK or Mahila Hasta Shilp Kendra (Women's Artwork Centre). MAHAK was a U.P. Labour Department initiative to promote women's handicrafts of various kinds in the Lucknow area. It grew out of the Mahila Kalyan Nigam (Women's Welfare Corporation), located near Hazratganj in Lucknow, which had already become involved in women's work. Preparations for establishing MAHAK were ongoing when I was in Lucknow and according to a May 1990 report in the *Times of India* (Lucknow), a pioneer center was indeed established in Kakori as a training and production unit. A few weeks before I left, my teacher became involved in a training/production scheme she said originated from the Mahila Kalyan Nigam. The scheme involved over thirty women producing chikan articles and was projected to last three months on a trial basis.

Chikan Products of the State Government

Government documents tout good design and fine-quality products as a hallmark of state government production centers and much of the work on display in both state and central handicrafts stores is certainly above average. However, there is not much exceptional work on sale, and in Delhi at least, chikan is not given pride of place in either the U.P. or the Central Cottage Industry Emporium, and is considerably overshadowed by other U.P. products like silk and zari, inlaid and carved boxes, and carpets.

The state appears to produce proportionately more "English goods" (like table linens) than are typically found in most Lucknow retail and wholesale stores, reflecting its orientation toward the tourist market in Delhi, and to a higher stratum of the middle classes within India that is more likely to consume these kinds of items (figure 6.1).

Officials at UPEC and in the hierarchy of the U.P. state government make a special point of the quality of government-produced chikan in contrast to the debased product of commercial enterprises. Many *mahajans* do indeed acknowledge that the government has a role in promoting the "art" of chikan. Their complaint, ironically enough, is that not enough is being done to cultivate better standards. This is a somewhat self-serving grievance, since any improvement in the standards of chikan embroidery that the government might effect would benefit the commercial sector (as the chief employer of embroiderers), without being directly paid for by *mahajans*. So, instead, *mahajans* criticize government-sponsored work as low-quality and portray government officials involved in chikan as corrupt and uninformed.

State Government Production Centers

At the time of my research, nearly two thousand embroiderers were listed on the government books as employees, finally exceeding the employment levels of the early 1950s. Of these two thousand, approximately three quarters were villagers. The number of formally registered employees does not reflect the total number of embroiderers who work on government goods, since enrolled embroiderers can take some work for their stay-at-home relatives.

Cloth was distributed at the production centers already tailored and printed and ready for embroidery. Work and wages were distributed at the centers on Tuesday and Saturday. An elaborate system of bookkeeping was used to keep track of work distributed, using issue slips matched with book entries to which embroiderers affixed their signatures or, more commonly, thumbprints. Few embroiderers paid much attention to the paperwork, and the claim that the system protected women from "malpractices" (*Lucknow City Magazine* 1988:18) seems lofty considering most women did not know what exact purpose it served. In fact, to the extent they did understand it, they viewed it as a means to reduce their wages, since deductions for late or shoddy work, and damaged material were calculated and entered in the process of filling in the women's wage slips.

In order to collect work from any center, women needed to pay an annual stamp fee of Rs. 10. They were only allowed to take a few items with them when they collected work so as to ensure an even distribution

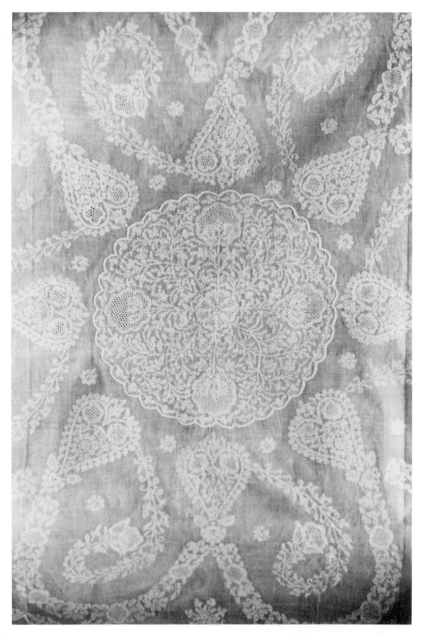

FIG. 6.1. A state government–produced tablecloth, embroidered in *bakhya* work.

of items and to deter subcontracting. The number of women from one family was limited at each center, again so as to ensure a fairer distribution of work. Although the government claimed to distribute work in an equitable fashion, more work was given to better workers, better workers being defined as those who did good work and finished it on time. The total value of material per woman was controlled in case it was lost or damaged. If a woman took four pieces one day and returned with only three, her pay was docked and she was given fewer items the next time. In fact, although limits were said to be placed on the amount of work going to any single person, several embroiderers in the town and the countryside said instead that some favored individuals were able to take large numbers of goods away with them.

Wages

Few argued that government wages per piece were higher than commercial wages. Records indicated that in 1989, nearly Rs. 200,000 a month was paid in wages. A table in an unpublished report on the activities of the UPEC centers purported to present an increase in total wages paid since 1986, but in actuality took no account of the opening of new centers and the increase in the number of workers, and even showed a decrease in the total outlay of wages between 1987 and 1989.[5]

In 1989–90, wages for a *bakhya kurta* were Rs. 7. The simplest *bakhya salwar-qamiz* brought in Rs. 15, a *murri salwar-qamiz* Rs. 25, and a *bakhya* sari Rs. 115. Wages for a *tepci sari* were Rs. 400. These rates were from 50 percent to nearly 100 percent more than the total wage for any given piece in the commercial sector, not counting the agent fees. In fact, of particular pride was the increase in wages to village women now receiving work directly instead of through agents. They saw the biggest difference in wages, getting Rs. 6.50 for *kurta* embroidery instead of less than a rupee in the commercial sector.

Since the difference in wages between a *sari* produced for the commercial sector and one made for the government was less than that between *kurtas* and *salwar-qamiz* in each sector, presumably women would opt to make *kurtas* and *salwar-qamiz* as much as possible. In fact, analysis shows that government wage rates were set so that if work were completed in the time allocated, whatever the item, women would make the same amount of money per month. Women rarely have much choice as to what kind of work they do, and on what kind of item they do it, but on one occasion I did see a woman reject a *sari* she was offered, stating that she would have preferred a smaller item. When women could choose, most likely they still preferred to make smaller items for more regular and swifter returns than to defer their wages several weeks while they finished a larger piece, in spite of efforts to equalize monthly wages.

The penalty system may also have affected women's choices over what work to do. The government set strict time limits upon completion of chikan articles, which varied according to the stitches required and the size of the piece. Time limits were imposed to prevent women from keeping *mal* for excessive lengths of time—occasionally even years. A *salwar-qamiz* was supposed to take only take a week, a *sari* two months, and a *tepci sari* six months at most. If the embroidery was not returned within these times, a deduction from wages was made. An embroiderer told me that if a *sari* was late by ten days (over the two month limit) a deduction of Rs. 20 was made, rising to Rs. 30 if an entire extra month went by.

Anything that takes much longer than a week to make is likely to be pushed aside in favor of more rapidly completed work. Thus, a woman was far more prone to incur a deduction if she took a *sari* to make than if she took a *kurta* or *salwar-qamiz*. Indeed, it was the women working on *saris* who complained the most about being unable to finish the piece and the likely cost to them of returning it late. Nor did the embroiderer simply miss out on some of her wages if her work was late, for once she erred by keeping an item for too long, her quota of embroidery articles was carefully controlled ever afterwards. A woman doing a piece of fine work that would take months to finish was allegedly given small pieces in the interim to tide her over financially. In truth, it was more likely she turned to the commercial sector for work, as the women doing the *saris* were apt to do. This strategy could cause problems when her fine work was due back at the government center, and she had had inadequate opportunity to work on it.

In an attempt to make sure that the wage paid by the government was actually what the embroiderer received, the government frowned upon any sharing or subcontracting of work. Subcontracting was viewed as an unqualified evil, and middlemen regarded even more sternly than commercial shopkeepers. If it was suspected that more than one woman had worked on a piece, the wage deduction was particularly severe, amounting to 50 percent of the total.

The first production center to open in 1986 was located near City Station in a part of the old city known as Crown Gate. Many of the supervisory staff were women, several of them with more than adequate skills in chikan who had been able to secure a staff position. Their official task was to monitor and to suggest ways to improve work, but their role more often inclined toward recommending penalties and deductions.

Production center number 1 focused on the production of so-called fine work and its workers were mostly from Daliganj. There were about

350 women registered at Crown Gate altogether, of which less than 50 lived outside the city. State and national award winners in chikan embroidery were partly drawn from this pool of employees. Sultana Begum, my teacher, her elder daughter and Kamrunissa Begum, among others, were enrolled at Crown Gate. All of them, with the exception of Asiya Khatun, had been award winners. Asiya said that between her and her mother they collected about eight pieces a month from the center, up to a maximum of twenty pieces per month.

Work here took longer to produce because the standard of work and degree of skill expected (on items like tablecothes, *topis*, and *saris*) were greater. It might take at least six months to make a fine tablecloth, 120 to 152 days to make a fine *sari*, 90 days to make a man's suit, and 106 days to make a fine *kurta*. One embroiderer showed me a *topi* that she said would take one and a half months to make, for which the wage would be Rs. 80.

The second production center, Koneshwar Temple, was named for its proximity to a temple on the corner of Napier and Hardoi Roads. While approximately one third of the women who worked for the center come from nearby locations, such as the Akbari Gate area at the southern end of the Chowk bazaar center, or elsewhere in the city, most came from villages up to fifteen kilometers to the west of Lucknow. No production center run by UPEC drew extensively upon the chikan-embroidering communities of the old city. Those urban women who did fine work for the government were associated exclusively with production center number 1.

The Koneshwar Temple center was smaller than Crown Gate and included an office for the staff, storerooms, and a hallway in which women gathered when waiting for work and wages. Besides the manager, the staff had the usual complement of embroidery specialists working as supervisors, including Nasim Bano, daughter of Hasan Mirza and sister of Akhtar Jahan. Although the kind of work distributed at the center was supposedly varied, in practice the type of embroidery most in demand was *phanda*.

About 360 women from different villages came to the center. The Tuesday crowds included women from Bijnor and Khushalganj. On Saturday, the women came from Gari Kanaura, a settlement near Talkatora. They traveled in groups and came on buses, *ṭāṅgās* (tongas horse-drawn carriages), and walked at least part of the way. The journey might take up to two or more hours en route. One woman who lived only five kilometers away complained that it cost her Rs. 4 or Rs. 5 rupees for the round trip. However, embroiderers came regularly, many of them once a week. Some did so reluctantly, forced into it after failing to get work from intermediaries. But even when they arrived, they were not assured of getting work. Some complained that while for the first few years of operation, center number 2 had provided them with plenty of work, in the last year, the supply had dropped.

The third center, in Kakori village, comprised two small rooms in a long building on one side of a dusty courtyard. At the time of my visit, the newly formed MAHAK project was to be housed in a nearby building in the same complex. The center gave out work to about five hundred local women. Most work done here was openly referred to as *āsān kam* (easy work) or *bakhya* work, as opposed to what the staff called *pakki chikan* or *asli chikan* (proper, real chikan).

In contrast to the women at centers 1 and 2, most women at Kakori said they were able to come every week on their customary day to collect and return work. However, this avowal was made in direct earshot of the center's manager, and so I do not know whether it truly reflected the embroiderers' situation.

I did not see center number 4 in Malyabad, so I have no knowledge of its physical appearance or its staff. Embroiderers from the nearby settlements of Mirzaganj and Kasmandi Kala said that the biggest drawback of the center was that it took time to go and wait for work to be given out. Only if a younger member of the family could be deputed to collect work was the effort worthwhile. Even then, work was scarce. In contrast to what I heard at other centers, some embroiderers said they were given thread as well as cloth by the people at the Malyabad center, and they added that thread could be replenished on request.

The Government as "Mahajan": *Limitations and Problems*

The state government programs were full of apparently good intentions, yet embroiderers still complained about them. Embroiderers were frustrated that there were no more centers and no more work for them. But with a limited budget and the GANGOTRI store monopoly, there seemed to be little chance of expanding the existing programs. Embroiderers were left largely dependent upon the *mahajan* and felt that their lives were not substantially affected by the efforts of the state. Bitterness and frustration overflowed at centers where women waited in vain to get work. Hardly anyone felt that the government was doing enough in terms of ensuring a constant supply of work to those enrolled at the centers. Instead, embroiderers felt that the amount of work had sharply decreased in the past few years.

The government's insertion into rural chikan production has been spurred in part by official distaste for subcontracting, since countryside embroiderers are rightly regarded as being under the thumb of the chikan middleman/middlewoman. Center staff openly criticized subcontracting and argued that it led some women to become chronically dependent upon others. In an overt effort to curtail subcontracting and to compel embroiderers to enter into face-to-face interactions over chikan, attendance at the centers was made mandatory if women were to receive any goods to embroider. The only people exempt from this requirement were women taking work for close family relatives—presumably because the burden of household duties prevented all the women of one household from making a collective visit to a center.

But instead of praising the centers for giving work directly to women previously at the lower reaches of the agent pyramid, these same women complained about the lengthy, time-consuming, and expensive journeys they had to make to avail themselves of this "benefit," without guarantee of work when they arrived. What is more, the staff at the production centers professed to encourage the better workers to become members, but better workers were more likely to include in their number the very agents the government was trying to circumvent. The commitment to quality could therefore mean that agent/embroiderers became the beneficiaries of production schemes, while women at the lowest levels continued to be forgotten.

Meanwhile, the better-skilled, urban embroiderers who also worked for the government (especially at center number 1), saw the government's efforts to take work directly to rural women as an attack on their own livelihoods, which were partially based on subcontracting work to villagers. Urban women resented the fact that rural women had been the beneficiaries of more recently opened centers, which they felt drained work directly from them. The government was therefore in the curious position of doling out work to the same embroiderers whose efforts at rural subcontracting they were attempting to frustrate.

Government wages were acknowledged to be higher than *mahajans'* wages, but the overwhelming complaint of embroiderers in 1989–90 was that there was simply not enough work from the public sector to keep them going. A particular complaint of the highly skilled was that while government wages were better than those from the *mahajan*, the amount and quality of work expected was greater. Thus, the differential between *mahajan* and government wage was, in fact, less than anticipated. "You can't pay Rs. 25 for a *salwar-qamiz* and expect it to be fine work," argued one woman.

All embroiderers disliked the policy of taking deductions from wages for work that had been shared, subcontracted, or delivered late. In this regard, *mahajans*, who paid less money but took fewer deductions, were preferred. I was surprised to see the number of deductions entered into a ledger at Crown Gate, considering this was a center for "fine work." Practically everything had been subject to a deduction, effectively reducing the wages to within the limits of commercial wages. These deductions were described as punishments for keeping work too long, sharing work, or simply doing it badly.

It is true that many embroiderers, even the best, were cynical about the need for good work. Any quality of work can be and is sold in shops, the women reasoned, so why should work of any kind be penalized? Moreover, women believed that deductions were less a matter of quality control than of extortion. All one had to do in order to avoid penalties was to pay a bribe, according to embroiderers. In short, embroiderers saw deductions as a systematic means of cheating them of their wages, used wantonly and without reference to the actual embroidery.

Deductions may also represent a real gap between the staff's genuine expectations of "good" work habits and the actual work practices of embroiderers. First, government officials believe any distribution of work among several women must always impact work negatively—which is by no means the case. Superior work can be, and customarily is, made by several women working together and in a sequence, in a single household. Second, production centers take the view that missing deadlines is evidence of indifference or laziness, when it is more likely that women have taken in more work from the commercial sector in the interim in order to make ends meet.

Mahajans too had complaints about the government production schemes but unsurprisingly their complaints were quite different from those of embroiderers. In contrast to the claims of the government staff, *mahajans* argued that government work was actually of poorer quality than work in the commercial sector. The reasons given for this were various; for example, that since the government paid better wages for the same work, women made no effort to do it any better; or that those in charge of government schemes were simply undemanding or indiscriminate in their standards. *Mahajans* rarely bothered to counter the claim that government wages were higher than in the commercial sector but qualified this by pointing out that they did not indulge in bribery or theft by making systematic cuts from the wages. All *mahajans* believed that corruption was rife in government circles, and that this contributed to the high cost of government articles, which they said were not so different from the ones they had to sell. They liked to contrast their "honesty" with the "dishonesty" of government staff. Officials were only interested in lining their own pockets, they argued, and even went so far as to invent names on government employment rosters to increase their own pickings.

Several *mahajans* also regarded government support as the cause of embroiderers' getting ideas "above their station." The embroiderers most likely to question their position and defy the *mahajans* were women who had received government awards. Of course, such behavior might be regarded as a victory of sorts for the women, but *mahajans* saw it as a breach of the proper social relations in the industry, in which embroiderers were expected to show deference to their employers. As they were singled out for patronage, women came to pay more attention to their government patrons than the *mahajans*. In other words, while women still needed the *mahajans*, the emergent sense of their own professional status affected their demeanor toward their employers.

Government efforts to help embroiderers are, in effect, little more than a transfer of authority from a *mahajan* to an equally lofty and unapproachable source. While government assistance fails to make a lasting difference in women's lives, the small stream of work it supplies keeps women involved in a world of chikan production that continues to benefit the *mahajan* more than it benefits them.

AWARD SCHEMES

Nowadays, *mahajans* occasionally commission embroiderers to make their finest work. There is no mass-market demand for the time-consuming, intricate work that the finest embroiderers can make. However, regular opportunities for demonstrating one's best work come in annual award competitions.

National Award for Mastercraftsmen

The national award was instituted in 1965 by the All India Handicrafts Board. The awards were intended for "distinguished craftsmen [sic] in the country in recognition of their valuable contribution to our cultural and aesthetic attainments. The Board has instituted these awards to honour and give recognition to exceptional merit in craftsmanship and designing" (India [Republic] All India Handicrafts Board 1965:19). National award winners are chosen on an all-India basis, with no fixed allocation of awards to any particular state or any particular craft. An initial field of nominees is determined by competition at the state level, after which names are forwarded to a central committee made up of "experts and knowledgeable persons in the field of arts and crafts" (Handicrafts India Yearbook 1990:389). This system of open competition replaced one in which nominations were fielded by institutions and government personnel involved in handicrafts development and promotion, for example, the state director of industries, state design centers and museums, and regional representatives of the All India Handicrafts Board (Fisher 1974). Reforms were introduced because a startlingly high number of nominees were already employees of the government, thus not craftspeople in urgent need of recognition and assistance. However, the case of chikan shows that reforms notwithstanding, winners usually have had some connection with government patronage, usually at the state level, beforehand.

Since the start of Mastercraftsmen National Awards, seven chikan embroiderers have won (Handicrafts India 1990 Yearbook:391–433). Craftspeople from Lucknow are overwhelmingly represented by chikan embroiderers. Two ivory carvers and a batik painter are the only other artisans from the city who have been chosen for national recognition.

In 1965, fourteen national awards were given out. The first award for chikan embroidery was given that same year to Fyaz Khan. One year later, he received one of the first three-year training schemes to be run by recipients of national awards. In following years, the numbers of awardees ranged from fifteen to twenty-five. In 1970, the number was cut to ten, but the cash prize increased from Rs. 1,000 to Rs. 2,500. In 1978, the figure of 15 was reinstated. The cash prize was raised again in 1981 to Rs. 5,000 and ten craftspeople per year were given merit certificates with prizes of Rs. 1,000 each. Since 1987, forty recipients have been selected each year, getting Rs. 10,000 along with the customary shawl and plaque (Handicrafts India 1990:389).

Hasan Mirza, the other great embroiderer of the mid-century, received his national award in 1969. By this point, it had become customary to reward a national awardee with his or her own training scheme. In 1974, Hasan Mirza's daughter, Akhtar Jahan, became a national awardee. There was then a dearth of awards for chikan artisans until the 1980s, when in fairly quick succession, Saliha Khatun (1981), Badar Anjuman (1983), Akhtar Jahan's sister, Rehana Begam (1985), and Shamim Jahan (1986) were honored. Nasim Bano, another sister of Akhtar Jahan, was reported to be receiving a national award in 1990. After Hasan Mirza, no man received national recognition for chikan. This appropriately reflects the current absence of men at the highest levels of chikan embroidery.

Uttar Pradesh State Award for Mastercraftsmen

The system of state awards was modeled on that of the national awards. Embroiderers submit their work and credentials to the local District Industry Commission (*Zilaudyog*) office, which is then responsible for recommending candidates to proceed to the next stage. Final selection of awardees is done by a committee of bureaucrats, previous award recipients, handicrafts promotion/literature professionals, and local dignitaries, and headed by the director of industries in Kanpur.

Awards are usually given out around March or April. Ten awards are made annually, with ten certificates of merit being given to runners-up. The awardees are given Rs. 5,000 in cash, and in keeping with the national award pattern, a plaque and shawl. The state merit winners are given Rs. 2,000. Again, like the national award, there is no fixed number of entries in any one craft, and no requirement that any particular craft be chosen in any given year. Conversely, there is no rule that limits the number of winners in any given craft each year. Since chikan is a prominent handicraft in Uttar Pradesh, many chikan embroiderers have been represented among awardees and merit recipients over the years, although exact figures are elusive. Recognition at the state level seems to be an almost standard precursor to getting a national award, although clearly not all state awardees become national awardees. Having won a national award, women no longer enter for the state awards, although there is technically no limit on the number of times one can be a contestant.

Entering and Winning

Women know little about the process of selecting and judging entries, and their own involvement in the process frequently stems from being told informally by a friend or official of the impending deadline for submitting samples of work. One might hear about an upcoming award or work opportunity when visiting the local District Industry Commission office, for example. But to make such a visit implies an existing relationship between the visitor and the staff. Indeed, anecdotes about embroiderers being invited in the course of such visits to submit entries belies the contention that awardees are plucked from a pool that is not unduly weighted toward artisans currently integrated into government patronage programs. Elite connoisseurs of fine chikan are often closely associated with the government. They are likely to be introduced to embroiderers via the award procedure or through officials working directly with embroiderers, and maintain contact with them through their efforts to promote the arts. A *daraz* artist said she had been encouraged to enter some articles of her work by a local dignitary whose wife was on award committees.

Although the AIHB award scheme is for craftspeople whose whole body of work constitutes a major contribution to their art, the focus of attention in both central and state competitions is a piece of embroidery specially made for the contest by the embroiderer. At the Crown Gate production center, for example, an embroiderer was making a piece that was to be entered into competition, for which she was also receiving a wage. I do not know what proportion of award contestants enter something for which they have already been paid directly by the government—it seems unlikely that most pieces can conform to these criteria since they are more elaborate and detailed than most customers demand, are probably priced well over what most buyers would be prepared to pay, and are hardly the run-of-the-mill production items found in GANGOTRI or CCIE. Whether artisans of any stripe are, or should be, paid for award competition entries seems to have been a contentious issue for some time (see Fisher 1974). Most women complained of never getting any kind of monetary compensation whatever for the pieces they had made. Award-winning pieces go into museum displays or collections, or into the hands of private patrons. Some embroiderers report being paid for their work by the recipient; more speak of giving, or being pressured to give, their work as a donation or gift.

Contestants enter work that is frequently stunning, elaborate, and very labor-intensive. They are rarely articles of clothing but look more like tablecloths or bedcovers, and most conform to the requirements of a display piece for wall mounting—square, oblong or circular, flat and untailored. Such pieces are the most expedient and inexpensive for the embroiderer to make, allowing her to dispense with the services of a master cutter and tailor, if not with the printer and washerman whose services are truly indispensable. Some embroiderers are able to amass a stock of such pieces for award competition, but given the fact that it takes at least half a year to make one truly top-quality piece, this is not an easy task.

If one looks at chikan on display in the handicrafts collections of the Central Design Centre Museum, Lucknow, and compares them with chikan at the State Museum, also in Lucknow, one sees a marked contrast between the framed and mounted chikan exhibits of the present and the elite chikan clothes of the past. Award competition has directed the very best chikan away from its uses as clothing and toward a new use as an object for display in the home or the museum.[6]

Winning an award opens the door for further economic opportunity. Skilled embroiderer Nur Jahan said that after she got a state award in 1988, her "interest grew" ("*shauq to bahut hua*"). "Shauq," she said, "grows when there is a reward for your work." The embroiderer becomes more widely known, her name, address, and perhaps her photograph appearing in an array of handicrafts manuals and volumes such as *Reference Asia*. The cash prize is an immediate windfall, but entry into new patronage circles, the opportunity to participate in exhibitions outside Lucknow, and to teach in government-sponsored training schemes, perhaps get a long-term government staff position, bring long-term financial rewards.

For example, a woman may now receive direct orders for work from individual patrons. Asiya and Saliha Khatun both agreed that private orders of work for Saliha had increased since she got her national award. Nur Jahan makes chikan on an occasional basis for a few relatives and private clients. For clients, her charge for a *kurta* is Rs. 40, considerably more than the wages from the private or the public sector. Many of Saliha Khatun's private clients have been directed to her by government officials at the Central Design Centre or the AIHB offices. The same is true of other women who make goods for private purchasers.

Very rarely, an embroiderer will receive a contract for her best work from an individual patron and will reproduce the caliber of work found in her award piece. Or she may continue to produce fine work on her own initiative, trusting that her new fame will bring a future customer to her. The work she makes is nominally free from the requirement that it should be easy to display, although in actual fact the kind of article produced is often of this type. *Saris*, however, are an alternative, which likewise require no services from the cutter and tailor. For these articles, the embroiderer will charge anywhere from about several hundred to thousands of rupees.

Embroiderers believed cheating and bribery were rife among officials associated with award competitions. Their fellow competitors were considered as susceptible to corruption as government staff. Even those who had got their awards felt that the recognition they deserved was either not forthcoming or was spoiled in some way. Many stories revolved around hopes of honor or patronage being built up, only to be dashed later. Nur Jahan was able to laugh about being summoned, along with other embroiderers, to New Delhi to display her talents to the prime minister. "We went to TeenMurti [the prime minister's residence]—that was back when the government really supported us—we picked up our thread and needles, then they said, 'Alright. We've seen it. That's fine.' We were stunned. We only picked up our needles, we didn't even do anything!" Other embroiderers were more bitter at having been asked to participate in presentations of work to various dignitaries, only to find that some other woman had gone in their place at the last minute. Anwar Jahan was particularly wounded that she had been deprived of the honor of winning her award when a runner-up's photograph was printed instead of her own in the awards booklet.

Women take the state and national awards very seriously, and cling to the tokens of recognition even when monetary rewards do not materialize. Saliha explained that award pieces are all done for *'izzat* (honor) and *t'arīf* (praise), or as Anwar Jahan, winner of a state award in 1985, said, "*ki government hameṅ inām degī, ki hamāre is meṅ nām paidā kare, hamārī 'izzat hogī*" ("[I did it] so that the government will give me a prize, that in this way my name will become known and I will be esteemed").

Embroiderers and the Judging of "Fine Chikan"

Perhaps the most significant aspect of the national award and state award selection procedures is their domination by government agencies and arts experts, with only a small role allocated for artisans in any decision making. In effect, conclusions about what the finest chikan is, and what is to represent that standard, are being made by uniquely positioned critics. The local government officers who act as the gatekeepers for the flow of entries to the selection committee will probably never consume the very best chikan. Yet they still exert a powerful influence over what is recognized as the best chikan, as well as over the fortunes of those who make it, through the exercise of their own culturally framed, critical abilities, and their patronage of specific embroiderers that has little to do with whether those embroiderers' work is "good" or not. Members of the final selection committee may possess some very fine chikan, but this may be a *result* of committee membership rather than its precursor.

Ironically, defining and rewarding what best represents the finest Lucknow chikan is kept out of the hands of the women who make it. A select few have their work, their skills, and their knowledge legitimized by receiving an award. Once they are so recognized, what these women profess to know about chikan becomes privileged through being repeated to nonembroiderers by word of mouth, or through published documents, as the "truth" about chikan. For example, a good proportion of chikan origin stories, and definitive statements about the number of stitches in chikan, come from government officials who ultimately derived them from embroiderers. The fact that knowledges are so variant and that many different chikan artisans have been rewarded in both national and state competitions means that no single definition, or story, can become authoritative. But the knowledges of those who neither win awards nor insert themselves as thoroughly into the network of government patronage, are still denied an important avenue of expression. This is an important point, since only the government provides a woman with the opportunity to express the full range of her knowledge and skill.

Award competition has transformed the production of fine work through replacing the links between patron, *mahajan*, and embroiderer (and other productive specialists) with a considerably more complicated arrangement of patrons, cultural critics, intermediate and low-level government staff, and the embroiderer (now disentangled from the wider productive network more decisively). In achieving the chance to become a named and individualized "artist,"[7] the embroiderer has lost her ability to define what fine chikan is.

TRAINING SCHEMES

The legimitization of knowledge is carried beyond award competition into training schemes. Although women saw these training schemes primarily as sources of money, they did also play a role in defining the best chikan, although none of the best chikan was produced in them.

The most common dividend from winning an award at either the state or national level is getting a training scheme. U.P. state government training schemes, led by mastercraftsmen, have been in operation at least since 1960. These are not intended to be permanent training programs with the broad objectives of retraining and building the skills of chikan embroiderers.[8] Instead, they involve setting up a mastercraftsperson with "apprentices" for one year. Comparable training schemes have been offered by the AIHB since 1965. In the year I was in Lucknow, three AIHB training schemes were in operation, one run by a former national award winner. Many women report having AIHB schemes who have not won national awards, although unlike Fisher (1974) I found no winner who had *not* got a training scheme.

Training schemes all run for one to three years. The intent is that craftsmen and craftswomen should transmit their specialized knowledge and skills to persons not in their family. Pupils in chikan training schemes are invariably girls, most of them Muslim, a minority Hindu. In 1989–90, the monthly stipend for the state award was Rs. 500 to the teacher and Rs. 50 for each of five girls. National schemes paid Rs. 1,000 to the teacher and Rs. 100 to the pupil, the girls numbering ten per year.[9] Unsurprisingly, embroiderers coveted the more lucrative AIHB schemes. Even potential trainees preferred to hold out for the Rs. 100 per month that came with the AIHB scheme, instead of the Rs. 50 of the state government alternative. In contrast, the stipends provided by the MAHAK scheme were the most generous of all, in which each girl was to get Rs. 10 and the the master Rs. 40 per day.

As I argued in the previous chapter, chikan knowledge is highly contextual, and so in order to learn, the girls must work upon distinct articles of embroidery. Herein lies an important financial benefit for the embroiderer. She may buy, at her own expense, material upon which the girls work, but she can sell it for herself once it is done. Some embroiderers use the girls to provide free labor doing, for example, *jali* on pieces from the *mahajan*. This work is counted, objectively, as experience for the trainees but it also benefits the embroiderer and *mahajan*, for obvious reasons.

With free labor and a monthly stipend at stake, competition for training schemes is fierce. Success or failure in obtaining schemes tends to be discussed in the idiom of pride and honor, but the desire for training schemes is, for most, a desire for money. As more and more women become award recipients, the pool for a limited number of training schemes becomes larger. Getting or not getting a scheme was increasingly at the whim of government officials who embroiderers felt had other interests in mind. "There's no benefit from those training schemes. It's all favoritism and bribery in the government," complained one. Officials were so distrusted that it was believed they gave schemes to cronies who did not even do embroidery. Stipends and subsidies for the training scheme premises (usually a part of the embroiderer's house) were supposedly either paid late, in part, or not at all. One said that two months of her stipend had never reached her, and so she had closed the scheme early. Some embroiderers seem to have had more than their share of schemes. One claimed to have had at least seven from both AIHB and state sources, although it is possible that she was counting multiple-year schemes as one scheme per year. Saliha Khatun said she had got state schemes for eight years, as well as one AIHB three-year scheme, but lately had no schemes at all. There seemed to be no official listing of state awardees, so claims were difficult to substantiate.

No one knows for certain how many girls go on to make chikan for a living, still less if any display outstanding abilities that will be recognized, at some future time, with an award. It is hard to gauge how effective the instruction is in the training schemes, assuming embroiderers share the goal of transmitting superior skills to a new generation. For the most part, embroiderers complained that *shauq* was rare and did not seem to have high expectations of their pupils. The fact that they view training schemes simply as an economic opportunity implies scant concern for the artistic or cultural contribution of these activities. Instead, the use of girls as free labor, or the stuffing of student rolls with the names of already skilled women and girls, indicates outright abuse.[10] Others, however, seemed to have enjoyed the experience and felt strongly about the respect and appreciation that being a teacher gave them. They may not have any more success at producing a new generation of skilled embroiderers, however, simply because training schemes are so short.

Co-opting girls into finishing commercial articles is a telling foretaste of the kind of work they will do once they complete their training—that is, the standard *murri* or *jali* work for the market. Apprenticeship with a mastercraftsperson prepares a girl well for working for a *mahajan* in the upper levels of the chikan market—as opposed, for example, to having only *bakhya* skills or no skills at all. However, these schemes do not appear to be a rich resource of chikan excellence and creativity. I am not sure to what extent training schemes are realistically thought to be seeding grounds for exceptionally skilled embroiderers, but the fact that an embroiderer is instructed to teach her pupils "all the stitches," implies that the programs' administrators have more than an education in basic *murri* in mind. The obvious avenue for promoting these newly acquired skills, government production, remains committed to conventional work distinctions (*bakhya, murri, jali,* and so on). A fundamental disjunction exists between the government as conservator and government as producer.

EXHIBITIONS

Exhibitions are settings for the display of a craftsperson's work and a chance for visitors to see the way they work. Opportunities to attend exhibitions follow routinely upon winning a national award but arise more sporadically for winners of state awards. In these cases, who goes is determined by local and mid-level officials of the AIHB and the U.P. state government. Ideally, the embroiderer has her travel and board expenses paid, plus a daily allowance. Chikan embroiderers usually take with them large bundles of commercial chikan bought from retail and wholesale stores in Lucknow, as well as a few fine chikan pieces they made themselves.

Some embroiderers are precluded by family circumstances or stricter observation of purdah from going to exhibitions. One was unable to participate in local exhibitions because of the disapproval of in-laws. Another embroiderer who had been offered exhibitions had a small child who could not travel with her. Still another was simply loathe to leave her house and do anything publicly. Others take as many opportunities as possible to advertise their skills and sell chikan.

A woman hears in spring about any shows coming up the following financial year. This amount of notice was important since it took a year to stockpile the necessary goods for a major exhibition outside Lucknow. The lion's share was made up of very ordinary chikan clothes purchased from local stores, with a handful of finer chikan articles like table linens and perhaps one or two more spectacular pieces. These last pieces obviously took time to make, but the main brake on women's buying up large amounts of ordinary work was lack of ready cash. Only buying over several months enabled the embroiderer to collect adequate stocks.

Exhibitions are the major money-spinner in the repertoire of income-generating activities connected with chikan. The competition for exhibition slots is as wracked with accusations and counter-accusations of bribery as those for awards and training scheme. A noteworthy barb directed at one woman by a rival was that she had slept with a government official in order to secure a stall at an exhibition.

The main limitation upon embroiderers who wish to exploit exhibitions is that only a few trips are fully subsidized by the authorities. The expense of sending a craftsperson to a show is not inconsiderable. One recipient told me that she got a first-class train fare, a fully paid-up hotel room, a Rs. 70 per diem allowance, and dearness allowance, depending upon the cost of living at the destination. The cost of shipping the exhibitor's goods is paid also, and he or she is accompanied by a government officer who is paid at the same rate. After the quota of free trips is used up, embroiderers generally cannot afford to pay the expenses of an independent trip to an exhibition.

Exhibitions may take an embroiderer as far away as Delhi, Goa, Madras, or Bombay. Undoubtedly, exhibitions permit the embroiderer to broaden her horizons, and become exposed to customers and clients from a much wider circle than that in Lucknow. Ironically, however, it is not her own fine products that are most in demand at these exhibitions, but the commercial work she brings with her. Without copious supplies of cheap *kurtas*, *salwar-qamiz*, and the like, which do not at all represent the kind of work the exhibitor is capable of, and which she likely had no hand in making, the embroiderer today will come away from the exhibition with some interesting experiences, but very little cash. Exhibitions, like training schemes, do not seem to contribute very greatly to the promotion and dissemination of fine chikan embroidery.

GOVERNMENT JOBS FOR SKILLED EMBROIDERERS

Checkers and finishers occupy formalized roles in the government domain, forming a low-level, female-dominated block. Highly skilled embroiderers are among those employed at government production centers, supervising and adjudicating work, making corrections and stock-keeping. In the family of Akhtar Jahan, two of her sisters were working for the government, Aphak Jahan at Moti Mahal and Nasim Bano at Koneswar Temple. Two of Badar Anjuman's sisters were supervisors at the DIC production center at Khanna Mill. Less skilled women may be picked out to take staff jobs also, in which case they are said to be trained to "judge quality," and to be able to either correct or order embroidery to be redone.

The relationship between permanently employed female staff and the women who take work on a piece-rate basis is analogous to that between female agents and their clients. But since many of the women employed as piece-workers by the government themselves have an agent background, the encounter between workers and staffers is perhaps better viewed as between erstwhile petty agents and potential large agents.

Many embroiderers are overtly critical of these lowly government functionaries and regard them as fundamentally antagonistic to their needs and interests, their being fellow embroiderers notwithstanding. Women staffers are the ones who make decisions to deduct from women's wages for late or inadequate work. They are self-styled, as well as government-designated "experts," whose judgments about the work of others is often resented. They are also employed on a time-wage basis and do not suffer from the fluctuations in the supply of work that are such an acute problem for women who habitually seek piece-work from the government.

SEWA LUCKNOW

SEWA Lucknow is what is known as an NGO, or nongovernmental organization. Women pay dues (Rs. 5 a year in 1989) to join and then become eligible to collect embroidery work, which they do at home. In 1989–90, SEWA Lucknow supplied work to around eight hundred city and village women. City workers for SEWA Lucknow mostly live in the Daliganj and Khaddra areas located close to the SEWA Lucknow office. This represents a very small proportion of all embroidery workers, but SEWA Lucknow is significant, first, because of its strong presence in these areas of the city where fine embroidery is concentrated, and second, because of the nature of its products and its market.

SEWA Lucknow is named after the well-known SEWA Ahmedabad. The name SEWA means "service" but is at the same time an acronym meaning "Self-Employed Women's Association." Initiated by Ella Bhatt in 1972, SEWA Ahmedabad is a women's organization that is now over twenty years old, dedicated to promoting self-awareness and economic self-improvement among its all-female membership.[11] Among the concerns that helped launched the organization were the recognition that women's work is not subsidiary but central, and that women needed recognition *as* workers, moreover as workers who could be organized. SEWA Ahmedebad held that female workers needed special support in the form of healthcare, childcare, skills training, legal aid, reliable work supplies, and, in general, assistance in dealing effectively with the public world.

In the 1980s, more SEWA organizations modeled on the SEWA Ahmedabad organization came into being throughout India. An umbrella organization, SEWA Bharat, was formed for all these groups. SEWA Lucknow came into being in this period and is affiliated with SEWA Bharat. Unlike the diverse occupational specialties represented by the SEWA Ahmedabad membership, SEWA Lucknow caters exclusively to chikan embroiderers. SEWA Lucknow does not seek to compete in the market dominated by the *mahajans*, but aims its products at an elite, metropolitan clientele already consuming various forms of Indian "ethnic art." SEWA Lucknow chikan has acquired a reputation for style and chic that is quite distinct from the prolific but conservative product of the commercial and government sectors. SEWA Lucknow goods are in large part the creation of a Delhi-based designer named Laila Tyabji, who has an extensive formal background in arts and crafts training, and is heavily involved in marketing and liaison with craftspeople. Her designs are not only radically different in appearance from mass-market styles, but their conception and production represent a sharp shift in the conventional distribution of creative energy in chikan production.

Unlike the government and *mahajans*, SEWA Lucknow does not use the existing structure of specialist occupations to make chikan. Rather the organization is striving to create an independent, largely self-contained productive structure that is staffed in its entirety by women. Like the state government, SEWA Lucknow's expressed goal is the economic betterment of embroiderers, through payment of better wages. But the organization gives more emphasis to empowering women than the government does. They try to do this by involving young women, usually the most socially and economically vulnerable, in the operations of the cooperative, familiarizing them with financial and manufacturing organization, supervision, and planning. They train and employ young women seamstresses, and have taught one older woman to be their garment cutter. The young women who make up the central staff travel to the organization's shows in Delhi and, more recently, Bombay, and take an active part in product marketing and administration. However, the undeniable assistance afforded some cannot be extended to the many, and the women who do work for SEWA Lucknow are mostly employed on a putting-out basis just as they are for the government and *mahajans*. Inevitably, some of the same ambiguities and conflicts that are evident in government policy are manifest in SEWA Lucknow's activity.

The administration of SEWA Lucknow consists of a committee that includes, among others, some government dignitaries involved in handicrafts or women's development, and fifteen chikan artisans, although day-to-day running of the current production center is completely devolved upon the resident director and staff. The history of the cooperative that follows is derived from interviews with Laila Tyabji and Runa Banerjee, the director of SEWA Lucknow.

The SEWA Lucknow organization developed out of a study made in 1979–80 for UNICEF's "The Year of the Child," by a Lucknow group called Literacy House. The study was of child labor in six industries in different areas of U.P., one of which was chikan embroidery. After making some sobering discoveries about the degree of exploitation of children, in particular, the women researchers became interested in forming a society to assist embroiderers. The first step was to work with UNICEF to extend educational assistance to embroiderers' children. The organizers of the school, who had been hoping all along to help embroiderers, applied for grant money and, in Banerjee's words, waited for signs of acceptance from the women themselves. Eventually, a society was formed in 1983 with donated funds. SEWA Lucknow officially came into existence in April 1984.

SEWA Lucknow started with only a handful of women, an investment of Rs. 10,000 and the goal of providing work for better wages than the *mahajans*. It did not start with the aim of carving out a distinct image and market share. The dramatic alteration in its product line came with the intervention of Tyabji as design consultant in the mid-1980s. In 1985, DASTKAR,[12] a crafts resource and sales center in Hauz Khas in New Delhi and a Registered Society for Crafts and Craftspeople with which Tyabji is associated, was asked to help SEWA Lucknow compete with the commercial chikan sector.

Tyabji's plan was to differentiate its chikan from all other chikan from other sources (Tyabji 1990). Far from sidelining the objective of providing better wages to the women affiliated with it, Tyabji argued that a strengthened and refined aesthetic vision could serve this aim. While it was impossible to compete with *mahajans* making a similar, but more costly product, a piece of work that cost appreciably more than a conventional *sari* or *salwar-qamiz*, but that looked distinct, was likely to find customers—especially, as it turned out, in the fashion centers of contemporary India. And, indeed, SEWA Lucknow clothing is markedly different—both in the use of embroidery and the style of the garments—from what is conventionally found in chikan.

The first tasks, undertaken in February 1986, were to select materials, design motifs, and stitch types, as well as to employ a group of embroiderers to put the ideas into practice. A student of fashion and various crafts at the Baroda Institute of Art and Design, and self-taught in embroidery,[13] Tyabji used this background to adapt and cost the articles she wanted the SEWA Lucknow embroiderers to make. She was depressed by the meager skills of embroiderers who remembered their grandmothers' making the stitches she was teaching them but never made them themselves. While satisfying an elite demand, SEWA Lucknow chikan is not made by an elite group of embroiderers. Indeed, the product line is designed with moderate to above average skills in mind, not necessarily the abilities of the most proficient, in recognition of the fact that those who stand to benefit from SEWA Lucknow's activities are unlikely to produce goods of consistently superb quality on a large scale. City embroiderers were given, and still are given, the most demanding work on *kurtas*, but most embroiderers spontaneously left *jali* and *hatkatti* undone on pieces that then had to be done by other women. I have explained in previous chapters that this practice represents a well-established separation in the phases of embroidery labor. It is not entirely clear that this was regarded as a further example of "debasement" by SEWA Lucknow, but it is an aim of the organization to encourage women to do *all* the work on a piece of chikan, in the fashion of the most skilled embroiderers. At the moment, the division of labor still stands, as many women in Khaddra are employed doing *jali* on already embroidered items.

While SEWA Lucknow continues to solicit funding from charitable sources, primarily the organization OXFAM, Banerjee hoped that SEWA Lucknow would become totally self-sufficient within a couple of years. In order to be fully self-sufficient, it was projected that sales had to reach Rs. 5 million. SEWA Lucknow sales have grown considerably since the early 1980s. After the first DASTKAR-sponsored sale in 1985, Rs. 43,000 worth of goods were sold and the first independent SEWA Lucknow show in Delhi in 1986 brought in nearly Rs. 200,000. By the time I left in 1990, the organization had sold Rs. 2 million worth of goods for the year. Most sales are made during a weeklong bazaar held in New Delhi in April at the Blind School in Sunder Nagar, at which between Rs. 1,000,000 and Rs. 1,500,000 worth of goods can be moved. A fall sale in Bombay was then added, and most recently, according to informal accounts from colleagues in India, a second sale in New Delhi.

The sales events are major expeditions for the SEWA Lucknow staff since many of them go along to take part in all aspects of organizing the bazaar, except for accounting and deliveries. Inside the large tent where the sale goes on, the scene is one of virtual chaos after a day or two. Clothes spill from hangers or are piled on the floor and tabletops as shoppers anxious to buy some SEWA Lucknow chikan mill around amid the scant pickings that remain unsold.

Back in Lucknow, a small store adjacent to the SEWA Lucknow headquarters caters to the local market, but local buyers are not regarded as the major consumer block for SEWA Lucknow goods. An exhibition in Halwasiya Market in Hazratganj was greeted enthusiastically, but was not repeated. In 1989, sales in Lucknow amounted to Rs. 20,000 or Rs. 30,000, and were not expected to rise any higher. On the other hand, some Lucknow residents complained that they did not have access to a wider SEWA Lucknow stock, from which they would gladly have bought. Instead, the organization focuses on building up stock for its major exhibitions outside Lucknow.

SEWA Lucknow's headquarters and its outreach projects are now centered in Khaddra. Today, eight hundred women work for SEWA Lucknow, of which half are city-dwellers in Khaddra and Daliganj, and half are villagers. School fees for children are also Rs. 5 per year. The school continues to operate, and has five hundred children enrolled. SEWA Lucknow also runs a creche (or day-care center) for very small children.

SEWA Headquarters, Lucknow

The SEWA Lucknow building consisted of a number of rooms used as workshops, storage areas, and offices on two sides of a small, partially roofed courtyard. Bundling and sorting of finished goods, or goods ready to be washed, also spilled out onto a front verandah. The building was set back from the road and shielded by several trees.

All administrative and financial operations went on cheek-by-jowl with sewing, printing, and embroidery. An entire room was occupied by about twenty or so manual sewing machines, at which girls worked a regular work-day. Next to that was a room in which women did hand sewing and hemming. In the courtyard, embroiderers and a female fabric cutter worked, and women looking for work waited to be attended to. Several young girls trained to check work for flaws also occupied the courtyard. The initials of every person who worked on a piece, the collar seamstress, the hem seamstress, the embroiderer, and so on, were written on the garment, so that if a mistake was found, the right person could be approached to account for and correct the error.

Adjacent to the courtyard was a narrow room where two male printers worked. The organization hoped one day to replace them with women, so that there would be no stage of SEWA Lucknow's production, save washing, that was not controlled and operated by women. In effect, all stages of chikan production, except washing and embroidery, had been centralized in this one, compact building. SEWA Lucknow was planning to open a village unit within the year. Although they were currently working with some village embroiderers, their intention was to set up a production center and school in a village where women were sufficiently organized and motivated to sustain them.

SEWA Lucknow Staff

Most women who are paid wages by SEWA Lucknow work for the organization on a putting-out basis. Work was picked up and returned on the third Wednesday in every month. However, a number of girls and young women had permanent staff positions and were being schooled in the philosophy of the group as well as in practical skills of administration, supervision, and quality control. A few older women were employed also, notably a middle-aged fabric cutter.

Women in pivotal supervisory positions were usually in their twenties, but SEWA Lucknow also permanently employed girls whose average age was thirteen years. All of these girls had received training from the center, either in embroidery or sewing, or had been taught other skills, such as reading. Some had also been instructed how to check and correct work, and had learned rudimentary organizational management. Even those who had specialized in sewing or embroidery and had no administrative skills spent their days at the center socializing with other girls their age. Some of them did embroidery and sewing work in the evenings after the center had closed, concentrating on quality checking during the day. Ongoing training and "refresher" programs were maintained for up to ten women at a time, with particular attention on assessing and improving skills when woman were first enrolled with the organization.

SEWA Lucknow Wage and Distribution Policies

Most embroidery and *daraz* work was done in embroiderers' homes. Machine and hand sewing was done on site for the most part but young women also took a portion (up to 50 percent of the amount of work they do during the day) home to work on in the evening. SEWA Lucknow estimates are that women can earn as much as ten to twenty times as much money making SEWA Lucknow chikan as they do in the commercial sector. Tyabji (1990) reckons that women may earn from Rs. 88 to Rs. 1,500 a month, depending upon how much, and what quality work they choose to do. She goes on to argue that women prefer the flexibility of doing embroidery on a take-out, piecemeal basis to becoming a permanent staff member with a salary. Among embroiderers, this was not entirely the impression I received—indeed there was some jealousy of the fact that several young women had secured full-time jobs with SEWA Lucknow at the inevitable expense of others.

Wages were generous compared to those paid in the commercial sector. *Turpai* stitchers were paid on average Rs. 30 for their work, *daraz* workers Rs. 75. Printing wages for the male employees were seventy-five paise per piece. For embroidery, women got up to Rs. 20 for working a *kurta* and wages were supposed to be raised by 10 percent per year. However, the work is more complex and detailed than commercial chikan, a point made by skilled embroiderers—candidates for state merits and state awards, for example—who might have sought SEWA Lucknow work but opted instead for government employment. They felt the extra work on a SEWA Lucknow piece effectively wiped out the elevated wages the organization paid, simply because it took more time to make.

SEWA Lucknow also adjusted wages according to the quality of work. For example, a novice *jali* embroiderer in Madeganj quoted some very low rates for the work she did, especially when compared to a relative who also worked for SEWA Lucknow. Besides the possibility that she was not being candid, the only explanation for this discrepancy was that her relative's pay reflected her greater experience and ability. Tyabji confirmed that wages were adjusted according to whether work was sub-par or showed evidence of creativity. These wage adjustment practices were, all in all, frustrating to embroiderers, who could not understand why equivalent work should be rewarded with different wages. One highly skilled embroiderer said, "I can't make SEWA out. I like their designs, but they pay different wages to people. I pay always the same, whatever the work. Also *mahajans*, if the work is good or bad, if it is for Rs. 20, that's what they'll pay. But if SEWA wants to give you less, they will. Whatever they want to give you, that's what you'll get."

Like the UPEC production centers, SEWA Lucknow is keen to discourage subcontracting. Women were encouraged to come personally to collect work, although *mal* was taken out to villages in a vehicle. Work could be taken for relatives, but each relative had to be a current member of SEWA Lucknow. Individuals were restricted to five items at any one time, although I was told by SEWA Lucknow workers in Khaddra that this rule was not always adhered to, and women could take away more, especially in the feverish period before the Delhi exhibition.

In spite of its more pointedly feminist orientation, and the prevalence of women in its organization, SEWA Lucknow was not universally approved by embroiderers. As with complaints about government schemes, embroiderers' disapproval and criticism stemmed from discrepancies in the organization's and the embroiderers' views of work and responsibility, as much as from deficiencies and iniquities in the organization. Complaints about SEWA Lucknow mirrored those about the government production centers—that there was not enough work and that one had to wait for it. Some grumbled that the staff were arrogant and obstructive, but others made a particular point of saying they were kinder than the government personnel. Embroiderers were also distrustful of the idea that one woman should be expected to do all the work on any given piece, instead of her customary speciality.[14]

Impact of SEWA Lucknow

What has been the influence of SEWA Lucknow on the industry as a whole and on embroiderers in general? SEWA Lucknow likes to point to its role in boosting women's self-awareness, as well as paying higher wages and improving skills. With the exception of the argument about consciousness, SEWA Lucknow's claims for itself sound very much like those made by the government for *itself*. However, its most obvious influence in Lucknow and outside has been in bringing about an aesthetic shift—now subtle, perhaps in future more marked—in clothing design.

SEWA Lucknow is not oriented toward overseas export and grounds itself firmly in the Indian market. Like the *mahajans*, SEWA Lucknow recognizes that its long-term stability and growth depend upon its satisfying a burgeoning middle-class consumer group. By doing this, it is more likely to maintain its own control over the volume of production and production schedules instead of finding itself captive to the fluctuating requirements of a fickle overseas market.

The new creative emphasis was, and is, most evident in two aspects of design. The first is the style of tailoring and stitching, which deliberately harks back to generously cut Mughal styles and employs more extensive use of *turpai* and *daraz* than commercial chikan. Their first, male master-cutter had to be fired because he would not, or could not, give up his customary way of cutting cloth to commercial specifications. Instead, a new, female cutter was trained who could work with the new designs (Tyabji 1990). The second aspect of design involves the application and choice of chikan stitches. Old, largely unused *murri* print blocks were bought from printers in Chowk. Block patterns were then applied in innovative and, to the embroiderers, sometimes startling, ways. The key to the use of embroidery in SEWA Lucknow clothing is not the fact that there is more *murri* proportionately to *bakhya*, but the fact that whether *murri* or *bakhya*, embroidery almost encrusts the garment. Embroidery is lavishly applied in large, bold motifs. Tyabji's (1990:3) reference to chikan as traditionally a "chiaroscuro" is not a casual one. Relief is an important effect in SEWA Lucknow clothing and it is best achieved not by the most delicate stitches an embroiderer can do, but by slightly thickened stitches, sometimes quite sketchily applied. Recalling the visual and tactile qualities of old chikan, *jali* and *hatkatti* feature far more prominently in the finished article than in most products of the market. Thus, SEWA Lucknow clothes represent a fusion of deliberate archaisms with innovations in stitch form and incidence.

An administrator at UPEC sounded one of the few sour notes expressed by anyone about SEWA Lucknow who was not directly employed by them. He said that SEWA Lucknow work was sometimes shoddy, that sizing and cutting were inferior and did not allow for shrinkage. He specifically faulted the dependence upon hand-labor at all stages of production, contrasting this with the move toward machine-cutting planned by the government. Even if these criticisms were fair, they miss the point of SEWA Lucknow's popularity, which is predicated on the handmade details that few other institutions or businesses attempt to duplicate.

By 1990, Tyabji had loosened her control of ongoing design, and stylistic decisions were taken at the local office more and more. However, Tyabji's input was still crucial, particularly in planning new trends and product ranges, or the use of new materials. Delegating more responsibility for design to the group is part of a general process by which it was hoped that local women would eventually take over SEWA Lucknow completely, making erstwhile designers and administrators redundant (Tyabji 1990). There did not seem to be much evidence that this would occur soon, or even that it would happen at all. Nor have other projects been launched along similar lines either by other design and development professionals, or by alumnae of SEWA Lucknow. Among the reasons given for these disappointments was the stifling influence of the *mahajans*, expressed in actual threats against SEWA Lucknow personnel. Tyabji also noted that Lucknow embroiderers were less motivated and more dependent than the Gujarati craftswomen she had worked with. SEWA Ahmedabad has been quite successful in instilling a sense of self-worth, as well as teaching the practicalities of organization and self-help to Gujarati women (see Westwood 1991; Bhatt 1987). Embroiderers in Lucknow do not seem to have responded so well to these kinds of stimuli.

On the other hand, SEWA Lucknow's effect on the appearance of chikan clothes is already being seen. The most striking achievement, design-wise, of SEWA Lucknow, is to have brought chikan into an elite *fashion* market, making desirable, wearable products at a rate much faster than that at which the conventional elite products of skilled embroiderers are made. Riding the crest of "ethnic chic," sophisticated marketing techniques including video advertising have been aimed at affluent women in Delhi and Bombay, convincing them that a piece of SEWA Lucknow chikan is an indispensable part of the cosmopolitan woman's wardrobe. This trend represents a "re-aestheticising" of chikan, subjecting it to the pressures of elite consumption and raising its profile to a degree unmatched since the early decades of the century.

Mahajans seem now to be catching on to this trend, and Banerjee told me that SEWA Lucknow had received requests from Chowk wholesalers to purchase their designs. Whether they had obliged, she did not say. However, a few weeks before I left, I saw a *tepci angarkhā* (long tunic), of an unmistakably SEWA Lucknow type, in an Aminabad chikan store. When I asked about it, I was told it was just a new design they were trying. Since that time, I have been told by visitors to Delhi and Bombay since 1992 that more SEWA Lucknow–type clothes have appeared. How profound this shift in design and embroidery working is is hard to evaluate and a few more years must pass before it is possible to say that SEWA Lucknow has truly transformed the appearance of chikan.

As for the higher reaches of the craft, and whether SEWA Lucknow's influence will extend there, is also to be seen. However, its appeal to the kind of affluent middle-class consumers who are also more likely to approach skilled embroiderers individually for work, is already apparent. For example, highly skilled craftswomen are already getting occasional orders from private patrons for *kurtas*, *angarkhas*, and so on that conform strikingly to the design principles of SEWA Lucknow clothing.

EMBROIDERERS, SKILLED EMBROIDERERS, THE GOVERNMENT, AND SEWA LUCKNOW

Skilled embroiderers, as a rule, spend only a small proportion of their productive lives making fine embroidery. Even those embroiderers who have received substantial government assistance through the demonstration of their own high skills are unable to support themselves upon the production of the very finest pieces they are capable of making. Elaborate pieces take months, maybe years of painstaking work to produce, they are costly, and they have limited consumer appeal.

No amount of government patronage seems adequate to support a woman who wishes to devote herself to making this kind of chikan exclusively. Instead, highly skilled embroiderers must rely on work from the very commercial sector in which their superior embroidery talents are not wanted. Indeed, many of the most skilled women make their living less from doing embroidery than from being agents, conveying *bakhya* and *murri* work to less skilled workers in the village or their immediate neighborhood, often on a large scale. Even training schemes and exhibitions that are intended to promote quality and tradition in the craft, and that are further sources of jobs and income for highly skilled embroiderers, seem more fitted to subsidizing the commercial sector.

There has probably never been a time in which the best embroiderers—male or female—made their living from the production of their finest work alone without doing simpler work or subcontracting in addition. But whereas in the past the commercial sector provided the opportunity to produce the spectacular as well as the commonplace articles of chikan, now the government is the major source of affirmation of high skills, and assures their continuance through the institution of award-giving.

The government has also emerged as an influential patron. New opportunities for highly skilled embroiderers contribute to their emergent sense of professionalism, denied while men still occupied the ranks of the most recognized and best-skilled embroiderers. Permanent jobs as staffers of production centers have raised women such as these to positions of tangible power over lower-level embroiderers, and award-winning has confirmed for them the reality of their high status, and with it the possibility that respect and recognition can be translated into cash.

The impact of SEWA Lucknow has been very different. For the skilled embroiderer, the most remarkable feature of the insertion of the SEWA Lucknow aesthetic into the world of chikan production is that it is only shallowly rooted in the actual practices of the best embroiderers in the city, despite its appeal to the kinds of patrons from whom skilled embroiderers expect to receive support and encouragement. The design impetus of SEWA Lucknow has been removed from a local context, and aesthetic decisions have been consolidated in the figure of the designer, and the complex artistic nexus of disputed contributions to the final product by the blockmaker, printer, and embroiderer has been dissolved. Should design decisions ever be turned over completely to the local unit, it would be interesting to see if the tension between these different actors (printer, blockmaker, and embroiderer) resurfaces.

The emphasis on empowerment and individual artistry, combined with a focus on clothing that strives deliberately to be chic, gives a coherence to the design output of SEWA Lucknow that is lacking elsewhere in the world of chikan. If a woman need only work for SEWA Lucknow, she would cease having to make the adjustments between cheap commercial work and very fine work that most skilled embroiderers negotiate all their working lives—although she would still have to settle for working at a level lower than the best work of which she was capable. But all the highly skilled embroiderers I knew denied they were at the time, or had ever been, involved with SEWA Lucknow. The goal of the organization, as I have said, is to achieve a consistent level and standard of production using the skills of the average embroiderer, not the very best. Placing younger girls and women in positions of power over other embroiderers may also have had a dampening effect on the involvement of the highly skilled. On the other hand, the government usually employs men in the most managerial levels, and their authority is, in comparison, easier to accept.

CONCLUSION

SEWA Lucknow and the collective activities of the U.P. and central governments occupy a separate sector in chikan production that is, at least in theory, opposed to the commercial one. Embroiderers who are able to get work from SEWA Lucknow or UPEC do so, since the wages may be more than double those paid in the private sector (for example, a sari from a prominent *mahajan* may bring an embroiderer Rs. 50, whereas the wages from UPEC would be Rs. 110–15).

For most embroiderers, SEWA Lucknow and the state government pale into insignificance next to the larger and more powerful commercial sector. Whatever the benefits or influences exercised by this separate, subsidized sector, women must still depend upon the *mahajan* for the core of their employment. The government, as manufacturer, has affected more women with varying skills than has SEWA Lucknow, but while it has largely emulated the product of the Chowk manufacturers, SEWA Lucknow has been influential in changing perceptions about chikan.

Both SEWA Lucknow and state production schemes have tried to reshape conventional productive arrangements. SEWA Lucknow aims to promote the singular craftsperson (in its efforts to get women to embroider the entire garment), while the government is content to go along with customary divisions of labor in embroidery. But both disdain (at least in principle) the parasitic agent and all multitiered productive arrangements, attacking these systems by restricting the numbers of articles a woman can take with her when she comes to collect work (and in the government case, exacting penalties if if is learned that more than one woman worked on a piece).

SEWA Lucknow more obviously views the individual as the only valid aesthetic actor, although the singular artist is celebrated in government rewards for the very best work and touted in handicrafts literature. There is little recognition, still less acceptance, of *atelier* arrangements for craft manufacture and learning. Finally, authority in both SEWA Lucknow and government schemes is concentrated at administrative and distribution centers, and little is devolved among embroiderers themselves. Women are outworkers, working for piece-wages just as they would in the commercial sector. The commercial sector, in turn, is a lasting source of work, however poorly paid it may be, for women who cannot live on the limited amount of chikan that is available to them through the government or SEWA Lucknow. Because neither organization has genuinely transformed women's working lives, yet perpetuates chikan as a major source of wages, government and SEWA Lucknow activities, in a perverse way, tend to entrench the arrangements of the commercial sector.

As Hjortshoj (1979:139–41, 182) has remarked, the power structure of contemporary Lucknow is quite different from what prevailed even half a century ago. Gone is the polyglot culture that dominated

Lucknow in the precolonial and colonial period, organized around a Muslim, Urdu-speaking core. Instead, tastes and ideas bear the stamp of a synthetic culture combining western and classical Hindu styles, the latter described by Hjortshoj (1979:140) as less "indigenous" than "Indological." In the wake of Indian independence, streets and landmarks were renamed, with figures largely drawn from the national independence struggle and Hindu legend for inspiration. This strategy indeed resulted in a partial obliteration of the evidence of British occupation— as well as of *nawabi* Lucknow. But this "Indianization" of Lucknow should in no way be conceived of as expressing real solidarity between Lucknow's new leaders and the masses. Conflicting interests often surface as communal difference. For example, Urdu, as an elite language, has all but disappeared. Practically all older embroiderers, even if they can read and write the Arabic script, are unable to read *nagari*, the official script of the U.P. government. I often found myself in the curious position of reading out loud to my teacher official communications sent to her from "her" government, that she was incapable of reading herself unless her daughters (schooled in Hindi) were present. The estrangement of the embroiderer and the government administrator, based in class, is experienced directly as differences of gender and culture, differences that the opposition of old and new cities seems, quite literally, to embody.

CONCLUSION

This book has uncovered some of the social world underlying a vast handicraft industry known primarily through its popular and ubiquitous products. As opposed to recapitulating existing stories of the exploitation of female labor, or analyzing chikan in the absence of its makers and users, I looked closely at the kinds of skills that are used in the production of chikan. Examining how these skills have changed, and how they are evaluated and transmitted, I have tried to show the complexity of chikan production, whether it is organized under *mahajans*, bureaucrats, or cooperatives. I have also demonstrated the most important ways in which the labor force is differentiated.

It seems clear that embroiderers' experiences as piece-wage workers are powerfully shaped by their gender. It would be hard to argue otherwise when an entire, and crucial, stage of production is almost completely populated by persons of one sex. Constraints upon female behavior, opportunity, and the devaluation of female productive activity all contribute to this state of affairs. Both women and men subscribe to the ideal that women's primary task is the care of the family and maintenance of the home. Waged work contradicts this ideal, since it challenges the complementary notion that men, and not women, bring earnings into the household. Besides their absorption in domestic duties, limitations on mobility and action outside the household caused by purdah observations force the physical isolation of women, and limit their knowledge of the market.

The simplest embroidery skills can be taught quickly and without marked interruption of household work—indeed, their acquisition may be regarded as simply a part of a domestic "education." Alternative job skills are scarce and hard to obtain. Government and NGO intervention has given women the chance to make more money with the skills they have, but in so doing has reinforced women's commitment to chikan, and with that their reliance upon agents and *mahajans* who are the only ones who can give them enough work to survive. Embroidery is regarded by manufacturers (and, one suspects, by Lakhnawis at large) as easy and undemanding work for a woman. With increasing economic pressure for women to find a source of cash, and with no caste obstacles to their doing embroidery, many women now find themselves in competition with each other for the meager rewards of an unreliable form of waged work. These conditions are more marked in the countryside, where the impetus toward employing more unskilled and pliant laborers is intensifying. Whatever the specific restrictions of purdah may be in these settings, its social effects of disempowerment and isolation are replicated through the atomization and dispersal of workers in many different villages.

The restructuring of the labor force that has created a female-dominated embroidery stage has occurred alongside an overall decline in the quality of chikan available on the market. Although artisans and *mahajans* alike are prepared to acknowledge the downgrading of skill in most phases of production besides embroidery, it is the embroidery stage (admittedly the central one) that is generally alluded to in discussions about decline. The devaluation (both ideologically and in terms of wages paid) of occupations as women enter them is not unique to chikan and is familiar enough in the United States and Europe (see Sacks 1989; Warren and Bourque 1991; Beneria and Roldan 1987). In the case of chikan, the employment of women at very low piece-wages has been a means of reshaping and sustaining a vigorous industry. Women are not unaware, and are often explicit about the fact that women work for wages that men would be unprepared to accept. But they do not specifically sanction the belief that women's work is fundamentally inferior to the work of men. The poor quality one sees in so many chikan garments for sale may not necessarily reflect technical and imaginative inadequacies, but instead the deliberate decision to do work to a lower standard than that which embroiderers are capable of.

Productive relations have taken center stage in this book. But I also wanted to find a way to bridge the gap between a focus on production and a focus on products. Chikan products are, and have been, very diverse, ranging from very coarse work to the exquisite embroidery that flourishes in the rarefied atmosphere of government-award competition and personal patronage. While I have highlighted the shifting proportions of cheap and fine work in the market, noting specifically the prevalence of cheap *bakhya*-work, it is a mistake to see chikan as an ancient, traditional art form that has been, or is being, corrupted by external influences.

First, chikan has been made for most of its history primarily for Indian consumers, and thus changes in production, as well as in taste, originate largely inside the country instead of outside. The makers of chikan are not quite so vulnerable as the makers of goods intended solely for export, whose livelihood can vanish as soon as new tastes are dictated. Nor are they in the same position as workers recruited into multinational firms, whose jobs disappear as capital moves from place to place. The product itself exhibits continuities in form and function that—alterations in styling, color, and fabric notwithstanding—mean that the embroiderer has not had to master radically different skills in order to remain employed. Now having found a place in the market for "ethnic chic," it is uncertain quite how long chikan as a fashion item will last. But it will probably not disappear as suddenly as some overseas fashion fads of the 1970s (Swallow 1982).

Secondly, cheap piece-work has been an element in chikan production for over one hundred years, perhaps throughout its existence in Lucknow. However, over time fine work has declined relative to cheap work, and there is a growing concordance in the symbolic roles of both fine and cheap chikan. Chikan's subtle powers to communicate *specifically* about status and identity in the particular context of Muslim-oriented, historic Lucknow, are no longer required. Instead, its contemporary appeal rests upon its embodying an authentic "slice" of Lucknow, whether it is *bakhya* work or a superb piece of *murri*. In this regard, chikan is like other handicrafts in India that are being revived as emblems of national and regional culture without explicit reference to the highly "modern" conditions of their production. This is most marked in the case of "ethnic chic," or the use of materials, designs, and styles lifted directly from artisanal traditions in the country, which has become very desirable in the last ten years or so among elite consumers, particularly in the metropolitan centers. Ethnic chic is predicated on the growing fashion market in India, and derives its energy from the "rediscovered" folk cultural heritage of India, particularly Gujarat and Rajasthan. Chikan, however, is a little different from mainstream ethnic chic in that it has not been totally subsumed by the fashion market. Instead, the banal *bakhya* work appeals strongly to more conservative buyers, from a range of social statuses in the middle class, living inside and outside the major cities. Indeed, were chikan to be swallowed up in the refined tastes of the metropolitan fashion market, the enormous industry that generates it would not survive. The trickle of work into embroiderers' homes fuels an industry that targets the sensibilities of the Indian equivalent of, so to speak, K-Mart shoppers, rather than those who shop on Fifth Avenue.

For the highly skilled, however, the new fashion market offers opportunities as well as liabilities. On one hand, their superior skills and creative abilities are more likely to be recognized as unconventional styles of chikan acquire a higher public profile. Accustomed to adapting prints and applying designs, embroiderers can quickly adjust to changing tastes in the fashion domain. However, the fashion market may be as volatile as it is in the West, and work that may increase at one time may become scarce at another.

So long as the government wants to present handicrafts as examples of national and transregional identities, there will be a stimulus for the creation of the finest work. But the whole enterprise is highly contradictory. Government sponsorship and patronage have given some among the highly skilled embroiderers a boost in their own efforts to differentiate themselves from the mass. At the same time, government production schemes attempt to cut out female agents, the same embroiderers who are lauded as national cultural treasures. It seems as though the socioeconomic base of fine work has not been fully understood. Even with all the help the government can give, no embroiderer can hope to live the life of an artist, devoted to her art. Fine work exists only because cheap work exists, and fine embroiderers exist through subcontracting cheap work. Recent reports of a decline in government production schemes may indicate a more widespread withdrawal of the state from its commitment to chikan.[1] If this withdrawal is also reflected in award schemes, training programs, and exhibitions, then it will profoundly affect the livelihood and creative activities of the highly skilled—if it has not already. The impact on the less skilled who have been getting work from the government is a little more difficult to judge, especially in the light of the fact that few had come to rely upon the UPEC production schemes exclusively for work.

I have argued that it is impossible to understand the organization of the embroidery stage, or the relationship of embroiderers to merchants, without reference to gender. But in chapter 4 I described some contradictory relations between female embroiderers and female chikan agents. How might we begin to think about how gender and class are related in the chikan industry?

Chikan embroiderers live at a distance from the shop but close to each other, and households and neighbors share in the daily round of managing work and family. In an effort to fuse elements of race, gender, and class into a coherent theoretical package, Karen Brodkin Sacks has proposed that the working class be defined as, *"membership in a community that is dependent upon waged labour, but that is unable to subsist or reproduce by such labor alone"* (Sacks 1989:543, emphasis in original). Describing and analyzing such a community would involve identifying networks, shared experiences and identities that define the boundaries of a world of production and reproduction. The problem with this approach is that it is not clear how it would encompass the fact that embroiderers are themselves differentiated and engaged in exploitative relations among themselves.

If there is one single point I wish to highlight, it is that female embroiderers cannot be regarded as a uniform group, whether in terms of the skills they possess, their status as workers, or their relationships to men. Using the distribution of discrepant skills as a guide, I have argued that female embroiderers diverge along important lines such as degree of skill, wages, observation of purdah, and their position in the chain of relationships linking *mahajans* to workers. Skill marks important boundaries in the chikan industry. *Bakhya* workers are the backbone of the industry but mostly cannot expect to learn better-paid *murri* skills. *Murri* workers are better paid but have less to offer in an industry where there is dramatic deskilling going on.

Women with higher skills, who also engage in subcontracting, are more likely to identify themselves as professional artisans and producers than the lesser-skilled women to whom they give out work. Among the most accomplished, this self-image—as I have pointed out—is also stimulated by government patronage. At these upper echelons, fine work is being made by women from families with continuous traditions of excellence in the craft over several generations. Women such as these have overcome the formidable obstacles of purdah, and, drawing upon the resources they have cultivated in organizing and controlling the household to which they have been confined, have carved out a niche in the industry that has hitherto been the province of men. But they have not used these opportunities to press for advantages for other embroiderers. Their energies are squandered on quarreling and competing with similarly skilled women in the struggle for government patronage. As agents, they control less-skilled women's access to work, perpetuate the conventional divisions of skill, and effectively keep their clients dependent upon them.

However benign the relationship between the agent and her "client" may be made to appear by either party, however much it might coincide with other community identities and networks, its antagonism ought not to be set aside while delineating women's oppression in chikan production. There is clearly much more research to be done on female agents, but their existence compels us to view with skepticism texts (e.g., Renuka 1980; Rai 1975) or manifestos in which gender is not only an unquestioned basis for collective identity but also for organization and struggle.

Curiously, the reality of differentation among female embroiderers has been recognized by researchers and development workers "on the ground" for some time, without its being openly acknowledged in most textual sources on chikan. For example, the involvement of the state government in schemes to supply work directly to rural women, and to minimize work-sharing and subcontracting within these schemes, is a direct response to the "nuisance" of female subcontractors. Yet the public version of why the government is involved in chikan production links the preservation of a national, cultural resource to the alleviation of the oppression of women conceived as a category. We encounter a similar situation at SEWA Lucknow. As with the state government organizations, SEWA Lucknow takes steps to reduce agent activities, and with its emphasis on work that can be done by the average embroiderer, effectively eliminates many of the most accomplished embroiderers (and subcontractors) from the mix. Simultaneously, SEWA Lucknow is explicit in its aim to achieve "female empowerment" without reference to divergent interests among embroiderers. These absences conceal important questions. Is the pursuit of rights for women hurt by admitting that all women are not the same? Does being a woman eliminate all other social identifications?

Feminist research has increasingly taken account of these questions (e.g., Johnson 1992; Naiman 1996). One implication is that while the full complement of women's work merits study, there is a particularly urgent need to understand the kinds of relations *among women* that waged work creates. A second implication is that having noted these discrepancies among chikan embroiderers, it is time to go beyond the familiar view of the chikan industry as one exclusively characterized by a stark division of female embroiderers and (versus?) male everybody-else. Studying female embroiderers was, for me, a decision shaped by the aesthetic centrality of the embroidery stage, the conundrum of female domination of the embroidery stage, and the fact that there was a small, but significant literature on chikan embroidery—a good proportion of it on the embroiderers. While female embroiderers are described as "invisible" in these texts, they are now, ironically, more visible than the male and female artisans who populate the stages prior to and following embroidery.

I do not mean to trivialize the embroidery stage in suggesting that our focus should move beyond it. I am also aware that just as women's embroidery and other forms of home-based production are regarded as insignificant and without great value (see Westwood 1991:299), so research into women's embroidery is often regarded as itself a form of "second-class" research. However, if we see women's domination of embroidery as an example of labor force restructuring, then it is critical to move outward from an almost exclusive focus on women to an intensive examination of the productive activities of the women *and* men on either side of them in the chikan production process.

This refocusing of the research problem does not mean that issues of gender are left behind. Indeed, the greatest mistake would be to assume that in studying the lives and work of related artisanal and technical specialists we need only deal with men. For example, many of the garments that are destined for embroidery are sewn by women, and female washerwomen play an important role in preparing chikan clothes for final sale. We simply do not know what other productive roles women have to play in the making of chikan, or how their own skills have changed over the years, but it is critical that we find out what they may be. Besides enriching the analysis of class in chikan production, such an approach would round out the portrait of gendered production that I have already sketched, by looking at ways in which productive tasks that surround embroidery are structured and interpreted.

APPENDIX

A *Short Description of Some Chikan Stitches and Terms*

Anokhī chikan ("Unique, special" chikan)
Exceptionally fine and exacting work, where the embroidery appears only on one side, no stitches being allowed to pass through to, or be visible on, the reverse.

Baldā
A stitch constructed on the base of a running stitch, which is then "over-sewn" by the thread winding under and over the base stitches. The over-sewing is especially compact and adheres tightly to the line traced by the understitches. It thus appears to be an effective "outlining" stitch.

Bakhyā
Bakhya is made on the reverse of the cloth. The needle picks up the cloth on alternate sides of the *patti* (leaf) to be embroidered with the thread intertwining as a series of crisscrosses in between. On the front, small contiguous stitches define the edge of the *patti*, and the cloth appears whiter and thicker where the threads cluster underneath. Run-of-the-mill *bakhya* work, though made with the same technique, owes its far different appearance from the *bakhya* stitches of the highly skilled to the more haphazard cross-hatching, in which the threads may barely cross each other at all, and the resultant broken or even completely discontinuous lines of stitches. *Bakhya* on straight lines appears continuous with the *patti* stitches on the obverse surface, but on the reverse appears, and is done, in a fashion broadly comparable to a backstitch. Some embroiderers distinguish between the two instances of *bakhya* as *sidhi* and *ulti bakhya*.

Bijlī (earring)
One of three stitches made by breaking threads in the cloth. *Bijli* is made by picking up two threads in the cloth with the tip of the needle. The needle is then twisted round and round until the threads break. The resultant hole is enlarged and its edges sealed with stitches fanning out

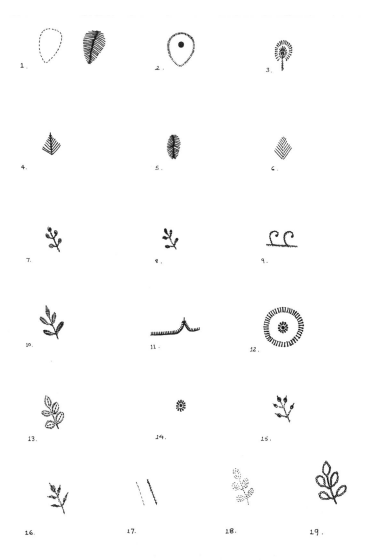

FIG. A.1. Sketches of some important chikan stitches.

1. Bakhya (front and back views). 2. Balda with rauzan (hul). 3. Bijli. 4. Cana ki patti. 5. Dhum. 6. Ghas ki patti. 7. Gol cikan. 8. Gol murri. 9. Jhumar. 10. Jora. 11. Kaj with nok. 12. Kangan. 13. Kauri. 14. Kil. 15. Lambi cikan. 16. Lambi murri. 17. Pencni. 18. Tepci. 19. Zanzira.

1.   2.   3.   4.

FIG. A.2. Some complex jalis.

1. Makra. 2. Bul-bul cashm. 3. Mandarasi. 4. Bank.

about 270° around the hole like spokes, the ones at the apex being longer than those at the sides. A final corona of overwrapped stitches like those found around *kil* completes the *bijli*.

Ćanā kī pattī (gram)

Similar to *ghas ki patti* (see below), except each new stitch is caught under the previous one to create a "spine" in the middle of the *patti*. No foundation stitches are used in *cana ki patti*.

Chiriyāgar

A whimsical style of chikan embroidery featuring animals, such as peacocks, lions, elephants, and so forth.

Dandī dār phandā

Basically, *gol cikan* (*phanda*), but with an elongated "neck" before the *gol* (nub) at the tip of the stemlet.

Dhūm

A complex interwoven stitch, underlain by running stitches defining the leaf, and then a cross-hatching done on top of them, creating closely spaced, angled stitches with a central spine, like a plait.

Ghās kī pattī (grass)

A complex stitch, *ghas* appears as angled, tapering stitches, wide at the base of the *patti*, and pointed at the top. The needle emerges from the cloth in the central "line" of the leaf, and defines the "frond" to the left edge first. The needle passes under the cloth to the right side, where the corresponding "frond" is traced from outer edge to center.

Hatkattī

A form of linear *jali*, made with a thick needle used to push aside the fabric threads to create a hole. Each hole is held open with tightly pulled stitches. *Hatkatti* is often used to embellish the spaces inside wide leaves and around motifs like *kil*.

Jalī (lattice, network)
There are many members of the *jali* group, of which a few are described. All are made inside the space of a *phul* (flower).

The most common *jali* is *sidhaur jali*, made diagonally to the base of the *phul*. The embroiderer first works a central line of holes made by pushing the fabric threads apart with a thick needle. The next line is built up "above" the first, with the stitches holding the holes open passing diagonally from one hole to another (holes and thread alternate like a checkerboard). *Sidhaur jali* has the most rounded or oval-shaped appearing holes of all the *jalis*.

Bank jali. This straight *jali* is made by drawing three to four threads from the cloth after scoring it with the needle. The embroiderer stitches first one way and then another to create an effect similar to some *turpai* (hand-hemming and seaming) techniques in tailoring.

Bul-bul cashm. Made in a similar fashion to *sidhaur* except perpendicular to the base of the *phul*. The holes are more squarish in appearance and each alternating hole has two threads from the fabric remaining, in the shape of an "x." As each line is worked, first two open triangles in the base of the hole are made, then the remaining triangles, and with them, the presence of the "crosshair" is revealed.

Makra (spider's web). In *makra*, each square hole (alternating once again with a square of fabric) has a single thread retained from the fabric suspended vertically across it.

Mandarazi. The most "checkerboard"-like *jali*, square holes alternate with solid squares of fabric.

Jhūmar (head ornament)
Very like *phanda*, but with each "stem" curving over at the head and culminating in a smooth knot.

Joṛā (a pairing, joining)
Often confused with *kauri* by even those familiar with chikan. The stitches were made in comparable ways, a fine and compact oversewing defining the two sides of the *patti*.

Kāj
Similar to "blanket stitch," the stitch was also used to "seal" the edges of material where it would be cut, to prevent fraying. Another name for the stitch was, in fact, *kat*. *Kaj* was almost always done upon a scalloped design, and was made up of two elements, *pasuj* and the covering stitch.

Kaurī (a cowrie shell)
Like *jora*, except *kauri* is made with more widely spaced base stitches, and in its final appearance is "open," in other words, there was a clear

space between its two sides. The leaf shape created has a distinctly tapered appearance and a pointed end. *Hatkatti* might be made in the space between the sides of the leaf.

Kherkī

Kherki involves breaking a couple of threads to make a center hole, with long, close clustered stitches surrounding it completely and circled themselves by the familiar *kil*-like spokes.

Kīl (nose-ring)

Kil is made up of a central, raised, smooth knob (the *gol*) and an outer array of small stitches like spokes, each made with one stitch being "overwrapped" by another.

Kaṅgan (bangle)

Kangan is essentially like *kil*, with an extra circle of "spokes" on the outside.

Murrī

Lambi murri (long murri) is distinguished by two vertical stitches at the point of each element of the *patti*, which are then oversewn at an angle.

Gol murri (round *murri*) is done in the same way, but the end is rounded or blunted, instead of pointed.

Nok (a point)

At the point of each scallop in *kaj*, the embroiderer makes a long single stitch, called a *nok*.

Pasūj

Pasuj is a form of basting, or foundation running stitch.

Pencnī ("penc"—twisting, weaving).

Pencni is constructed on the base of a running stitch, which is then "oversewn" by the thread winding under and over the base stitches.

Phandā/ćikan

Gol cikan (round cikan) is made by creating a raised knot (*gol*) at the end of a stem.

Lambi cikan (long cikan) is made like *gol chikan*, except a single stitch is placed at its apex to make it seem pointed.

Rojan/hūl (a hole)

The hole in the cloth is made as in *bijli*. It is sealed with small over-wrapping stitches that are only visible underneath the cloth. *Rojan* usually appears as a circular hole in the middle of an open *patti*, for example, one embroidered in *balda*.

Tepcī

Tepci is a very fine stitch made with a small number of threads lightly skimming the surface of the cloth. In construction, it is most like a running stitch, with the needle passing in and out of the cloth so that the thread goes alternately over the top and underneath it. *Tepci* may be made so as to appear the same on either the obverse or reverse of the cloth. In the version I was taught, the needle picks up less material as it travels underneath than it does when it traverses the top.

Urmā (see *pencni*)

Zanzīrā (a necklace)

Made like western chain stitch, except the looped part is at the base of each stitch, instead of at the apex.

NOTES

INTRODUCTION

1. In 1990, one rupee was equal to approximately six cents.

CHAPTER 1. CHIKAN IN HISTORICAL CONTEXT

1. Definitions include "form of embroidery done on some white washing material such as muslin, calico, linen or silk" (Watt 1903:398); "white cotton threads on colourless muslin" (Pande 1968:43). Naqvi's (1971:40) definition is almost the same as Watt's, with the addition of a statement about the thread that is used—"white cotton threads of bleached raw silks like Muga or Tasar."

2. *Katao* (also known as *daraz*)—a form of appliqué, is often encountered in the literature under chikan, although *daraz* specialists think of it as a distinct specialty. The inclusion of *katao* in the flat-stitch category may derive from the similarities in effect, if not in technique, between *katao* and *bakhya*, namely, that appliqué as well as *bakhya* creates areas of relative opacity on the finished piece.

3. Dhamija (1964:25) writes that chikan was also introduced to elites in Delhi and Rampur after artisans left Bengal, but that it has not survived into the present day.

4. Carved stonework may be referred to as "*jali*," the same name as a long-established female embroidery specialty.

5. Irwin's translation, cited in Oldenburg (1984:16). She and Hjortshoj (1979) both observe that many merchants and shopkeepers of Lucknow utter this couplet upon commencing business in the morning.

6. Watt dubs *tepci* "a cheap imitation of bukhia" (i.e., *bakhya*) Perhaps what he means is that the surface similarity of the stitches allows *tepci* to function as an expedient version of *bakhya*, in which no herringbone is used.

7. I am using "distinction" in the light of Bourdieu's (1984) book of that name, in which it means both relative superiority and cultural differentiation.

CHAPTER 2. THE DIVISION OF LABOR

1. Like Kumar (1988:13), I found that a common way to refer to artisans was to use occupational descriptions of the type, "he/she makes [the item]." The formative element *wālā* was frequently used in epithets like *chapwālā* (printer) or *sil'āīwālā* (stitcher).

2. A *mahajan* quoted in *Lucknow City Magazine* (1988:20) says, "First we purchase cloth, then raw material, then get the cutting done. Then printing is done by blocks. Then it is sent for embroidery and then the network. Then we get it washed properly and after packing and decorating it is sent for marketing." Like the *mahajans* I interviewed, this individual constructs an active role for the manufacturer in the production process by stressing how "we get (the particular process) done," along with the activities that are indeed the province of the *mahajan*.

3. Chikan was exempted from sales tax in Uttar Pradesh in 1952. A prominent *mahajan*, Chandra Prakash Garg of one of the Chhangamal stores, said his father had successfully petitioned the state government on this issue, arguing that chikan deserved exemption on the basis of its being a cottage industry.

CHAPTER 3. EMBROIDERERS IN SOCIAL PERSPECTIVE

1. Underreporting women's work is a problem in other parts of the Third World (see, for example, Beneria 1982 and Weiss 1991:73–75).

2. As Kumar (1988:14) notes, it is difficult to describe relative wealth or deprivation in the Indian context. However, embroiderers do not hesitate to make the subjective assessment that they are poor. While living standards vary, many embroiderers live without private household supplies of water or electricity. If food is prepared in the middle of the day, it is served to men and then perhaps to children. Women forego it. Consumer goods are sparse in embroiderers' homes and clothing is frequently old or used.

3. For women and girls who do not wear *burqas*, and for all women inside the house, proper and respectful (as well as respectable) attire includes a *dupatta* (scarf) to cover the chest (Jeffrey 1979). In actual practice, however, the *dupatta* is not always worn carefully. It may be not worn at all within the walls of the house where men are absent, although a piece of cloth must always be close to hand in case covering is needed quickly. The *dupatta* can also be used to cover the head, when the *azān* (call to prayer) is heard or as a partial concealment when a woman does not want to "suit up" in her *burqa* for a short trip outside the house. Although Muslims are stereotypically expected to wear *salwar-qamiz* or very voluminous pants in this region, some Muslim women wear *saris* by choice. This obviates the need for a *dupatta*.

CHAPTER 4. WORK AND WAGES

1. Note that this differs from Kumar's (1988:13) findings in Banaras, where karigar was used only with reference to the "art or craft aspect of the work."

2. For a discussion of comparable attitudes among Spanish embroiderers, see Lever 1988:4.

3. Some reported having to pay for colored *kacca* thread when its use was required. But white *kacca* thread is by far the most commonly employed in all chikan work. For those who execute any of their own work, white *kacca* thread

costs between Rs. 40 to Rs. 50 per kilo, but one kilo lasts several months.

4. The agent may have obtained the *sari* directly from a shop—although it would be unusual for a manufacturer to give out just one piece of embroidery. Alternatively, she may have obtained it from yet another agent, or the *sari* may have been part of a larger (though not necessarily an enormous) bundle of work. Rs. 90 is quite a good wage for work in the private sector, and may itself imply that the woman was not dealing with another agent. As in many exchanges I had with women engaged in all levels of agent activity, she did not elaborate further on the precise networks in which she was involved.

5. This statement is, I believe, deceptively simple. For one thing, agents often get both *bakhya/murri* and *jali* done on a garment—each phase of embroidery being done by different sets of people. The wage bundle per piece must be divided into two portions, one for the *murri* embroiderer, and one for the *jali* embroiderer, besides the portion that is set aside for the agent.

6. In fact, the "standard" rate for *kurtas*, according to most agents, is Rs. 1 or Rs. 2, *irrespective* of the work on it. The challenge here is to resolve two contradictory phenomena—the agent's quotes, which will probably downplay their own amount of profit-taking, and the *mahajan's* quotes, which will be pitched higher so as to distract from the low wages conventionally paid.

7. "*Kurta*" was sometimes used indiscriminately to refer to women's and men's tailored apparel. *Salwar-qamiz* often went by the term, "ladies suit," while a *kurta* and *pajama* set (in which the embroidery was almost exclusively concentrated on the *kurta*) was termed "gents suit").

8. This was the only case in which a family of daughters had presented an opportunity, rather than a liability, to their parents.

CHAPTER 5. SKILL AND KNOWLEDGE IN FINE CHIKAN EMBROIDERY

1. For a discussion of the symbolic nature of cotton cloth in India, see Bayly (1986).

2. *Ulti bakhya* is used in other contexts to refer to regular *bakhya*.

3. The correct way to count *bakhya* stitches is to count the number of herringbones on the back of the patti.

4. James Kippen (1988:53), in writing about *tabla* (drum) music in Lucknow, refers to *saf* as an adjective used by (mostly Muslim) instrumentalists to point out "clear articulation" in another's performance—*unkā hāth bāhut ṣāf hai* (his hand is very clear).

5. Some women distinguish the two kinds of *murri* using the terms *gol/lambi murri*, and others do so with *mundi/nukili murri*. A woman will use one set of terms or the other, but not both. In both the *murri* and the *phanda* cases, the *gol* element may be left out, and *lambi* being used as the qualifier of the variant stitch. This not seem to be the case with *mundi/nukili*.

6. *Bijli* (earring), *kangan* (bangle), *kil* (nosering), *karan* (earring), *zanzira* (necklace), and *jhumar* (head ornament). Embroiderers of Madeganj also referred to *kangan* as *barī kīl*, and *kil* as *ćoṭī kīl*.

7. *Ghas* (grass), *cana* (gram), *dhaniya* (coriander), *bajrā* (a kind of millet), *khājuri* (khajur—date). *Tilkadī hatkatti* (sesame), *sabudānā hatkatti* (sago).

8. Paine's (1987) compilation of "basic stitches" includes *rehat*. *Rehat* was also said by Kanis Usgar to be "like *pencni*" and was used in *daraz* work.

9. The last part of this comment is reminiscent of Vygotsky's (1978:90) description of how properly organized learning stimulates internal developmental processes.

10. This manner of dealing with the thread has also been observed among tailors (Yusuf Ali 1900:70, cited in Bayly 1986:296).

11. I am using the term "Orientalist" in Said's (1978) sense, and as it has been used subsequently in the literature on colonial and postcolonial South Asia.

12. It is hardly surprising this advice should be repeated in Rastogi's article, since it is an interview with Saliha herself. However, its appearance in Pande (1968) seems to suggest that this is more widely recognized as good technique.

13. In written sources, what Saliha termed *taj mahal* is most often called *madrasi jali* (Naqvi 1971; Pande 1968).

14. Hoey (1880) distinguished between *bel* and *buta*. Round motifs are conventionally referred to as *buti* today, denoting a smaller form than that implied by *buta*.

15. Ayub Khan also referred to *daurukhī* chikan, in which the work can be viewed as well from the back as from the front.

16. Radha Rastogi, in her article about Saliha Begum in a 1988 issue of *MARG*, refers to her making a piece of *anokhi* chikan at that time.

CHAPTER 6. DEVELOPMENT SCHEMES
AND STATE PATRONAGE

1. Indian members of this diverse group were very few; in fact, only two of the eight members of the judging committee were Indian. Indians featured most prominently in the exhibition as producers, possessors, or sellers of handicrafts, or as the donors of prizes. Except for an earlier catalog of art manufactures that was written for the Glasgow International Exhibition by T. N. Mukharji of the Indian Museum, Calcutta (Mukharji 1888) and the work of perhaps one of the most outstanding figures in the history of Indian art criticism, Ananda Coomaraswamy, judgments about Indian handicrafts were made almost exclusively by Europeans.

2. Source: AIHB annual reports, 1962 and 1963.

3. Production worth Rs. 12,925 is recorded in the report, which is a very low figure compared to those of previous years. Sales, curiously, amounted to Rs. 53, 940.

4. Source: Undated report of the Uttar Pradesh Niyatri Nigam Limited (UPEC).

5. Source: Undated report of the Uttar Pradesh Niyatri Nigam Limited.

6. Note, however, that in the Delhi Exhibition of 1903, the pieces that featured "almost every stitch" were *rumals* and handkerchiefs (Watt 1903:402).

7. Compare Ritzenhaler (1979) on the rise of the named artist in the U.S. Southwest.

8. Programs of this sort are run by UPEC. Chikan training schemes administered by UPEC were said to have been in operation in 1978–79 and 1979–80, but I did not meet anyone connected with them.

9. There was some disagreement about stipends in oral accounts. One embroiderer said Rs. 1,000 was the stipend for instructors in AIHB schemes, while another said it was only Rs. 850. Whether the fact that the first embroiderer was male and the second female had anything to do with this discrepancy, I do not know.

10. In his study of the AIHB and training schemes in several crafts, Fisher (1974) wrote that some artisans improperly included their own family members in training schemes. In this way, the full proceeds from a scheme could be channeled to a single family, and the skills of a mastercraftsperson not disseminated to unrelated students. Although I knew that daughters of artisans helped make the goods that were supposedly the products of a training scheme, I did not come across a case where a close family relative had been blatantly added to a register.

11. A thorough history of the SEWA Ahmedabad organization can be found in Rose (1992). SEWA Ahmedabad is not the only women's organization of its type in India but is one of the most famous.

12. DASTKAR was founded in 1981 by Tyabji and five other women with craft and development experience. DASTKAR's special aim is to help craftspeople link up with new, urban markets. In 1990, it was working with about seventy-five crafts groups. The organization offers advice and information, and gives workshops on business, design, and public relations. DASTKAR attempts to promote cooperative and self-help organizations for artisans and extends marketing opportunities through placing direct orders with artisan groups and giving access to the Hauz Khas craft village for shows (Handicrafts India 1990:355).

13. Tyabji told me that her understanding of chikan was shaped by her own analysis of pieces in her possession, whence she derived the figure of twenty-one stitches. That her figure differs from those of other embroiderers means little, because they are all different. But what is important is that her figure was derived from her own analysis of embroidery, not from indigenous reports.

14. In theory, girls and young women who had learned a range of stitches in the government training schemes should have found a perfect niche in SEWA Lucknow, but there was never any mention of government scheme "graduates" involved in the organization.

CONCLUSION

1. Source: *Times of India* (Lucknow), December 15, 1994.

GLOSSARY OF
SELECTED TERMS

The system of transliteration used in this book is derived from John T. Platts (1977 [1884]) *A Dictionary of Urdu, Classical Hindi and English* (Delhi: Oriental Books Reprint Corporation).

The words and definitions given here are either of special importance to the subject at hand, or recur throughout the text. Meanings are, for the most part, derived from the context in which they were encountered in speech. Other meanings can be found through consulting Platts's book (1974).

For those unfamiliar with Urdu or Hindi, the most important point to note about sounds are as follows. Vowels ā, ī and ū are elongated. Consonants ṭ, ḍ and ṛ are retroflex, ṅ is nasalized, ć is pronounced rather like the 'ch' in chair. An 'h' following a consonant as in dh, kh, bh and ph, indicates aspiration.

'ādat	habit, custom
angarkhā	a long man's tunic
āsān	easy
aṣlī	real, true
bādlā	gold or silver thread, stitching with metal thread
bārīk	thin, fine
barsāt	rainy season
bhaṭṭī	oven
bīćwālā	go-betweens, agents
burqa'	women's concealing garment
būṭā	large flower design
būṭī	small flower design
ćālū	ordinary, commonplace
ćhapwālā	printer
ćogā	long garment, cloak
ćūnā	lime-paste, ingredient in pan
ćuṅgī	duty, tax
ćuṭkī	tight pinching by the finger
ćunnī	small scarf, mantle

darzī	tailor
dehāt	countryside, rural
dhobī	washerman
dimāg	brain, imagination
dūkān	shop
dūkāndār	shopkeeper
dupaṭṭā	woman's scarf
fardī	stitching with metal thread, as badla
fursat	leisure, free-time
galī	lane, narrow street
ganj	market
gulābī	pink (dye used in chikan)
ḥajj	pilgrimage to Mecca
hāth kā kām	handwork
havelī	mansion
'Id u'l-fitr	festival to mark the breaking of the fast of Ramadan
'īdgah	grounds where the festival of Id is observed
ilāćī	cardomam, occasional ingredient in *pan*
imāmbārā	a building associated with Shia mourning ritual commemorating the martyrdom of the Prophet's grandsons
'izzat	honor
jāmdānī	cloth in which flower designs are woven
jāt	caste, occupational category
kaććā	uncooked, unfinished
kām	work
kāmdānī	light embroideries with gold and silver wire
kārhai	embroidery
kārīgar	worker, artisan
karkhānā	workplace, workshop
kurtā	shirt
kurtewālīṅ	women who distribute *kurtas*, agents
kaṭā'o	appliqué work
katthā	catechu, ingredient in *pan*
kharāb	broken, no good
khatam	finished, dead, gone

mahājan	businessman, merchant, man of substance
moṭā	thick, bulky, coarse
mahīn	fine, thin
maidān	field
māl	goods, material
man	mind, imagination
melā	festival, exhibition
mohallā	neighborhood, locality
Muḥarram	first month of Islamic year, important to Shias for commemoration of death of the Prophet's grandsons
mustaqil	permanent, enduring
mukesh	stitching with metal thread, as *badla* and *fardi*
mulmul	muslin
nawāb	lord, governor; title of rulers of Awadh
nīl	blue (dye used in chikan)
pallū	border (of a sari)
pakkā	cooked, finished
pān	betel leaf, betel nut, and condiments
pān-dān	container for ingredients of *pan*
pardā	seclusion of women (purdah)
pardanishīn	state of being in *parda*
pareshānī	troubles, distress
patlā	slender, thin
pattī	leaf
phūl	flower
ra'īs	gentry, well-off people
Ramadan	month of fasting for Muslims
rekhtī	speech style of Lucknow courtesans
rozā	fast
rūmāl	square of cloth
ṣāf	clear, clean, distinct
sāṛī	woman's wrapped-style garment
shāh	king
salwār-qamīz	woman's tunic and pants
sharm	shame, sense of shame
shauq	passion, love, interest
sīdhā	straight
ta'rīf	praise
ta'alluqāt	relationships

ta'alluqadār	landholder
ṭabiyāt	disposition, inclination
tāgā	thread
ṭānkā	stitch
tez	smart, sharp, feisty
ṭhappākar	blockmaker
ṭhekedār	contractor, agent
ṭolā	district, neighborhood
ṭopī	cap
turpāi	hand-seaming and hemming
'ulamā	learned men, religious scholars
ulṭā	reversed
ustād	master
zamīndār	land-holder
zardozī	heavy embroidery with gold and silver wire
zarī	gold thread

BIBLIOGRAPHY

Abidi, Nigar Fatima. 1986. Home-based production: A case study of women weavers in a village of eastern Uttar Pradesh, India. In Amit Kumar Gupta (ed.), *Women and Society: The Developmental Perspective*. New Delhi: Criterion. pp. 324–55.

Abu-Lughod, Lila. 1986. *Veiled Sentiments: Honor and Poetry in a Bedouin Society*. Berkeley: University of California.

Adams, John and Linda Paul. 1987. The Informal Sector in India: Work, Gender and Technology. In James Warner Bjorkman (ed.), *The Changing Division of Labor in South Asia: Women and Men in India's Society, Economy and Politics*. New Delhi: Manohar. pp. 33–52.

Ahmad, Imtiaz. 1978a. Endogamy and Status Mobility among the Siddiqui Sheikhs of Allahabad, Uttar Pradesh. In Imtiaz Ahmad (ed.), *Caste and Social Stratification among Muslims in India*. New Delhi: Manohar. pp. 171–206.

Ahmad, Imtiaz. 1978b. *Caste and Social Stratification among Muslims in India*. New Delhi: Manohar

Alam, Muzaffar. 1986. *The Crisis of Empire in Mughal North India: Awadh and the Punjab, 1707–1748*. Delhi: Oxford University Press.

All India Handicrafts Board. 1959. *Report of the Working Group on Evaluation of Progress of Handicrafts during the Second Five-Year Plan, 1956–61*. New Delhi: All India Handicrafts Board.

——. 1963 [1959] *Report of the Working Group on Evaluation of Progress of Handicraft Industries*. Delhi: All India Handicrafts Board.

——. *Annual Reports*, 1959–1975. Delhi: All India Handicrafts Board.

Ansari, Ghaus. 1960. *Muslim Caste in Uttar Pradesh*. Lucknow: Ethnographic and Folk Culture Quarterly.

Appadurai, Arjun. 1986a. "Is Homo Hierarchicus?" *American Ethnologist* 13: 745–61.

——. 1986b. "Introduction: Commodities and the Politics of Value." In Arjun Appadurai (ed.), *The Social Life of Things: Commodities in Cultural Perspective*. Cambridge: Cambridge University Press. pp. 3–63.

Appadurai, Arjun and Carol A. Breckenridge. 1987. "Public Culture in Twentieth-Century India." Paper presented at the University of Pennsylvania Ethnohistory Workshop, September 1987.

Banerjee, Nirmala. 1985. Women Workers in the Unorganized Sector: The Calcutta Experience. Hyderabad: Sangram Books.

Barnett, R. 1980. North India Between Empires: Awadh, the Mughals and the British, 1720–1801. Berkeley: University of California Press.

Baud, Isa. 1987. "Industrial Subcontracting: The Effects of Putting Out System on Poor Working Women in India." In Andrea Menefee Singh and Anita Kelles-Viitanen (eds.), *Invisible Hands: Women in Home-Based Production.* New Delhi: Sage. pp. 69–92.

———. 1992. *Forms of Production and Women's Labor: Gender Aspects of Industrialisation in India and Mexico.* New Delhi: Sage.

Bayly, C. A. 1983. *Rulers, Townsmen, and Bazaars: North Indian Society in the Age of British Expansion, 1770–1870.* New York: Cambridge University Press.

———. 1986. "The Origins of Swadeshi (Home Industry): Cloth and Indian Society, 1700–1930." In Arjun Appadurai (ed.), *The Social Life of Things: Commodities in Cultural Perspective.* Cambridge: Cambridge University Press. pp 285–321.

———. 1989. *New Cambridge History of India, Vol II.* Cambridge: Cambridge University Press.

Bean, Susan. 1989. "Gandhi and Khadi, the Fabric of Indian Independence." In Annette B. Weiner and Jane Schneider (eds.), *Cloth and Human Experience.* Washington, D.C.: Smithsonian Institute Press.

Becker, H. 1982. *Art Worlds.* Berkeley: University of California Press.

Benegal, Som. 1963. *The Story of Handicrafts.* Delhi: All India Handicrafts Board.

Beneria, Lourdes and Shelley Feldman (eds.). 1992. *Unequal Burden: Economic Crises, Persistent Poverty, and Women's Work.* Boulder, Colo.: Westview.

Beneria, Lourdes and Martha Roldan. 1987. *The Crossroads of Class and Gender: Industrial Homework, Subcontracting, and Household Dynamics in Mexico City.* Chicago: University of Chicago Press.

Bennholdt-Thomsen, Veronika. 1981. "Why Housewives Continue to Be Created in the Third World Too." In Maria Mies, Veronika Bennholdt-Thomsen, and Claudia von Werlhof (eds.), *Women: The Last Colony.* Delhi: Kali for Women. pp. 159–67.

Bhatt, E. 1987. "The Invisibility of Home-Based Work: The Case of Piece Rate Workers in India." In Andrea Menefee Singh and Anita Kelles-Viitanen (eds.), *Invisible Hands: Women in Home-Based Production.* New Delhi: Sage.

Bhatty, Z. 1978. "Status and Power in a Muslim Dominated Village of Uttar Pradesh." In Imtiaz Ahmad (ed.), *Caste and Social Stratification among Muslims in India.* New Delhi: Manohar. pp. 207–24.

———. 1980. "Muslim Women in Uttar Pradesh: Social Mobility and Directions of Change." In Alfred de Souza (ed.), *Women in Contemporary India and South Asia.* New Delhi: Manohar.

———. 1981. *The Economic Role and Status of Women in the Beedi Industry in Allahabad, India.* Saarbrücken, Germany, and Fort Lauderdale, Fla.: Verlag Breitenbach.

———. 1987. "Economic Contribution of Women to the Household Budget: A Case Study of the Beedi Industry." In Andrea Menefee Singh and Anita Kelles-Viitanen (eds.), *Invisible Hands: Women in Home-Based Production.* New Delhi: Sage. pp. 35–50.

Birdwood, George Christopher Moresworth, Sir. 1880. *The Industrial Arts of India.* London: Chapman.

Blacking, John. 1973. *How Musical is Man?* Seattle: University of Washington Press.

Boris, Eileen and Cynthia Daniels. 1989. *Homework: Historical and Contemporary Perspectives on Paid Labor at Home.* Urbana: University of Illinois Press.

Boris, Eileen and Elisabeth Prügl (eds.). 1996. *Homeworkers in Global Perspective: Invisible No More.* New York: Routledge.

Bourdieu, Pierre. 1984. *Distinction: A Social Critique of the Judgement of Taste.* Cambridge, Mass.: Harvard University Press.

Breckenridge, Carol A. 1989. "The Aesthetics and Politics of Colonial Collecting: India at World Fairs." *Comparative Studies in Society and History* 31(2):195–216.

Brown, Judith M. 1985. *Modern India: The Origins of an Asian Democracy.* Delhi: Oxford University Press.

Buechler, Hans. 1989. "Apprenticeship and Transmission of Knowledge in La Paz, Bolivia." In Michael W. Coy (ed.), *Apprenticeship: From Theory to Method and Back Again.* Albany: State University of New York Press. pp. 31–50.

Bunzel, Ruth. 1929. *The Pueblo Potter: A Study of Creative Imagination in Primitive Art.* New York: Columbia University Press.

Cable, Vincent, Ann Weston, and L. C. Jain. 1986. *The Commerce of Culture: Experience of Indian Handicrafts.* New Delhi: Lancer International in Association with Indian Council for Research on International Economic Relations.

Castaneda, Carlos. 1968. *The Teachings of Don Juan: A Yaqui Way of Knowledge.* New York: Simon & Schuster.

———. 1970. *A Separate Reality.* New York: Simon & Schuster.

———. 1972. *Journey to Ixtlan.* New York: Simon & Schuster.

Census of India 1971. Series 21, Uttar Pradesh.

Census of India 1981a. Series 22, Uttar Pradesh. District Census Handbook: Lucknow District. Volume 36.

Census of India 1981b. Series 22: Uttar Pradesh. Part X-A. Town Directory. pp. 62–63.

Census of India 1991. Series 25, Uttar Pradesh. Provisional Population Totals.

Chattopadhyaya, K. 1963. *Indian Handicrafts.* New Delhi: Allied Publishing.

———. 1964. "Origin and Development of Embroidery in Our Land." *MARG* 17(2):2–4.

———. 1977. *Indian Embroidery.* New Delhi: Wiley Eastern.

———. 1980. *India's Craft Tradition.* New Delhi: Publications Division, Ministry of Information and Broadcasting, Government of India.

———. 1985. *Handicrafts of India.* 2nd ed. New Delhi: Indian Council for Cultural Relations.

Cohn, Bernard S. 1983. "Representing Authority in Victorian India." In Eric Hobsbawm and Terence Ranger (eds.), *The Invention of Tradition.* Cambridge: Cambridge University Press. pp. 165–210.

———. 1984. "The Census, Social Structure and Objectification in South Asia." *Folk* 26:25–47.

———. 1989. "Cloth, Clothes, and Colonialism: India in the Nineteenth Century." In Annette B. Weiner and Jane Schneider (eds.), *Cloth and Human Experience*. Washington, D.C.: Smithsonian Institution Press. pp. 304–55.

Cole, J. R. I. 1989. *Roots of North Indian Shi'ism in Iran and Iraq: Religion and State in Awadh, 1722–1859*. Delhi: Oxford University Press.

Collins, Jane L. 1990. "Unwaged Labor in Comparative Perspective: Recent Theories and Unanswered Questions." In Jane L. Collins and Martha E. Gimenez (eds.), *Work without Wages: Comparative Studies of Domestic Labor and Self-Employment*. Albany: State University of New York Press. pp. 3–24.

Collins, Jane L. and Martha E. Gimenez (eds.). 1990. *Work without Wages: Comparative Studies of Domestic Labor and Self-Employment*. Albany: State University of New York Press.

Coomaraswamy, A. 1964 [1913]. *The Arts and Crafts of India and Ceylon*. New York: Noonday.

Cooper, Eugene. 1980. *The Wood-Carvers of Hong Kong: Craft Production in the World Capitalist Periphery*. Cambridge: Cambridge University Press.

———. 1989. "Apprenticeship as Field Method: Lessons from Hong Kong." In Michael W. Coy (ed.), *Apprenticeship: From Method to Theory and Back Again*. Albany: State University of New York Press. pp. 137–48.

Coy, Michael W. (ed.). 1989. *Apprenticeship: From Theory to Method and Back Again*. Albany: State University of New York Press.

Dhamija, Jasleen. 1964. "The Survey of Embroidery Traditions: Chikankari." *MARG* 17(2):25–26.

di Leonardo, Michaela. 1991. "Gender, Culture and Political Economy: Feminist Anthropology in Historical Perspective." In Michaela di Leonardo (ed.), *Gender at the Crossroads of Knowledge*. Berkeley: University of California Press. pp. 1–50.

Dongerkery, Kamala S. 1951. *The Romance of Indian Embroidery*. Bombay: Thacker and Co.

Dow, James. 1989. "Apprentice Shaman." In Michael M. Coy (ed.), *Apprenticeship: From Theory to Method and Back Again*. Albany: State University of New York Press. pp. 199–210.

Engineer, Asghar Ali (ed.). 1987. *The Shah Bano Controversy*. Hyderabad: Orient Longman.

Etienne, Mona. 1980. "Women and Men, Cloth and Colonization: The Transformation of Production-Distribution Relations among the Baule (Ivory Coast)." In Mona Etienne and Eleanor Leacock (eds.), *Women and Colonialism: Anthropological Perspectives*. New York: Praeger. pp. 214–38.

Ewing, Katherine P. (ed.). 1988. *Shari'at and Ambiguity in South Asian Islam*. Berkeley: University of California Press.

Feld, Steven. 1990 [1982]. *Sound and Sentiment*. Philadelphia: University of Pennsylvania Press.

Feldman, Shelley. 1992. "Crisis, Islam and Gender in Bangladesh: The Social Construction of a Female Labor Force." In Lourdes Beneria and Shelley Feldman (eds.), *Unequal Burden: Economic Crises, Persistent Poverty and*

Women's Work. Boulder, Colo.: Westview Press. pp. 105–30.

Feldman, Shelley and Florence E. McCarthy. 1984. *Rural Women and Development in Bangladesh.* Oslo: NORAD.

Fernea, Elizabeth. 1969 [1965]. *Guests of the Sheik: An Ethnography of an Iraqi Village.* New York: Anchor/Doubleday.

Fisher, Allyn Johnston. 1972. "The All India Handicrafts Board and the Development of Handicrafts in India." Ph.D. dissertation, Indiana University.

Fisher, Michael H. 1987. *A Clash of Cultures: Awadh, the British and the Mughals.* New Delhi: Manohar.

Fortes, Meyer. 1938. *Social and Psychological Aspects of Education in Taleland.* London: Oxford University Press.

Fox, Richard D. (ed.). 1970. *Urban India: Society, Space and Image.* Durham, N.C.: Duke University Press.

Freitag, Sandria B. 1990. *Collective Action and Community: Public Arenas and the Emergence of Communalism in North India.* Berkeley: University of California Press.

Ganju, Sarojini. 1980. "The Muslims of Lucknow." In Kenneth Ballhatchet and John Harrison (eds.), *The City in South Asia: Pre-Modern and Modern.* Atlantic Highlands, N.J.: Humanities Press. pp. 279–98.

Ghosal, S. 1923. *Uttar Pradesh District Gazetteer.* Lucknow: Government of Uttar Pradesh.

Gilsenan, Michael. 1983. *Recognizing Islam: Religion and Society in the Modern Arab World.* New York: Pantheon.

Gold, Anne Grodzins. 1988. *Fruitful Journeys: The Ways of Rajasthani Pilgrims.* New Delhi: Oxford University Press.

Goody, Esther N. 1982. "Introduction." In Esther N. Goody (ed.), *From Craft to Industry: The Ethnography of Proto-Industrial Cloth Production.* Cambridge: Cambridge University Press. pp 1–37.

Gould, Harold A. 1965. "Lucknow Rickshawallas: The Social Organization of an Occupational Category." In Ralph Piddington (ed.), *Kinship and Geographical Mobility.* Leiden: E. J. Brill. pp. 24–47.

———. 1974. "Cities on the North Indian Plain: Contrasting Lucknow and Kanpur." In C. Maloney (ed.), *South Asia: Seven Community Profiles.* New York: Holt, Rinehart & Winston. pp. 258–93.

Grunebaum, Gustave Edmund. 1951. *Muhammedan Festivals.* New York: H. Schuman.

Handicrafts India Yearbook. 1989. New Delhi: Handicrafts India.

———. 1990. New Delhi.

———. 1991. New Delhi.

Hannerz, Ulf. 1980. *Exploring the City.: Inquiries toward an Urban Anthropology.* New York: Columbia University Press.

Hasan, Amir. 1983. *Palace Culture of Lucknow.* Delhi: B. R. Publishing Corp.

———. 1990. *Vanishing Culture of Lucknow.* Delhi: B. R. Publishing Corp.

Hjortshoj, Keith. 1979. *Urban Structures and Transformations in Lucknow, India.* Ithaca, N.Y.: Cornell University Press.

Hoey, William. 1880. *A Monography on Trade and Manufactures in Northern India.* Lucknow: American Methodist Press.

Hopkins, Nicholas S. 1978. "The Articulation of the Modes of Production: Tailoring in Tunisia." *American Ethnologist* 5(3):468–83.

Hossain, Hameeda. 1987. "Capitalist Penetration into Handicrafts Manufacture: An Historical Review of Women's Work for the Market in Bangladesh." In Andrea Menefee Singh and Anita Kelles-Viitanen (eds.), *Invisible Hands: Women in Home-Based Production*. New Delhi: Sage. pp. 165–74.

Irwin, John and Margaret Hall. 1973. *Indian Embroideries*. Ahmedabad: Calico Museum of Textiles.

Jain, Devaki. 1980. *Women's Quest for Power: Five Indian Case Studies*. Ghaziabad: Vikas Publishing House.

Jalees, Faridha. 1989. *Glittering Threads: A Socio-Economic Study of Women Zari Workers*. Ahmedabad: SEWA Bharat.

Jeffrey, Patricia. 1979. *Frogs in a Well: Indian Women in Purdah*. London: Zed Press.

Johnson, Patricia Lyons (ed.). 1992. *Balancing Acts: Women and the Process of Social Change*. Boulder, Colo.: Westview Press.

King, Anthony D. 1976. *Colonial Urban Development*. London: Routledge and Kegan Paul.

Kippen, James. 1988. *The Tabla of Lucknow: A Cultural Analysis of a Musical Tradition*. Cambridge Studies in Ethnomusicology. Cambridge: Cambridge University Press.

Knighton, William. 1855. *The Private Life of an Eastern King*. New York: J. S. Redfield.

———. 1865. *Elihu Jan's Story: or the Private Life of an Eastern Queen*. London: Longman, Green, Longman, Roberts and Green.

Kooiman, Dick. 1983. "Rural Labour in the Bombay Textile Industry and the Articulation of Modes of Organization." In Peter Robb (ed.), *Rural South Asia: Linkages, Change and Development*. London: Curzon. pp. 130–62.

Kostoff, S. 1991. *The City Shaped: Urban Patterns and Meanings through History*. Boston: Little, Brown.

Kumar, Nita. 1988. *The Artisans of Banaras: Popular Culture and Identity, 1880–1986*. Princeton, N.J.: Princeton University Press.

Lateef, Shahida. 1990. *Muslim Women in India: Political and Private Realities 1890's-1980's*. Delhi: Kali for Women.

Lave, Jean. 1982. "A Comparative Approach to Educational Forms and Learning Processes." *Anthropology and Education Quarterly* 13:181–88.

Lave, Jean and Etienne Wenger. 1991. *Situated Learning: Legitimate Peripheral Participation*. Cambridge: Cambridge University Press.

Lever, Alison. 1988a. "Capital, Gender and Skill: Female Homeworkers in Rural Spain." *Feminist Review* 30 (Autumn 1988):3–24.

———. 1988b. "Women's Employment in the Informal Sector: San Santiago, Spain." *Social Justice* 15(3–4):87–113.

Llewellyn-Jones, Rosie. 1985. *A Fatal Friendship: The Nawabs, the British and the City of Lucknow*. Delhi: Oxford University Press.

Lown, Judy. 1990. *Women and Industry: Gender at Work in Nineteenth Century England*. Minneapolis: University of Minnesota Press.

Lucknow City Magazine. 1988. "Charm of Chikan." September.

Mandelbaum, David G. 1988. *Women's Seclusion and Men's Honor: Sex Roles in North India, Bangladesh and Pakistan.* Tucson: University of Arizona Press.

Marglin, Stephen. 1990. "Losing Touch: The Cultural Conditions of Work Accommodation and Resistance." In Frederique Apfell Marglin and Stephen Marglin (eds.), *Dominating Knowledge: Development, Culture and Resistance.* Oxford: Clarendon. pp. 217–82.

Marriott, McKim. 1976. "Diversity without Dualism." In Bruce Kapferer (ed.), *Transaction and Meaning: Directions in the Anthropology of Exchange and Symbolic Behavior.* Philadelphia: Institute for the Study of Human Issues.

Martin, E. 1982. "The End of the Body?" *American Ethnologist* 19(1):121–40.

Marx, Karl. 1976 [1867]. *Capital: A Critique of Political Economy.* Vol. 1. Harmondsworth, U.K.: Penguin.

Mathur, R. S. 1975. *Report on Chikan Handicraft, Lucknow.* Technical Report No. 2. Lucknow: Giri Institute of Development Studies.

Mehta, Rustam J. 1960. *The Handicrafts and Industrial Arts of India.* Bombay: D. B. Taraporevala.

Meer Hassan Ali, Mrs. 1973 [1832]. *Observations on the Mussulmauns of Lucknow.* Delhi: Manohar.

Messick, Brinkley. 1987. "Subordinate Discourse: Women, Weaving and Gender Relations in North Africa." *American Ethnologist* 14(2):210–25.

Metcalf, T. R. 1964. *The Aftermath of Revolt: India 1857–1870.* Princeton, N.J.: Princeton University Press.

Mies, Maria. 1982. *The Lace Makers of Narsapur.* London: Zed Press.

————. 1988. "Capitalist Penetration and Subsistence Production: Rural Women in India." In Maria Mies, Veronika Bennholdt-Thomsen, and Claudia von Werlhof (eds.), *Women: The Last Colony.* Delhi: Kali for Women. pp. 27–50.

Mies, Maria, Veronika Bennholdt-Thomsen, and Claudia von Werlhoj (eds.). 1988. *Women: The Last Colony.* Delhi: Kali for Women.

Mitra, Asok. 1969. "The Present State of Handicrafts." *MARG* 22(4):58–60.

Mukerjee, Radhakamal and Baljit Singh. 1961. *Social Profiles of a Metropolis: Social and Economic Structure of Lucknow, Capital of Uttar Pradesh, 1954–56.* New York: Asia Publishing House.

Mukharji, T. N. 1974. *Art-Manufactures of India.* New Delhi: Navrang.

Naiman, Joanne. 1996. "Left Feminism and the Return to Class." *Monthly Review* 48(2):12–28.

Naqvi, S. M. 1971. "Stitches Employed in Lucknow Chikan." *Bulletin of Museums and Archaeology in U.P.* 5:40–49.

Oldenburg, Veena Talwar. 1984. *The Making of Colonial Lucknow, 1856–1877.* Princeton, N.J.: Princeton University Press.

Omvedt, Gail. 1992. "The 'Unorganised Sector' and Women Workers." *Guru Nanak Journal of Sociology* 13(1):19–61.

Ong, Aihwa. 1987. *Spirits of Resistance and Capitalist Discipline: Factory Women in Malaysia.* Albany: State University of New York Press.

Paine, Sheila. 1989. *Chikan Embroidery: The Floral Whitework of India.* Princes Risborough, Aylesbury, Bucks, U.K.: Shire.

Pande, M. C. 1968. "Chikankari of Lucknow." *Bulletins of Museums and Archaeology in U.P.* 2:43–55.

Papanek, Hanna. 1982. "Purdah: Separate Worlds and Symbolic Shelter." In H. Papanek and G. Minault (eds.), *Separate Worlds: Studies of Purdah in South Asia.* Columbia, Mo.: South Asia Books. pp. 3–53.

Phillips, Anne and Barbara Taylor. 1980. "Sex and Skill: Notes toward a Feminist Economics." *Feminist Review* 6:79–88.

Polanyi, M. 1967. *The Tacit Dimension.* Garden City, N.Y.: Anchor.

Prügl, Elisabeth. 1996. "Home-Based Producers in Development Discourse." In Eileen Boris and Elisabeth Prügl (eds.), *Homeworkers in Global Perspective: Invisible No More.* New York: Routledge. pp. 39–59.

Rai, Prabha. 1975. "Unorganised Labour Force." *Social Welfare* 22(6–7):16–18, 93.

Rastogi, R. 1981. "Chikankari." *The India Magazine.* November 1981:63–67.

Renuka. 1980. "Working Women." *How* 3(5):1–3.

Risseeuw, Carla. 1987. "Organisation and Disorganisation: A Case Study of Women Coir Workers in Sri Lanka." In Andrea Menefee Singh and Anita Kelles-Viitanen (eds.), *Invisible Hands: Women in Home-Based Production.* New Delhi: Sage. pp. 177–205.

Ritzenhaler, Robert. 1979. "From Folk Art to Fine Art: The Emergence of the Name Artist among Southwest Indians." In Justine Cordwell (ed.), *The Visual Arts: Plastic and Graphic.* The Hague: Mouton.

Rizvi, S. H. M. and Shibani Roy. 1984. *Muslims: a Bio-Cultural Perspective.* Delhi: B. R. Publishing.

Robinson, Francis. 1974. *Separatism among Indian Muslims.* Cambridge: Cambridge University Press.

———. 1983. "Islam and Muslim Society in South Asia." *Contributions to Indian Sociology* 17(2):185–203.

Rose, Kalima. 1992. *Where Women are Leaders: The SEWA Movement in India.* London: Zed Books.

Ruswa, Mirza. 1961. *Umrao Jan Ada: The Courtesan of Lucknow.* Delhi: Orient.

Sacks, Karen Brodkin. 1989. "Toward a Unified Theory of Class, Race and Gender." *American Ethnologist* 16(3):534–50.

Sahai, Indu. 1973. *Family Structure and Partition: A Study of the Rastogi Community of Lucknow.* Lucknow: Ethnographic and Folk Culture Society of U.P.

Saraf, D. N. 1982. *Indian Crafts: Development and Potential.* New Delhi: Vikas.

Saraswati, Baidyanath. 1986. "Crises in Aesthetic Culture." *Man in India* 66(2):166–79.

Sarkar, Sumit. 1973. *The Swadeshi Movement in Bengal, 1903–1908.* New Delhi: People's Publishing House.

Schildkrout, Enid. 1983. "Dependence and Autonomy: The Economic Activities of Secluded Hausa Women in Kano." In Christine Oppong, (ed.), *Female and Male in West Africa.* London: Allen and Unwin. pp. 107–26.

Sharar, Abdul Halim. 1975. *Lucknow: The Last Phase of an Oriental Culture.* Transl. E. S. Harcourt and Fakhir Hussain. London: Elek.

Sharma, Ursula. 1980. *Women's Work and Property in North-west India*. London: Tavistock.

———. 1986. *Women's Work, Class and the Urban Household: A Study of Shimla, North India*. London: Tavistock.

Sharma, V. C. 1959. *Uttar Pradesh District Gazetteer*. Volume 37. Lucknow. Government of Uttar Pradesh.

Singh, Shanta Serbjeet. 1987. "The Apna Utsav Syndrome." *Seminar* 329 (January 1987):72–75.

Singh, Andrea Menefee and Anita Kelles-Viitanen. 1987. *Invisible Hands: Women in Home-Based Production*. New Delhi: Sage.

Sleeman, William Henry. 1858. *A Journey through the Kingdom of Oude, 1849–1850*. 2 vols. London: R. J. Bentley.

Spear, Percival. 1984. *A History of India*. Volume 2. Harmondsworth, U.K.: Penguin.

Srinivasan, Nirmala. 1981. *Identity Crisis of Muslims: Profiles of Lucknow Youth*. New Delhi: Concept.

———. 1989. *Prisoners of Faith: A View from Within*. New Delhi: Sage.

Stoller, Paul and Cheryl Olkes. 1987. *In Sorcery's Shadow: A Memoir of Apprenticeship among the Songhay of Niger*. Chicago: University of Chicago Press.

Swallow, D. A. 1982. "Production and Control in the Indian Garment Export Industry." In Esther Goody (ed.), *From Craft to Industry: The Ethnography of Proto-Industrial Cloth Production*. Cambridge:Cambridge University Press.

Taylor, James. 1851. *A Descriptive and Historical Account of the Cotton Manufactures of Dacca, in Bengal. By a resident of Dacca*. London: John Mortimer.

Tyabji, Laili. 1990. "SEWA Lucknow and DASTKAR." Text of talk delivered to the Crafts Council of India Ahmedabad.

Victoria and Albert Museum. 1951. *Indian Embroidery*. London: Her Majesty's Stationery Office.

Vatuk, Sylvia. 1982. "Purdah Revisited: A Comparison to Hindu and Muslim Interpretations of the Cultural Meaning of Purdah in South Asia." In H. Papanek and G. Minault (eds.), *Separate Worlds: Studies of Purdah in South Asia*. Columbia, Mo.: South Asia Books. pp. 54–78.

von Werlhof, Claudia. 1988. "Women's Work: The Blind Spot in Political Economy." In Maria Mies, Veronika Bennholdt-Thomsen, and Claudia von Werlhof (eds.), *Women: The Last Colony*. Delhi: Kali for Women. pp. 13–26.

Vreede-de-Stuers, Cora. 1968. *Parda: A Study of Women's Life in Northern India*. Assen, Netherlands: Van Gorcum.

Warren, Kay B. and Susan C. Bourque. 1991. "Women, Technology and International Development Ideologies: Analyzing Feminist Voices." In Michaela di Leonardo (ed.), *Gender at the Crossroads of Knowledge*. Berkeley: University of California Press. pp. 278–311.

Watt, Sir George. 1904. *Indian Art at Delhi, 1903, Being the Official Catalogue of the Delhi Exhibition 1902–1903*. London: John Murray.

The Wealth of India: A Dictionary of Indian Raw Materials and Industrial Products. 1953–1981. Vols. I–XI [A–Z]. New Delhi: Council of Scientific and Industrial Resources.

Vygotsky, L. 1978. *Mind in Society: The Development of Higher Psychological Processes*. Ed. Michael Cole, Vera John-Steiner, Sylvia Scribner, and Ellen Souberman. Cambridge, Mass.: Harvard University Press.

Weiner, Annette B. and Jane Schneider. 1989. *Cloth and Human Experience*. Washington, D.C.: Smithsonian Institute Press.

Weiss, Anita. 1991. Walls within Walls. Boulder, Colo.: Westview Press.

———. 1996. "Within the Walls: Home-Based Work in Lahore." In Eileen Boris and Elisabeth Prügl (eds.), *Homeworkers in Global Perspective: Invisible No More*. New York: Routledge. pp. 81–92.

Weston, Ann. 1987. "Women and Handicraft Production in North India." In Haleh Afshar (ed.), *Women, State and Ideology: Studies from Africa and Asia*. Albany: State University of New York Press. pp. 173–84.

Westwood, Sallie. 1991. "Gender and the Politics of Production in India." In Haleh Afshar (ed.), *Women, Development, and Survival in the Third World*. Delhi: Manohar.

Wilkinson-Weber, Clare M. 1994. "Embroidering Lives: Women's Work and Skill in an Urban Industry." Ph.D. dissertation, University of Pennsylvania.

———. 1997. "Skill, Dependency, and Differentiation: Artisans and Agents in the Lucknow Embroidery Industry." *Ethnology* 36(1): 59–65.

Yusuf Ali, A. 1900. *A Monograph on Silk Fabrics Produced in the North Western Provinces and Dudh*. Allahabad.

INDEX